The Ultimate Guide:
Literature for Teens

The Ultimate Guide: Literature for Teens

Sharron L. McElmeel

2021
Reading Trove Publishing

For all educators in classrooms and libraries that share a love of literacy with scholars of all ages. Readers are leaders.

Copyright © 2021 Sharron L. McElmeel
All Rights Reserved
No part of this book may be reproduced, or stored in a retrieval system, or transmitted in any form or by any means, electronic, mechanical, photocopying, recording, or otherwise, without express written permission of the publisher.

ISBN: 978-0-578-24740-3 (paperback)

Cover design by: Art Painter
Library of Congress Control Number: 2018675309
Printed in the United States of America

Reading Trove Publishing
A division of McBookwords, L.L.C.
3000 N Center Point Rd
Cedar Rapids, IA 52411-9548

Table of Contents

Introduction ix
Chapter I - Thoughts and Ideas 1
  Points of View - Consideration 1
  Teen Reading Survey 2
  Building a Community of Readers Ways and Means 3
    Written Surveys 4
  The Development of Children's and Young Adult Literature 5
    In the Spotlight: S. E. Hinton 6
  Classics That Are Touchstones in Children's Literature 7
    Picture Books 7
    Chapter books 7
    Classics 7
  Children's Authors Too Good to Miss 7
    Ideas to Use with Teen Readers 9
  What Is Teen Literature 10
    Characteristics of a Teen Novel 11
    Teen Novels Too Good To Miss: 1960–2019 12
    Ideas to Use with Teen Readers 14
  Significant Authors 15
    Winners of the Margaret A. Edwards Award 2021- 2005 15
    In the Spotlight: Steve Sheinkin 16
  Awards and Recognition 17
    The Michael L. Printz Award 17
    The John Newbery Award 17
  Multicultural Awards 18
    Coretta Scott King Award 18
    The Coretta Scott King-(CSK) Virginia Hamilton Award for Lifetime Achievement ... 19
    The Pura Belpré award 19
    The American Indian Youth Award 19
  Awards Sponsored by ALA Divisions or Others 20
    Robert F. Sibert Award 20
    Odyssey Award for audio books 20
    Prestigious awards 20
    Other Awards 21
    State and Regional Choice Awards 22
    In the Spotlight: Laurie Halse Anderson 23
    In the Spotlight: Kekla Magoon– 2021 Margaret A. Edwards Award winner 24
  Collection Development and Selection 25
    Professional Reviewing Sources: A Selected list 27
    Ideas to Use with Teen Readers 29
  School and Public Library Cooperation in a Teen World 30
    School Libraries 30
    Public Libraries: Their Role 32
    School and Public Library Cooperation 32
  The Culture of Teens and Reading 34
  Graphic Novels and Manga 37
    In the Spotlight: Gene Luen Yang 38
    Resources for Using Graphic Novels 39

  Manga and Anime.. 40
  Ideas to Use with Teen Readers... 42
  Using Graphic Novels in Chemistry Class-A First Foray... 42
  An Example: Options for the Chemistry Classroom.. 42
  Ideas to Use with Teen Readers... 43
 Picture Books for Teens 44
  Uses and a Selected List.. 45
  The POWER of ONE BOOK 48
  Using Picture Books 49
  Ideas to Use with Teen Readers... 55
  Read a picture book and share one new fact that you learned........................... 55
 Adult Books and the Teen Reader.. 55
  Alex Award.. 56
  New Adult (NA) Fiction 58
  Good Reads... 58
 Contemporary Literature for Teens – Fiction.. 60
  Major Subject Groups in Contemporary Realistic Fiction 60
  Other Literary Subjects 62
  Authors to Watch... 63
  In the Spotlight: Angie Thomas 64
 Poetry and Full-Length Works in Verse 66
  Verse Novels in the Classroom 66
  Prose & Poetry Connections... 67
  Poetry Blasts, Jams, and Slams 67
  In the Spotlight: Kwame Alexander 68
  Opportunities for Community Service in Literacy – World-Wide Poetry and Literacy 69
 Mysteries and Suspense.. 70
  In the Spotlight: Nancy Werlin.. 74
  Edgar Allan Poe Award.. 75
 Folklore /Mythology 76
 More Subjects (Genres or Categories) 77
 GLBTQ Literature for Teens - The History 78
  In the Spotlight: Alex Gino 79
  How to Feature GLBTQ books... 80
 Diversity Concerns 80
  Resources for Understanding and Keeping Up with Multicultural Concerns 82
  Publishers to Watch... 82
  Teaching Tolerance.. 83
  Dr. Seuss and Other Classics to Re-evaluate... 83
 Censorship Issues & Banning Books... 86

Chapter II – Finding Books.. 92
 Publishers... 92
  The Largest Trade and Educational Publishers 92
  Other Publishers 93
 The Bibliographies 94
 *Books * Books * Books*.. 94

Chapter III – A Patchwork of Ideas 141
 Literary Quotes 141
 Reading and Vocabulary... 142
  Vocabulary and You — See How You Read.. 142
 Thematic Lists 143

- A List — Thinkers and Inventors 143
- *Book Packages* 145
  - Civil Rights 146
  - Discrimination in America 146
  - Family Dynamics 148
  - Finding Who We Are 148
  - On the Homefront – World War II 149
  - Black Panthers and Their Voice in America's Culture 150
- *Capsule Packages* 151
  - Time Warp Titles 151
  - Coming of Age – Dealing with Sexual Violence, Racism, Poverty … 151
  - Soldiers & Spies in Plain Sight – Revolutionary War 152
  - Hidden Secrets – Forbidden Records 152
- *Instead of Book Talks - Instead of Book Reviews Instead of Anything Else* 153
  - Literary Triads 153
  - Quotes – What Do You Make of It? 154
  - Book Pairings 155
- *But We Have to Teach the Classics* 155
  - Classic: *Romeo and Juliet* by William Shakespeare 155
  - Classic: *Macbeth* by William Shakespeare 155
  - Classic: *To Kill a Mockinbird* by Harper Lee 156
  - Classic: *1984* by George Orwell 156
  - Classic: *The Great Gatsby* by F. Scott Fitzgerald 156
  - Classic: *The Scarlet Letter* by Nathaniel Hawthorne 156
  - Classic: *Lord of the Flies* by William Golding 156
  - Classic: *Of Mice and Men* by John Steinbeck 157
  - Classic: *The Kite Runner* by Khaled Hosseini 157
  - Classic: *The Odyssey* by Homer 157
  - Classic: *Catcher in the Rye* by J.B. Salinger 157
  - Need more examples or suggestions? 157
- *Searching for Balance* 158

About the Author 159

Introduction

Ever since S.E. Hinton's *The Outsiders* was published in 1967, teen readers have demanded books that reflect their lives. They want to read about young people who are facing the same challenges that they are facing – sometimes in a realistic world and sometimes in a world of fantasy. As they age and mature, they seek books that address the changes they are encountering - changes in relationships, life choices, coming to terms with their lives and existence. They want to be valued and significant. No one book can do total justice to the immense world of publication of books for teens. What twenty-year-old people read as teens have changed tremendously. This book does not intend to be a comprehensive guide to the history of the evolvement of teen literature. Most books included or mentioned will have been published within a five-year publication window, and literature for teens is the focus on the book's three sections.

The first section will present thoughts and ideas related to various points of view regarding topic issues within the lexicon of teen literature. The narratives will present thoughts regarding the specific topic within the lexicon with the intent to promote thinking and discussion regarding that topic. The narrative is not intended to be the definitive statement on the topic addressed but rather to present one line of thought on the topic, to raise questions, and to promote the discussion of options. As the topics are discussed and addressed refinements of the thinking will emerge. Are picture books valuable tools for sharing with teen readers? What responsibility do educators have in regard to curating selections that are inclusive and avoid racist language and images? Should LBGTQ literature be included in classroom and library collections? What is choice reading? What emphasis should be given to informational reading versus fiction reading?

The second section will be comprised of briefly annotated bibliographies that represent some of the best books published during the past five years. The books listed will include fiction, Nonfiction (informational), graphic novels (both fiction and Nonfiction), and will include titles in all the major forms of writing. Some of the special topic narratives in section one will also include some titles that fit within the focus topic, e.g. picture books, LBGTQ titles, and so forth.

The third section will be a collage of collected strategies and ideas for infusing literature into various areas of the curriculum. Thematic booklists, strategy procedures for sharing literature and books in the classroom, connecting fiction with information titles, and promoting writing with mentor texts.

Much as quilters choose pieces of cloth, to create a tapestry that holds memories and symbols to be made into rich and treasured quilts, we ask that readers of this guide to choose the various pieces of writings available, to weave a tapestry. This rich tapestry of literature will bring experiences, vicarious or real, evoking memories, and building knowledge that will allow the literature to enrich lives and promote curiosity and life-long learning.

Chapter I - Thoughts and Ideas

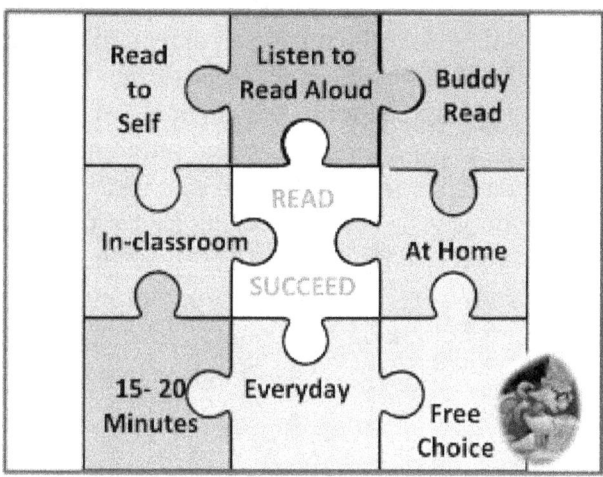

Points of View - Consideration

It is important that thoughts and ideas related to various points of view regarding topic issues within the lexicon of teen literature be presented and discussed with the intent of promoting thinking and discussion regarding each selected topic. The narrative is not intended to be the definitive statement on any topic addressed but rather to present one line of thought on the topic, to raise questions, and to promote the discussion of options. As the topics are discussed and addressed refinements of the thinking will emerge. The topics selected are not the only topics that we might want to examine. There are important questions to answer in regard to promoting literacy and reading in relation to curriculum, research, and recreation – all seem to involve choice and motivation.

How do we select books to recommend to readers? Are picture books valuable tools for sharing with teen readers? How do we determine what books and reading material teens are interested in reading? What are some ideas for building a positive environment for literacy? How do we identify books targeted to teens (young adult literature)? What responsibility do educators have in regard to curating selections that are inclusive and avoid racist language and images? Should LBGTQ literature be included in classroom and library collections? What is choice reading? What emphasis should be given to informational reading versus fiction reading? How do we determine what we could or should be recommending to teen readers? What place does motivation play in building a community of readers? All topics related to literature for teens should encompass the element of choice and motivation.

Teen Reading Survey

One of the first pieces of advice given to educators working with readers is to know your students and put the right book in their hands. Give them books they are interested in reading and books which have an appeal to their interests. Putting the right book in the hands of the right teen is often listed as one of the key factors for moving a potential reader to the ranks of avid reader. One of my colleagues commented to a parent during a teacher conference that their child did not read much. The parent responded that his son did read – and read a lot. The child just did not read the books she (the teacher) or his mother choose for him to read. The child was more interested in Nonfiction titles – history, sports, and related topics. No, *Little House on the Prairie* (by Laura Ingalls Wilder) for him. He wanted real accounts not fictionalized accounts. That conference gave the teacher a new perspective. Choice was a key to motivating and creating readers.

Curriculum sometimes mandates specific book titles but often that is discretionary in terms of what titles are chosen. If one articulates what the goal is for asking a student to read a specific book there can be choices within the curriculum and still retain the ability to achieve the goal. With that said it is also the responsibility of educators to encourage and promote reading of a wide and broad range of high-quality literary and informational texts. Refer to http://www.corestandards.org for more information regarding the standards for various aspects of literacy education; and for content curriculum standards that will correlate with the goals to promote reading. The reading material should include a wide and diverse range of stories, dramas, poems, and myths.

> Common Core State Standards Initiative. (2021). (Website) http://www.corestandards.org/

To provide a selection from which teen readers might choose, educators might wish to design a survey of interests that could yield information that might assist in suggesting books of interest to an individual teen or a group of teens. Frankly I find both paper and pencil surveys and electronic surveys time-consuming and ineffective. If you wish to create a survey, I certainly won't discourage surveys, if you feel they are helpful, but taking the time to match survey to individual students is time consuming.

A more effective technique might be genuine conversations about books, either individually, or group discussions. What books are they most interested in reading? What was the last book they read that they really liked? Why? With genuine conversations in which you are actively involved you will be able to provide suggestions, and schedule booktalks that will introduce large groups to a select group of books. A most important aspect of encouraging reading is choice. We need to be open to providing that choice. Authentic discussions will open possibilities for matching the right book with the right reader.

Building a Community of Readers
Ways and Means

1. Accessibility: Create an environment making high interest books in a variety of formats, easily available to the reader. Take the materials to them if necessary.
2. Choice: Always provide reader's choice regarding what to read and in what format they would prefer to read. Graphic novels (could be fiction or Nonfiction), fiction, Nonfiction, or even picture books might be appropriate material. Keep the focus on the goal and objective.
3. Be prepared to suggest new, more challenging reading experiences based on the reader's interests.
4. Be a model of what it is to be a reader.
5. Read aloud to readers – it is never too early or too late to read aloud to any reader, young or old.
6. Provide opportunities for readers to read on their own an with each other.
7. Promote conversations about reading. Allow each reader to voice their views orally and in writing. These conversations might be oral dialogues, written reviews posted online or on bulletin boards, and so forth. Literary Triads may also be an ongoing procedure that you might employ (See appendix).
8. Energize the literature by encouraging creative responses in the form of writing (plays, parodies, sequels, reviews, more research into a topic), speaking (conversations, formal presentations about a book, i.e. booktalk), dramatization (plays, pseudo interviews with characters, authors, radio broadcasts), and employ the visual arts to advertise the book, create a book jacket, illustrate a scene from the book). Allow a variety of ways that students might choose to share the book or the information they gained through the book.
9. Encourage interaction with others in the community that support the building of an inclusive environment of literacy throughout the school, neighborhood, and community of literacy (school and public librarians, classroom teachers and professors, storytellers, bookstore staff, local authors, afterschool tutors, language specialists, and others).
10. Create reading clubs/discussion groups.
11. Encourage the connection between reading and writing. Acquaint readers of all levels with the idea of writing and sharing (publishing their work). Invite local authors and writers of all types (publicity material, public relations materials, manuals) to share tips and tricks.
12. Connect readers to opportunities for all type: journalists, fiction writers, technical writers, research writers, and so forth. Create or improve manuals for sewing machines, welders, all types of gadgets)

Those interested in automobiles might write an instruction manual providing instruction regarding changing oil, or changing a headlight (specific model). Write the manual for some gadget or write a script and create a YouTube video. Check out copyright considerations.
13. Build and encourage reading confidence with opportunities to read aloud, participate in readers' theater, story times, etc.
14. Be alert of opportunities to promote and sell books and reading. Share connections wherever possible.
15. Create opportunities for readers to emerge as readers by engaging them in planning and executing the plans for literacy related activities, programs, and performances. Create a poetry slam, assist with selecting readings for theatrical performances, invite community members for dramatic readings.

Written Surveys

If you still feel the need to survey your students in a formal way you will find some prototypes here:

Findley, Jennifer. (2020, July 14). Free Digital Reading Interest Surveys. *Teaching with Jennifer Findley*. (Blog). https://jenniferfindley.com/free-digital-reading-interest-surveys/ -- designed for upper elementary but easily adaptable.

Studylib. (2013-2021). Adolescent Reading Profile Survey. *Studylib* (Web document). https://studylib.net/doc/7142134/adolescent-reading-profile
Create your own electronic survey at
https://www.surveymonkey.co.uk/r/9NVPTK7 - check their prototype and explore the site for yourself.

The Development of Children's and Young Adult Literature

The concept of children's literature did not exist prior to the 18th century. Young readers took books that appealed to them from the adult lexicon and read the tales of Gulliver and the Lilliputians, Robinson Crusoe, and other tales of adventure. The first person to write and publish books for children was John Newbery (1713-1767). Newbery is recognized as the first publisher of books for children when he published, *A Little Pretty Pocket Book* which is often cited as the first children's book. In the years that followed there were books with Mother Goose verses, fairy tales, myths and legends collected by the Grimm Brothers, and Charles Perrault, and later books we now call classics, such as *Treasure Island*, *Peter Pan*, and *Tom Sawyer*. Don't kid yourself regarding the folk and fairy tales being primarily for young children. If you are in doubt read an early version of *Cinderella* as retold by the Grimm Brothers. In the Grimm retelling the stepsisters cut off their heel, or toes in order to fit into the glass slipper. When their bleeding appendages alert the guards on the way to the palace, each respective stepsister is returned to their home. Eventually *Cinderella* is identified, and on the day of the marriage – the stepsisters attend the ceremony. The birds (already present in the story) fly down and peck the stepsisters' eyes out. Hardly a story for the very young.

By the mid-twentieth century well-known and revered authors/ illustrators such as Virginia Lee Burton, Eric Carle, Ezra Jack Keats, Dr. Seuss, Steven Kellogg, Lee Bennett Hopkins, Jan Brett and Maurice Sendak emerged as iconic authors/illustrators. These giants of children's literature emerged with touchstone titles that set the pace for today's books. That era (the mid-60s) saw the beginning of the golden age of picture books, the gorgeous, illustrated books, the toy books, and the televised or full-length movies of children's books. The emergence of books marketed to the teen reader was not far behind. The current era is a period where there is a lot of cross age appeal of titles. Young adult books, such as the Harry Potter series are being read by adults, pictures books are being created for more sophisticated older readers, and many popular novels are being made into movies for all ages. And while books written for and marketed to young adults are being read by adults, books written for and marketed to adults are being read by young adults. The focus is on the appeal, interest, and format factor. The resurgence of children's books, and an interest from readers of all ages, has been launched by highly successful movies made from extremely popular novels: *Holes* (Louis Sachar), *Because of Winn Dixie* (Kate Dicamillo), *Harry Potter*, Books 1-7 (J.K. Rowling), and *The Hunger Games* Trilogy (Suzanne Collins). And graphic novels are no longer the shunned relative in the family of literature for young readers.

In the Spotlight: S. E. Hinton

In the Spotlight

S.E. Hinton

The book often credited with establishing the YA body of literature, was S.E. (Susan Eloise) Hinton's *The Outsiders* (Viking, 1967). She was a teenage, female writer who at the time she was writing the ground-breaking coming of age novel, she was flunking her high school writing class. She had not intended to publish the book, but her younger sister wanted a car so the two of them could have some fun. She convinced Susan to give her manuscript to a friend's mom, a literary agent. The friend's mom submitted Hinton's manuscript to a publisher. The book was accepted and published when Susan was just 17. She became the first recipient of the Margaret A. Edwards award for her contribution to literature for young adult readers.

Books by S.E. Hinton

The Outsiders (Viking, 1967)	*Taming the Star Runner* (Delacorte, 1988)
Tex (Delacorte, 1979)	*Hawkes Harbor* (Tor Books, 2004)
Rumblefish (Delacorte, 1975)	*That Was Then, This is Now* (1971)

Before the era when Hinton's book was published the books for the teen reader were aged-down sappy and romantic books written about prom queens, high school crushes, and the obligatory books about sports. But the books specifically for young adults and geared toward the interests of young adults and their contemporary lives did not become a focus until the popularity of S.E. (Susan Eloise) Hinton's books, beginning with *The Outsiders* (Viking, 1967). Perhaps the popularity was enhanced because Hinton was a teenager at the time that she wrote the book. She started the book as a fifteen-year-old and did most of the writing at age 16.

For more information read this interview with Hinton from 2018, and comments from Debbie Reese:

Parr, Ali. (2018, January 25). *12 Fascinating Facts About S.E. Hinton's Outsiders.* Mental Floss. (Interview). http://bit.ly/sehinton-interview and

Reese, Debbie. (2020, October 16). Anti-Indigenous Content in S.E. Hinton's *The Outsiders.* American Indians in Children's Literature. http://bit.ly/Outsiders101

Classics That Are Touchstones in Children's Literature

Picture Books

The Cat in the Hat by Dr. Seuss
The Snowy Day by Ezra Jack Keats
Where the Wild Things Are by Maurice Sendak
The Very Hungry Caterpillar by Eric Carle
The Polar Express by Chris VanAllsburg
The Lion and the Mouse by Jerry Pinkney
Knuffle Bunny by Mo Willems
Goodnight Moon by Margaret Wise Brown
Frog and Toad (series) by Arnold Lobel

Chapter books

Henry and Mudge by Cynthia Rylant
Ramona by Beverly Cleary
Charlie and the Chocolate Factory by Roald Dahl
Charlotte's Web by E.B. White
Sadako and the Thousand Paper Cranes by Eleanor Coerr and Ronald Himler
The Cay by Theodore Taylor
At least one childhood series, such as *Nancy Drew*, *The Hardy Boys*, *The Boxcar Children*, or *The Babysitter's Club*
The Black Cauldron by Lloyd Alexander
Roll of Thunder, Hear My Cry by Mildred Taylor
Where the Red Fern Grows by Wilson Rawls
The Giver by Lois Lowry
Walk Two Moons by Sharon Creech

Classics

Mary Poppins by P.L. Travers
Wizard of Oz by L. Frank Baum
The Secret Garden by Frances Hodgson Burnett
Anne of Green Gables by Lucy Maud Montgomery
Little Women and Little Men by Louisa May Alcott
Winnie the Pooh by A. A. Milne
Alice in Wonderland by Lewis Carroll

Children's Authors Too Good to Miss

- ❏ Adler, David
- ❏ Alexander, Lloyd
- ❏ Alexander, Sue
- ❏ Aliki
- ❏ Asch, Frank
- ❏ Avi
- ❏ Aylesworth, Jim
- ❏ Base, Graeme
- ❏ Blume, Judy
- ❏ Bond, Michael
- ❏ Brett, Jan
- ❏ Brown, Marc
- ❏ Brown, Marcia
- ❏ Bunting, Eve
- ❏ Burton, Virginia. Lee
- ❏ Byars, Betsy
- ❏ Carle, Eric
- ❏ Carlson, Nancy
- ❏ Carroll, Lewis
- ❏ Casanova, Mary
- ❏ Christopher, Matt

- ❏ Cleary, Beverly
- ❏ Cole, Joanna
- ❏ Collier, Chris.
- ❏ Collier, James Lincoln
- ❏ Cooney, Barbara
- ❏ Coville, Bruce
- ❏ Creech, Sharon
- ❏ Crews, Donald
- ❏ Cummings, Pat
- ❏ Curtis, Christopher Paul.
- ❏ Cushman, Karen
- ❏ Dahl, Roald
- ❏ dePaola, Tomie
- ❏ Diaz, David
- ❏ DiCamillo, Kate
- ❏ Dillon, Diane
- ❏ Dillon, Leo
- ❏ Duncan, Lois
- ❏ Fisher, Aileen
- ❏ Fitzhugh, Louise
- ❏ Fleischman, Paul
- ❏ Fleischman, Sid
- ❏ Fox, Mem
- ❏ Fox, Paula
- ❏ Freedman, Russ.
- ❏ Fritz, Jean
- ❏ Gag, Wanda
- ❏ Galdone, Paul
- ❏ George, Jean Craighead
- ❏ Goble, Paul
- ❏ Hahn, Mary D.
- ❏ Haley, Gail
- ❏ Hamilton, Virginia
- ❏ Henkes, Kevin
- ❏ Henry, Marguerite
- ❏ Hobbs, Will
- ❏ Hopkins, Lee Bennett
- ❏ Hughes, Langston
- ❏ Hyman, Trina Schart
- ❏ Janeczko, Paul
- ❏ Johnson, D.B.
- ❏ Keats, Ezra Jack
- ❏ Kellogg, Steven
- ❏ Kimmel, Eric A.
- ❏ Kjelgaard, J.
- ❏ Konigsburg, E.L.
- ❏ Kurtz, Jane
- ❏ L'Engle, Madeleine
- ❏ Lawlor, Laurie
- ❏ Lawson, Robert
- ❏ Lewis, C. S.
- ❏ Lindgren, Astrid
- ❏ Lobel, Anita
- ❏ Lobel, Arnold
- ❏ Lowry, Lois
- ❏ MacLachlan, Patricia
- ❏ Marshall, James
- ❏ Martin, Bill Jr.
- ❏ Martin, Jacqueline Briggs
- ❏ Mayer, Mercer
- ❏ McCloskey, Robert
- ❏ McKissack, Patricia
- ❏ McPhail, David
- ❏ Milne, A. A.
- ❏ Mora, Pat
- ❏ Most, Bernard
- ❏ Nelson, Kadir
- ❏ O'Dell, Scott
- ❏ Oxenbury, Helen
- ❏ Park, Linda Sue
- ❏ Paterson, Katherine
- ❏ Paulsen, Gary
- ❏ Peck, Richard
- ❏ Peet, Bill
- ❏ Pinkney, Brian
- ❏ Pinkney, Jerry
- ❏ Polacco, Patricia
- ❏ Potter, Beatrix
- ❏ Prelutsky, Jack
- ❏ Ransome, James
- ❏ Rey, H. A.
- ❏ Rey, Margret
- ❏ Ringgold, Faith
- ❏ Rohmann, Eric
- ❏ Ross, Tony
- ❏ Rubel, Nicole
- ❏ Ryan, Pam Muñoz
- ❏ Rylant, Cynthia
- ❏ Sachar, Louis
- ❏ Sachs, Marilyn
- ❏ San Souci, Robert
- ❏ Say, Allen
- ❏ Sayre, April Pulley
- ❏ Scieszka, Jon
- ❏ Sendak, Maurice
- ❏ Seuss, Dr.
- ❏ Shannon, David
- ❏ Sierra, Judy
- ❏ Silverstein, Shel
- ❏ Simon, Seymour
- ❏ Sis, Peter
- ❏ Small, David
- ❏ Smith, Cynthia Leitich
- ❏ Sneve, Virginia Driving Hawk
- ❏ Soentpiet, Chris
- ❏ Spier, Peter
- ❏ Spinelli, Jerry
- ❏ Steptoe, John
- ❏ Stevens, Janet
- ❏ Stevenson, James
- ❏ Taback, Simms
- ❏ Taylor, Mildred
- ❏ Taylor, Theodore
- ❏ Uchida, Yoshiko
- ❏ Van Allsburg, Chris
- ❏ Viorst, Judith
- ❏ Voigt, Cynthia
- ❏ Waber, Bernard
- ❏ Watson, Wendy
- ❏ White, E. B.
- ❏ Wiesner, David
- ❏ Wilder, Laura Ingalls
- ❏ Wiles, Deborah
- ❏ Willard, Nancy
- ❏ Willems, Mo
- ❏ Williams, Vera
- ❏ Wood, Audrey
- ❏ Wood, Don
- ❏ Wright, Betty Ren
- ❏ Yates, Elizabeth
- ❏ Ylvisaker, Anne
- ❏ Yolen, Jane
- ❏ Young, Ed
- ❏ Zemach, Margot

Ideas to Use with Teen Readers

Invite teen readers to take these quizzes with you.

Children's Book Quiz. Quiz Zone. http://bit.ly/Childlitknowledge

Braingle: 'Characters from Children's Literature' Trivia Quiz: http://bit.ly/ChildLitCharacters

Broke by Books. The Ultimate Classic Children's Literature Trivia Quiz: How well do you remember? https://brokebybooks.com/take-the-ultimate-childrens-literature-trivia-quiz Scroll down to the fourth section "And now on to the questions!" 20 questions. Answer key is at the end of the quiz.

Making an Interactive Quiz using Power Point

Ask a student to use the Broke by Books quiz questions (or make up original questions) to create an interactive quiz using power point. For a tutorial watch:

SlideUpLift. (2020, April 29). How to Create an Interactive Quiz in PowerPoint. https://youtu.be/6rBhVEx6eEs

What Is Teen Literature

Once child labor laws came and kept children out of the workforce, and compulsory education laws were enacted, society began to recognize that children were just not little adults. But still there were only two distinct age groups children and adults. But by the end of World War II this changed, at least in the Western world. The in-between stage (those between the age of 12-18) of being a teenager became part of our culture – and then the distinction of being a pre-teenager (ages 8-12). Recognition of this new class of individuals brought about a group of young people who were in school, but they also had leisure time-time for recreation and for mischief.

Over the history of literature, the first books were meant for adults, but for lack of anything else to read, were often read by children. Eventually John Newbery came along and spurred publication for children. So young readers read the scant children's books and then moved directly into adult books. But with the emergence of the teenage class so also grew a desire for books related to teen life. The first few books for teenagers included *A Tree Grows in Brooklyn* (1943) and the shocking *Seventeenth Summer* (1942), plus lots of other sentimental aged-down topics. The emphasis on books that would appeal directly to teenagers did not come until 1967 when S.E. Hinton's *The Outsiders* was published. Hinton's book was quickly followed by Paul Zindel's *The Pigman* (1969). Writing for young adults slowly grew to prominence up to the publication of Robert Cormier's *The Chocolate War* (1974). By then the emergence of the young adult novel (then called adolescent literature) was a thriving part of the publication (and library) world.

Eventually teenagers entered the workforce. They no longer toiled at industrial jobs (now forbidden by child labor laws) but worked at low-paying jobs no one else wanted and reading time decreased despite the increase in publication. Publishers began to actively court readers to the young adult body of literature and expanded the readership group to target "Tweens" – those readers from 8-12. In recent years, the teen culture changed as its desire toward ultimate consumerism required more than just pocket change. Today, most teens are back in the work force doing the low-paid jobs no one else wants in order to pay for the things they want to buy. With less free time, the reading of the young adult novel has declined despite the increase in its production. At the beginning of a new millennium, advertisers have developed a new group of "clients" to whom they are targeting their advertising: the "Tween"-the group that ages 8–12.

Young adult literature is characterized somewhat different than the strictly adult level novel. However, over time the subject and treatment of those subjects have also changed over time and writers are constantly pushing the envelope in terms of how a subject is treated, and especially the subject itself. For example, John Donovan's *I'll Get There, It Better be Worth the Trip* (1969) brought the topic of gay and lesbian teens into YA fiction. The topic is now not a question of "Am I gay?" but rather how is life as a gay teen. The issues faced are dealt with more openly and with a first-person perspective. Acceptance of this topic within the young adult literature world came full-blown when books with gay characters began to be recognized by award lists.

Four books with gay characters have won the Michael L. Printz Award since 1999. And more recently books such as Rainbow Boys (2001) by Alex Sanchez and Boy Meets Boy (2003) by David Levithan. Other ground-breaking subjects have been addressed by such writers as Laurie Halse Anderson who successfully wrote about a 14-year-old girl, Melinda Sordino, who battles depression after being raped by an older teen. *Speak* (1999) has sold more than 3 million copies and continues to be a popular read. These topics, once taboo in the world of teen literature began to emerge as topics teens wanted (and needed) to read about.

Characteristics of a Teen Novel

So, what defines young adult literature? There will be differences of opinion but in general these are the general elements that determine young adult literature versus children's or adult literature.

- Books are written about and for young adults between the ages of 12 and 18.
- Books in the young adult lexicon, includes those borrowed from children's literature or adult literature, and in many forms, i.e. comics, magna, Internet sites, or teen generated writings including fan fiction.
- Includes some classics that while not written for teens specifically are deemed necessary reads prior to entering adulthood, i.e. classics such as Shakespeare.
- A developing body of interesting Nonfiction both aimed at teenagers, adopted by teens from the adult world, or forced upon teens in school, including library databases and research tools on the Internet
- The broad category of literature also includes music, dancing, movies, YouTube, and television adopted by teenagers as their own.
- YA literature also the part of high culture including drama, art, music, dancing, television, and the Internet that adults think teenagers should experience.

While the characteristics listed below are typical of most young adult novels, the absence of one characteristic does not necessarily keep the novel from being designated as being part of this body of literature. Many books are characterized by the emotional and social appeal to young adults.

- Written from the perspective of a young adult character (often the narrative is written in first person).
- Majority/main characters are approximately the age of the intended reader (or slightly older).
- Characters engaged in activities with which young readers can identify.
- Must include characters that the reader will care about.
- Ends with a sense of hope.
- Young person responsible for own destiny. Formula fiction and much of the mainstream fiction for young adults finds a method of absenting the parents from the picture so that the youthful characters can figure out and be responsible for solving their own problems.
- Fast-paced narratives reach for fast action and powerful images.

- Much of the literature deals with real-life and realistic teen experiences with gangs, sexual experiences, teen problems, conflict, relationships, rebellion, and other problems teens often encounter.

But even as we list these characteristics, we recognize that these characteristics are often pushed to the edge by the writer. In the past decade, several popular books are thought to end unhappily. Those titles include The Fault in Our Stars (2012) by John Green, and Eleanor & Park (2012) by Rainbow Rowell, and Heartless (2016) by Marissa Meyer - thus these books might be considered to abandon the criteria of ending with a sense of hope. And of course, books such as Neverwhere (1996) by Neil Gaiman and his depiction of the city under London symbolically depicts teens who have fallen between the cracks but abandons realistic life as teens know it. Other books which abandoned realism followed and appealed to the teen reader because of the other criteria they embodied. The absence of one characteristic does not remove a book that fits the majority of the other characteristics.

Teen Novels Too Good To Miss: 1960–2019

1960s

Knowles, John. *A Separate Peace.*
Lee, Harper. *To Kill A Mockingbird.*
L'Engle, Madeleine. *A Wrinkle in Time.*
Hinton, S.E. *The Outsiders.*
Lipsyte, Robert. *The Contender.*
Potok, Chaim. *The Chosen.*
Zindel, Paul. *The Pigman.*
Cleaver, Vera and Bill. *Where the Lilies Bloom.*
Armstrong, William. *Sounder.*

1970s

Plath, Sylvia. *The Bell Jar.*
Gaines, Ernest. *The Autobiography of Miss Jane Pittman.*
Anonymous. *Go Ask Alice.* - Actual author is Beatrice Sparks
Mathis, Sharon Bell. *A Teacup Full of Roses.*
Potok, Chaim. *My Name is Asher Lev.*
White, Robb. *Deathwatch.*
Kerr, M.E. *Dinky Hocker Shoots Smack.*
Green, Betty. *Summer of My German Soldier.*
Childress, Alice. *A Hero Ain't Nothin' But A Sandwich.*
Peck, Robert Newton. *A Day No Pigs Would Die.*
Sleator, William. *House of Stairs.*
Cormier, Robert. *The Chocolate War.*
Blume, Judy. *Forever.*
Yep, Lawrence. *Dragonwings.*
Guest, Judith. *Ordinary People.*
Peck, Richard. *Are You in the House Alone?*
McCaffrey, Anne. *Dragonsong.*
Cormier, Robert. *I Am the Cheese.*
Duncan, Lois. *Killing Mr. Griffin.*
McKinley, Robin. *Beauty: Retelling...*

1980s

Adams, Douglas. *A Hitchhiker's Guide to the Galaxy.*
Walker, Alice. *The Color Purple.*
Cisneros, Sandra. *The House on Mango Street.*

Voigt, Cynthia. *Dicey's Song.*
Paulsen, Gary. *Dogsong.*
Card, Orson Scott. *Ender's Game.*
Paulsen, Gary. *Hatchet.*
Myers, Walter Dean. *Fallen Angels.*

1990s

Avi. *The True Confessions of Charlotte Doyle.*
Lowry, Lois. *The Giver.*
Crutcher, Chris. *Ironman.*
Pullman, Philip. *The Golden Compass.*
Thomas, Rob. *Rats Saw God.*
Hesse, Karen. *Out of the Dust.*
Levine, Gale Carson. *Ella Enchanted.*
Soto, Gary. *Buried Onions.*
Sachar, Louis. *Holes.*
Hickham, Homer. *Rocket Boys/October Sky.*
Rowling, J.K. *Harry Potter and the Sorcerer's Stone.*
Myers, Walter Dean. *Monster.*
Curtis, Christopher Paul. *The Watson's Go to Birmingham.*
Curtis, Christopher Paul. *Bud, Not Buddy.*

2000s

Anderson, Laurie Halse. *Speak.*
DiCamillo, Kate. *Because of Winn-Dixie.*
Philbrick, Rodman. *The Last Book in the Universe.*
Peck, Richard. *A Year Down Yonder.*
Crutcher, Chris. *Whale Talk.*
Howe, James. *The Misfits.*
Brashares, Ann. *Sisterhood of the Traveling Pants.*
Taylor, Mildred. *The Land.*
Park, Linda Sue. *A Single Shard.*

Giff, Patricia Reilly. *Pictures of Hollis Woods.*
Avi. *Crispin: The Cross of Lead.*
Johnson, Angela. *The First Part Last.*
Moriarty, Jaclyn. *The Year of Secret Assignments.*
Paolini, Christopher. *Eragon.*
Farmer, Nancy. *House of the Scorpion.*
Riordan, Rick. *The Lightning Thief.*
Sonnenblick, Jordan. *Notes from the Midnight Driver.*
Schmidt, Gary D. *The Wednesday Wars.*
Collins, Suzanne. *The Hunger Games.*
Applet, Kathi and David Small. *The Underneath.*
Frost, Helen. *Crossing Stones.*
Korman, Gordon. *Pop.*
McCormick, Patricia. *Purple Heart.*
Smith, Sherri L. *Flygirl.*

2010s

Bray, Libba *Going Bovine.*
Murray, Liz. *Breaking Night.*
Donoghue, Emma. *Room.*
Green, John and Levithan, David. *Will Grayson, Will Grayson.*
Collins, Suzanne. *Mockingjay.*
Perkins, Stephanie. *Anna and the French Kiss.*
Sepetys, Ruta. *Between Shades of Gray.*
Whaley, Corey. *Where Things Come Back.*
Mafi, Tahereh. *Shatter Me.*
Lu, Marie. *Legend.*
Green, John. *The Fault in Our Stars.*

Danforth, Emily M. *The Miseducation of Cameron Post.*
Maas, Sarah J. *Throne of Glass.*
Rowell, Rainbow. *Fangirl.*
Han, Jenny. *To All the Boys I've Loved Before.*
Lockhart, E. *We Were Liars.*
Niven, Jennifer. *All the Bright Places.*
Albertalli, Becky. *Simon vs. The homo Sapiens Agenda.*
Tahir, Sabaa. *An Ember in the Ashes.*
Murphy, Julie. *Dumplin'.*
Nijkamp, Marieke. *This Is Where It Ends*
Chokshi, Roshani. *The Star-Touched Queen*
Yoon, Nicola. *The Sun Is Also a Star.*
Silvera, Adam. *The Both Die at the End.*
Thomas, Angie. *The Hate U Give.*
Lee, Mackenzi. *The Gentleman's Guide to Vice and Virtue.*
Lee, Stacey. *The Downstairs Girl.*
Stone, Nic. *Dear Martin.*
Reynolds, Jason. *Long Way Down.*
Acevedo, Elizabeth. *The Poet X.*
Adeyemi, Tomi. *Children of Blood and Bone.*
Pan, Emily X.R. *The Astonishing Color of After.*
Ribay, Randy. *Patron Saints of Nothing.*

These books listed are not necessary the award list books from that decade or year. They are just one person's idea of the books that they think are the best. Any one person who creates a list will find their own personal favorites listed on that list.

Ideas to Use with Teen Readers

Invite teen readers to create a young adult quiz.

As examples, use the quizzes for children's literature.

Making an Interactive Quiz using Power Point. For a tutorial watch:
SlideUpLift. (2020, April 29). How to Create an Interactive Quiz in PowerPoint. https://youtu.be/6rBhVEx6eEs

Significant Authors

Several authors have emerged in the young adult field. Among these authors are the winners of the Margaret A. Edwards Award. The Edwards Award honors authors who have contributed significantly to the body of young adult literature. Consult the Awards list for specific titles cited. The author list includes S.E. Hinton who was the first to be given this award.

Winners of the Margaret A. Edwards Award 2021- 2005

- Kekla Magoon (2021)
- M. T. Anderson (2019)
- Angela Johnson (2018)
- Sarah Dessen (2017)
- David Levithan (2016)
- Sarah M. Draper (2015)
- Markus Zusak (2014)
- Tamora Pierce (2013)
- Susan Cooper (2012)
- Sir Terry Prachett (2011)
- Jim Murphy (2010)
- Laurie Halse Anderson (2009)
- Orson Scott Card (2008)
- Lois Lowry (2007)
- Jacqueline Woodson (2006)
- Francesca Lia Block (2005)

See a complete list of winning authors and books at YALSA. (1996-2021). *Margaret A. Edwards Award.* http://www.ala.org/yalsa/edwards

In the Spotlight: Steve Sheinkin

Steve Sheinkin

The selection of Steve Sheinkin as the 2020 Margaret A. Edwards award winner is significant in that his reputation as a young adult writer is in the realm of well-researched Nonfiction (information) books.

    Bomb: The Race to Build – and Steal – the World's Most Dangerous Weapon. Roaring Brook Press, 2012.
    Lincoln's Grave Robbers. Scholastic Focus, 2013.
    The Notorious Benedict Arnold: A True Story of Adventure, Heroism, & Treachery. Roaring Brook Press, 2010.
    The Port Chicago 50: Disaster, Mutiny, and the Fight for Civil Rights. Roaring Brook Press, 2014.

For more information about the author Steve Sheinkin go to his website at http://www.stevesheinkin.com

ABOUT

You know the part about the textbook writing (full confession on file here). So let's move on to other stuff about me.

I was born in Brooklyn, NY, and my family lived in Mississippi and Colorado before moving back to New York and settling in the suburbs north of New York City. As a kid my favorite books were action stories and outdoor adventures: sea stories, searches for buried treasure, sharks eating people... that kind of thing. Probably my all-time favorite was a book called *Mutiny on the Bounty*, a novel based on the true story of a famous mutiny aboard a British ship in the late 1700s.

I went to Syracuse University and studied communications

Awards and Recognition

The American Library Association (ALA), and its subdivisions, sponsor many of the prestigious awards given to books for young readers (ages 12-18). Among the most revered for young adult literature is the Michael L. Printz Award established in 2000 and the John Newbery medal. The Newbery Award was first awarded in 1922 to honor excellence in children's literature (with children being defined as ages 8–14). The Newbery Award was funded by Frederic G. Melcher and administered from the beginning by the ALA. Several other awards have been established honoring books and authors in the area of young adult literature.

Some of those awards recognize individual awards while others recognize a body of work by a specific author. Most of the awards established by the ALA or the National Council of the Teachers of English are chosen based on literary merit. However, individual state awards are most often guided by popular appeal to readers and are often chosen directly by the target audience of readers.

The Michael L. Printz Award

The Michael L. Printz award winners have included *Looking for Alaska* by John Green (Dutton, 2005), which was made into a Hulu original movie, airing first in 2019.

Recent award winners include:
- 2021: *Everything Sad is Untrue (a true story)* by Daniel Nayeri (Arthur A. Levine)
- 2020: *Dig* by AS King (Dutton).
- 2019: *The Poet X* by Elizabeth Acevedo (HarperTeen)
- 2018: *We Are Okay* by Nina LaCour (Dutton)
- 2017: March by John Lewis, Andrew Aydin, and Nate Powell (Top Shelf)

The John Newbery Award

The John Newbery Award has been given since 1922. The focus has changed from didacticism to books that seem to truly reflect the interests (along with literary merit) of readers. The books are not restricted by age level but only by criteria regarding the author and language, and publication date. Books eligible include everything from picture books to full-length novels and books of information. The critical element being that the book is deemed to be the most distinguished contribution to American Literature, published in the preceding year.

The most recent decade of award winners include:
- 2021: *When You Trap a Tiger* by Tae Keller (Random House Children's Books)
- 2020: *New Kid*, written and illustrated by Jerry Craft (HarperCollins)
- 2019: *Merci Suárez Changes Gears*, written by Meg Medina (Candlewick)
- 2018: *Hello, Universe* by Erin Entrada Kelly (Greenwillow Books)
- 2017: *The Girl Who Drank the Moon* by Kelly Barnhill (Algonquin Young Readers/Workman)
- 2016: *Last Stop on Market Street* by Matt de la Peña (G.P. Putnam's Sons)
- 2015: *The Crossover* by Kwame Alexander (Houghton Mifflin Harcourt)
- 2014: *Flora & Ulysses: The Illuminated Adventures* by Kate DiCamillo (Candlewick)
- 2013: *The One and Only Ivan* by Katherine Applegate (HarperCollins)
- 2012: *Dead End in Norvelt* by Jack Gantos (Farrar Straus Giroux)

Multicultural Awards

In recent decades there have been several awards established to focus on diverse writers and books. Often under-represented in the realm of prestigious awards, several councils or subdivisions within the ALA or other organizations sought to establish awards that focused on the diverse population or type of books that they sought to elevate into the mainstream of the YA lexicon. The Ethnic & Multicultural Information Exchange Round Table (EMIERT) of the ALA (http://www.ala.org/rt/emiert) is the official sponsor of many of these awards.

Coretta Scott King Award

The Coretta Scott King (CSK) award is presented to an author (or illustrator) of African descent who promotes understanding of the American dream. The award was established in 1970. Past winners include: Heart and Soul: The Story of America and African Americans by Kadir Nelson and Elijah of Buxton by Christopher Paul Curtis. In 2020 the author winner was Jerry Craft for his graphic novel New Kid (HarperCollins, 2019); and Kadir Nelson was given the 2020 illustrator award for Kwame Alexander's *The Undefeated* (Versity/Houghton Mifflin, 2019). In 2021 Jacqueline Woodson was an author award recipient for Before the Ever After (Nancy Paulsen Books). Frank Morrison's illustrations for Carole Boston Weatherford's *Respect: Aretha Franklin, the Queen of Soul* earned Morrison a CSK award for illustration.

The Coretta Scott King-(CSK) Virginia Hamilton Award for Lifetime Achievement

The CSK lifetime achievement award was established in 2010 and awarded every two years. During the years between, an educator is named in recognition of the award winner's contributions to the field as a practitioner. The first author award winner was Walter Dean Myers and in 2012, the winner was Ashley Bryan. In 2014, Patricia and Fredrick McKissack were honored. In 2016, Jerry Pinkney, 2018 Eloise Greenfield and in 2020, Mildred D. Taylor. The Ethnic & Multicultural Information Exchange Round Table (EMIERT) of the ALA (http://www.ala.org/rt/emiert) is the official administrator of the CSK awards.

The Pura Belpré award

The Pura Belpré Award honoring a Latino/a that best represents and celebrates the Latino culture became an annual award in 2009. The award is administered by the Association for Library Service to Children (ALSC) a division of ALA. Past winners include **Under the Mesquite** by Guadalupe Garcia McCall, *Return to Sender* by Julia Alvarez, and in 2020 the author award winner was Carlos Hernandez for *Sal and Gabi Break the Universe* (Hyperion, 2019). 2021 marked the first year that the Pura Belpré award was given in a young adult category. The 2021 award winner in the YA division was Yamile Saied Méndez, author of *Furia* (Algonquin Young Readers).

The American Indian Youth Award

The American Indian Youth Award seeks to honor the very best writing and illustrations of books by and about Native Americans and indigenous people of North America. The award is presented in each of three categories- picture book, middle school, and young adult. The first award winner (2006) in the YA category was Joseph Bruchac for *Hidden Roots* (Scholastic, 2004). The award is given in each even numbered year. The most recent award (2020) was presented to Cynthia Leitich Smith for *Hearts Unbroken*. (Candlewick Press, 2018). Smith has also recently been named as the editor of a new Native-focused publication imprint for HarperCollins Children's books. The imprint Heartdrum launches in Winter 2021. Smith is a member of the Muscogee Creek Nation and the author of several books that reflect the diversity of Native people. Of some significance is that the Randolph Caldecott Award – given annually for the most distinguish illustrated book, was given in 2021 to Michaela Goade, the illustrator for Carole Lindstrom's book *We Are Water Protectors* (Roaring Brook Press, 2020). Both Goade and the subject of the book are deeply connected to the Indigenous people in North America.

Awards Sponsored by ALA Divisions or Others

Few books of information have been honored with the major awards: four biographies, two books of poetry (including Paul Fleischman's *Joyful Noise: Poems for Two Voices* in 1989), and one book of history have garnered the Newbery Award.

Robert F. Sibert Award

In 2001 ALA members responded to the growing oversight by establishing the Robert F. Sibert Award to celebrate the best informational book published in the preceding year. Past winners have included *An American Plague: The True and Terrifying Story of the Yellow Fever Epidemic of 1795* by Jim Murphy (2004) and *Almost Astronauts: 13 Women Who Dared to Dream* by Tanya Lee Stone (2010). In 2019, Joyce Sidman was given the award for *The Girl Who Drew Butterflies: How Maria Merian's Art Changed Science* (Houghton Mifflin Harcourt, 2018). In 2020, the award went to *Fry Bread: A Native America Family Story* by Kevin Noble Maillard, illustrated by Juana Martinez-Neal (Roaring Brook Press, 2019). Both the 2019 and 2020 are pictures books that have great utility for use with young adult readers.

Odyssey Award for audio books

In 2008, ALSC and YALSA named the first Odyssey winner for excellence in audio books for children/young adults. In 2020 the award when to the full-cast audio version of Jarrett J. Krosoczka's biographical, *Hey, Kiddo: How I Lost My Mother, Found My Father, and Dealt with Family Addiction*, produced by Scholastic Audiobooks.

Prestigious awards

These awards are among the most prestigious include the following awards from the ALA:

    Michael L. Printz Award
    John Newbery
    Robert F. Sibert Award
    Margaret A. Edwards
    Coretta Scott King – Virginia Hamilton
    Coretta Scott King
    Schneider Family Book Award
    Pura Belpré

ALA awards and those from divisions and councils within the ALA organization are generally named during the ALA mid-winter conference. The actual award is presented to recipients during the annual ALA conference each year during the summer (generally June or July) of each year.

Other Awards

ALA, and its various divisions, are not the only organizations recognizing outstanding young adult books. The Assembly on Literature for Adolescents (ALAN) honors an individual who has made an outstanding contribution to the field of young adult literature. The ALAN award is typically awarded during the annual National Council of Teachers of English (NCTE) conference. Previous winners have included: Michael Cart, John Green, and Nikki Grimes. ALAN Award winners listed at http://www.alan-ya.org.

The Boston Globe-Horn Book Awards are jointly sponsored by the Boston Globe and the Horn Book and announced in October of each year. The categories include picture books, fiction and poetry, and nonfiction. The 2020 winner in fiction and poetry is Kacen Callender for *King and the Dragon Flies* (Scholastic), a book for intermediate and middle school readers. In the nonfiction category the winning title was Infinite Hope: *A Black Artist's Journey from World War II to Peace* (Dlougy/Atheneum), an autobiographical book written and illustrated by Ashley Bryan for middle school/high school readers. It is significant that the winning title in the nonfiction section was a biography and the two honor books were a memoir and another biography. *Ordinary Hazards: A Memoir* by Nikki Grimes (Wordsong/Boyds Mills) and *It Began with a Page: How Gyo Fujikawa Drew the* Way by Kyo Maclear (Harper/HarperCollins) were both honored in 2020.
http://www.hbook.com/boston-globe-horn-book-awards/

National Book Awards-Young People's Literature are presented each year and includes a winner, finalists, and the organization publishes a longlist of the titles considered for the award. In 2020 the winner was *King and the Dragonflies* by Kacen Callender (Scholastic). The award is announced in November. https://www.nationalbook.org/

Golden Kite Award is presented by the Society of Children's Book Writers & Illustrators (SCWBI). It is an award given, since 1973, by peers for outstanding work in seven categories including: Young Adult Fiction and Nonfiction Text for Older Readers. Recent winners include *Boots on the Ground* by Elizabeth Partridge (Viking); and Jane Yolen has been honored for *Mapping the Bones* (Philomel). https://www.scbwi.org/

The Charlotte Huck Award which was established in 2014 focus on transformative texts that instills compassion, imagination, and wonder. The 2021 winner*: I Am Every Good Thing* by Derrick Barnes, Illustrated by Gordon C. James (Nancy Paulsen Books). Award is administered by the National Council of the Teachers of English.

The Orbis Pictus Award was established in 1989 and is the oldest children's book award for nonfiction. The 2021 Winner: *Above the Rim: How Elgin Baylor Changed Basketball* by Jen Bryant; illustrated by Frank Morrison (Abrams). Award is administered by the National Council of the Teachers of English.

NCTE Award for Excellence in Poetry for Children has been given since 1977. The award given by the National Council of the Teachers of English is not restricted by the age group intended as the audience of the book, nor by format. Some years the books/author chosen might be targeted to any relevant age group other than adult. In 2021 Janet S. Wong was given the NCTE Award for Excellence in Poetry for Children.

State and Regional Choice Awards

Most often the state and regional awards are choice awards selected through a combination of teens and adults. Nominations come from teens, and adult professionals (librarians and classroom teachers) narrow the list. Teens read and vote for the winner from the narrowed list. Selected State/Regional Choice Awards-Gateway (links) to websites available at http://www.mcbookwords.com/authorlinks/bookawards.html

In the Spotlight: Laurie Halse Anderson

Laurie Halse Anderson

Laurie Halse Anderson has been honored with the Margaret A. Edwards Award in recognition of her powerful novels: *Catalyst*; *Fever 1793*; and *Speak*. She has written other powerful novels: *Chains* (slavery during the Revolutionary War). period. *Forge* (2010) continues the story started in *Chains*.

Catching up with Anderson's writing:

The Impossible Knife of Memory (2014) Anderson focuses on the Iraq war and a soldier's PTSD. *Speak* has been released in a 20th anniversary edition, and also issued as a graphic novel with illustrations by Emily Carroll – *Speak: The Graphic Novel* (Farrar, Straus and Giroux, 2018).

Anderson's 2020 title is *Wonder Woman: Tempest Tossed,* with art by Leila Del Duca (DC Comics, 2020). Reviews of the book refer to the book as reimagining the origins of Wonder Woman, all while speaking of refugee experiences, teenage activism, and the teen experience of finding love and stimulating change.

Keep up with Anderson's writing adventures on Twitter, twitter.com/halseanderson and on her website at:

https://madwomanintheforest.com

**In the Spotlight: Kekla Magoon–
2021 Margaret A. Edwards Award winner**

Kekla Magoon

Each year a young adult author is honored for their significant and lasting contribution to the lexicon of literature for teens. Kekla Magoon was honored in 2021 with this award in recognition of: *X: A Novel* (co-written by Ilyasah Shabazz – Malcolm X's daughter, Candlewick Press), *How It Went Down* (Henry Holt & Co.); *The Rock and the River* (Aladdin); and *Fire in the Streets* (Aladdin).

Magoon was born in Michigan, lived several childhood years in Cameroon (where her dad grew up), but says she grew up in Fort Wayne, Indiana where she wrote her first novel in high school. Several degrees later, and several jobs as a fund raiser for various organizations, Magoon now lives in Vermont where she is a member of the faculty at the Vermont College of Fine Arts. In 2019, the second book in the How It Went Down Series, *Light It Up*, was published by Henry Holt & Company. 2021 brought *The Highest Tribute: Thurgood Marshall's Life, Leadership, and Legacy* and a title in Chelsey Clinton's "She Persisted" series: *Ruby Bridges*.

Revolution in Our Time: The Black Panther Party's Promise to the People (Candlewick, 2021) examines the revolutionary socialist movement that drew thousands of members (mostly women) during the Civil Rights era.

Learn more about Kekla Magoon on her website at http://www.keklamagoon.com.

Kekla Magoon's 2021 book *Revolution in Our Time: The Black Panther Party's Promise to the People* examines the long history of the struggle for a voice from slavery to Black Lives Matter.

Collection Development and Selection

One of the most important professional activities a teacher or librarian can and should do in regard to selection of literature that will be recommended to young readers is to thoroughly vet the selection for accuracy, lack of bias, and literary merit. There are many books being self-published and self-promoted. In general, those selections have not been vetted by anyone other than a small group of the author's associates and friends. Some have garnered much acclaim but the majority fall short. Young readers should be offered the best we can offer.

Generally, that means leading teens to materials that will interest them, is well written, and has value to the reader. Online sites often have reviews written by consumers who pan a book for reasons that are very personal to them. Some amateur reviewers on sales sites miss the purpose of the book. In the children's arena: Karen Katz wrote and illustrated a delightful interactive book intended for infants, *Where Is Baby's Belly Button?* (Little Simon, 2000). The reviewer said, "There is no mystery. There is no twist. Baby's belly button is right where it's suppose (sic) to be, on Baby's stomach. Right where it clearly SHOWS you it is on the COVER OF THE BOOK." And then the reviewer went on to say, "…you would have to be an infant to not immediately understand where Baby's belly button is." Well, yes, that is the intent of the book. Not too difficult to understand that this reviewer clearly wasn't familiar with the idea of interactive concept books for the very young reader or that the intended audience was an infant, not adult reviewers.

But it is not only the online amateurs that sometimes miss the mark with concepts and purpose of a book. Some established reviewing sources use volunteer reviewers as well. And it is good to know about the expertise of the reviewer. A reference book intended to connect common food dishes to episodes in middle school/YA books (and a myriad of information about each author) was panned by a *School Library Journal* reviewer who said, "Not to imply that children's authors are unhealthy eaters, but desserts are plentiful and most of the entries will not accommodate a health-conscious diet." Clearly the book's purpose was far from one that was intended to promote a healthy diet, or even actually making the dish – it was a reference book about authors that used a common connection to food to comment on episodes in the books the author wrote, or personal anecdotes about the author's life. But this reviewer wanted a health-conscious recipe book. Professional reviewers generally know that they should review the book they have in their hand not the book the reviewer thinks the author should have written.

> *The Guardian* (2014, September 14). headline. https://www.theguardian.com/childrens-books-site/2014/sep/06/review-the-giver-lois-lowry (Online).

When first published some reviewers criticized the ambiguity of Lois Lowry's ending to her award-winning novel, The Giver (1993). Some reviewers wanted the ending tied up in a secure and complete resolution. Later when the book was made into a well-received movie (2014) a reviewer for The Guardian, said "The ending of The Giver is powerful because we have a choice in what it means" (2014). Sometimes time changes the way we view a book or the lens through which we view a title. That was certainly true in 2021, regarding the books by Theodor Seuss Geisel. Times change the way we do look at a specific book. It is our role to curate the best selection of titles for young adult readers, based on what we know now. What we assumed or knew (or didn't know) in the past should not determine what we read now.

In general, those who justify keeping out-of-date materials, books that would not ever be selected today, by saying things such as "they are good example to use in the teachable moment." Or perhaps "Those books need to be discussed and the discussion will benefit readers in a way that cannot be duplicated otherwise." Philosophically, many will agree with those statements but... then one much ask the tough questions: How do those discussions occur? Are the discussions part of the curriculum or are they left to happenstance? Who is involved in those discussions? Who is in charge of monitoring who "needs" to have those discussions? Is it better to put a negative example in front of readers and say this is not right; or is it better to model the appropriate behavior and inclusive attitudes as the norm. Does offering negative examples tend to normalize the behavior? At what age do young learners question behavior modeled in books, or do they accept the behavior as acceptable and normal at any age? All questions that we need to think about.

In a Bookbub compilation of funniest online book reviews (Schlesinger, 2020) *we* see that Madeline wants someone to explain the plot of this book (or why there is no plot) and explain why people think it is so amazing. She's reviewing *The Catcher in the Rye* by J.D. Salinger. Another reviewer simply says of *Wuthering Heights* by Emily Brontë, "Vile people are mean to one another. The end."

Bookbub
Schlesinger, Tara Sonin. (2020, March 18). 17 of the Funniest Online Book Reviews. *Bookbub* (Online).
https://www.bookbub.com/blog/funniest-online-book-reviews)

Another reviewer judged a book (*Twilight* by Stephenie Meyer) by its cover and was disappointed. "MISLEADING COVER – with the cover art, you'd think that this is a gothic novel. A big no!"

Needless to say, certified librarians have dealt with the issue of selection in courses intended to help them examine the pros and cons of relying on reviews and patron opinions, their community needs, and maintaining a balanced collection. In general, school librarians concentrate more on collections that support the school's curriculum while public librarians see teen needs in a larger framework of community information needs. Classroom teachers do not have that same level of global responsibility but in a sense their selection concerns are even greater as many of the books they select are often directly recommended to readers, and often are an integral part of the prescribed curriculum. In a sense all educators stand in a loco parentis role. This presents an additional element to our choices. From a teen's point of view – they just want the books that they are interested in reading. It is our job to find them, offer them, and encourage reading.

In terms of selecting books, we can only do our best. However, we must be aware of the resources and their limits and the expertise they employ. Most of us should be able to recognize the misguided reviews by those who are expressing a very personal opinion about a book rather than actually assessing the book itself. But even professional reviewing sources have limitations. Here are some notes that might be helpful.

Professional Reviewing Sources: A Selected list

VOYA (Voices of Youth Advocates) magazine.

- Published six times a year.
- Reviews programs and facilities, but primary focus is materials, i.e. books – including graphic novels, serial publications, and the Internet
- Reviews are written by volunteers and teens
- Reviews include a popularity rating as well as a quality rating
- Since volunteers are reviewers there is an uneven quality in the reviews.

School Library Journal

- Reviews materials for all ages, with a category for 5th grade and up, and adult books for young adult readers, reference materials, audio books, and other media.
- Has employed editors, reviews are largely written by volunteer reviewers
- Since volunteer educators are reviewers there is an uneven quality in the reviews.

Booklist

- Professional reviewers
- Only reviews materials that warrant a positive review.
- Reviews are more annotative in nature.
- Does not waste space reviewing materials that would get a negative review.

Kirkus Reviews

- Focus is on public libraries
- Reviewers are anonymous and paid but are mostly working professionals.
- The anonymity allows reviews to be sharper and more direct.
- Includes positive and negative reviews.

School Library Connection

- A merged publication – School Library Monthly and Library Media Connection.
- Uses volunteer reviewers – often educators/librarians, and a panel of working professionals who serve as editors and advisory board.
- Categories for all ages of school-aged readers
- A bi-monthly publication
- Focus is on curriculum applications

Publishers Weekly

- Is an international news publication (print and online)
- Is a news periodical for the publishing and bookselling industry
- Includes book reviews, often prepublication
- Business news often announces book deals and forthcoming titles
- Has bestseller lists
- Provides commentary and feature article about topics of interest, i.e. most-read children's and YA stories, Book Deals.

Horn Book for Children

- Does have reviews for older readers; focus is on the younger reader
- Professional reviews
- Articles about books and authors
- Reprints annually the acceptance award speeches of the major award recipients, i.e. Caldecott, Newbery, Printz Award.

Amazon and Barnes & Noble (Internet sites)

- Pays for professional review reprint rights from many of the sources listed above.
- Includes publisher's annotations about the book, and sometimes includes an official synopsis from the bookseller.
- Often has access to a short biographical sketch or to an author's page uploaded by the respective author.

The customer reviews should not be considered on par with the professional reviews reprinted by arrangement with the professional reviewing sources. Bibliographic information on these sites is often incorrect (publisher, copyright date, and so forth.

Internet Sites

Some internet sites provide book lists, reviews, author interviews, and author information. Check out these sites

- Reading Rants-- http://www.readingrants.org/
  The site has been up for over 20 years commenting on books and provides lists and commentary about all things literary. Long-time project of Jennifer Hubert, a middle school librarian at a progressive independent school in Manhattan. Sign up for e-mail updates.
- Richie's Picks -- http://richiespicks.com
  This is a wiki site that has Richie Partington sharing his picks in terms of books – mostly YA titles. He has an index of his reviews by alphabetical sections. He has a Facebook page, and has over 2000 reviews on Good Reads. For a time, he was an associate lecturer at San Jose State University in California, School of Library and Information Science (SLIS).
- Goodreads -- https://www.goodreads.com/
  A site that generates many lists based on reviews from readers who regularly use and contribute to the site. The site collects comments and allows visitors to set their own reading goals and challenges, to track their progress, to recommend books. A search for a subject will yield lists to explore. As with all user contributors the reviews and comments are uneven depending on the lens through which the reader is viewing the book.

Ideas to Use with Teen Readers

Blogs that Might be of Interest

Feedspot hosts a blog that lists the Top 100 Young Adult Book Blogs and Websites to Follow.
Access this list at https://blog.feedspot.com/young_adult_book_blogs/ .
Ask readers to visit the *Feedspot* list, explore one of the listed blogs, and write a review of the blog they have explored.

School and Public Library Cooperation in a Teen World

Libraries are libraries – whether public or school based. And most patrons view the institutions as being the same only differing in location and space. True, there are similarities in function and mission. Both seek to provide literacy services to their patrons. However, there are vast differences.

School Libraries

Until the 1960s, school libraries were virtually non-existent. If teachers in schools had access to libraries, it was generally a classroom library with relatively few titles. By the 1970s many urban schools and some rural schools had begun to develop central libraries; recognizing that a central library could expand the availability of books to students, without the unnecessary duplication that seemed to be inherent in establishing classroom libraries. In addition, classroom libraries were not equipped to maintain inventory control nor reliably allow access for home use. Anecdotes testify to the problems brought about with classroom libraries that lacked control and a balanced selection process.

One such situation occurred in a school that had a well-stocked and functioning central library as well as classroom libraries that had been established in prior years and still not dismantled. The teacher in the classroom came to the central library requesting a specific title: *Nadia the Willful* by Sue Alexander. The title was not in the central library's collection. The teacher was very upset that the central library did not have the title, as they were sure it had been in the collection the previous year. The trade book had been used in a compare/contrast exercise with a selection in the 7th grade literature compilation text. The teacher was less than pleasant inferring that the librarian had weeded a perfectly good title that several teachers in the building used regularly. The teacher eventually borrowed a copy of the book from a fellow teacher who had the title in their classroom library. A month or so later, the teacher's classroom associate reported that the teacher had actually found the title in question in their own classroom library – stuck on a closet shelf. This anecdote exemplifies two problems:

- Money spent in the duplication of the same title for several classrooms (and used just once or twice a year).
- Lack of control of those titles that are in the classroom.

Multiply this many times over and there is a huge waste of time, money, and actually of books.

Another incident occurred when an advanced placement (AP) literature teacher at the secondary level had a classroom library, funded in part by the school parent organization. The books were selected by the specific AP teacher. When the students complained about the titles available and the fact that they wanted to select more interesting titles from the high school's central library, the teacher denied their request. The reasoning:

- There were 100 or so titles in the classroom library
- The teacher had read those 100 titles and she needed to have read the titles in order to create questions that would help her determine if the student had actually read the book or not.

The problem here of course is that the 100 titles were all ones that mirrored the teacher's interests and preferences for reading. The actual subjects were very limited. Historical fiction was completely absent as was any title with a science theme. Sports themed titles were minimal, and there were no informational titles. Biographies were available but the subjects featured people that were over exposed throughout the school years – and none that featured any subjects that infused a different degree of interest or a new and interesting perspective on a familiar person's life. Generally, the collection was devoid of diverse topics or subjects. In short, the students were not at all interested in the titles that the teacher was interested in reading. These students were high-level students who were interested in many aspects of research, exploration, and so forth – and the meager collection in the classroom did not address many of those interests.

Brian Seto McGrath addresses the concerns regarding the pros and cons of maintaining both classroom libraries and a viable central library. Don't miss this article from the *School Library Journal*.

McGrath, Brian Seto. (2018, September 11). Love Them or Hate Them, Classroom Libraries Can Provide Partnership Opportunities. (Online) http://bit.ly/schoollibraries101

School libraries have a focus that differs from that of public libraries. Whereas both seek to maintain an up-to-date balanced collection that serves their respective patrons. However, school libraries have a task of directly serving students with school assignments, collaborating with teachers to identify materials that complement the assignments they create to meet curriculum standards (goals and objectives), and establishing a collection that supports the school's curriculum at each level, while maintaining a balanced perspective of any subjects in the curriculum, providing both fiction and informational titles. In addition, the librarian is charged with providing books that promote reading for enjoyment and which also allows patrons to learn, to be entertained, and to develop a deeper understanding of a particular topic. The books selected must offer a balance of depth of content and readability so as to facilitate the patrons' development of reading comprehension and fluency, expanding vocabulary, and expanding awareness of writing techniques. School libraries are also tasked with organizing digital databases for their school, databases that provide access to hundreds of research aids for students seeking entertainment and information.

There is much information regarding the support of reading achievement by way of centralized school libraries, libraries that are staffed with certified librarians, and supported with clerical help, and a budget to develop a suitable collection.

Citations or links to research regarding the impact of certified librarians and curated central libraries are available on various sites on the Internet.

> Lance, Keith Curry, and Kachel, Debra E. (2018, Mar 26) Why school librarians matter: What years of research tell us. Phi Delta Kappan: The Professional Journal for Educators. https://kappanonline.org/lance-kachel-school-librarians-matter-years-research/ . This article includes references to a plethora of other research articles supporting libraries and librarians in the schools.
>
> Merga, Margaret Kristin. (2019) How do librarians in schools support struggling readers? English in Education: Research Journal of the National Association for the Teaching of English. 53:2, 145-160. DOI:10.080/04250494.2018.1558030. Available online at https://www.tandfonline.com/doi/full/10.1080/04250494.2018.1558030 . This site is a gateway site with links to many ideas and support for valuing librarians and libraries and their role in creating readers.
>
> Librarians' role in creating readers from the:
> National Library in New Zealand. Gateway site at https://natlib.govt.nz/schools/reading-engagement/libraries-supporting-readers/librarians-role-in-creating-readers

Public Libraries: Their Role

Public libraries have by nature a more diverse demographics regarding their patron base. A community's public library serves the very young, and their patrons ranges through all age levels to seniors who seek the resources of a library. A public library's resources are not concentrated on the student user. However, in many larger public libraries, there are designated young adult librarians. And where there are such young adult librarians, they try to build activities to attract their young patrons to the library. The activities include book clubs, discussion groups, cultural activities, and service projects. Often the library establishes as teen advisory group that proposes and advises regarding activities that might be of interest to their demographic. Teens look to the public library both to augment the selections in their school library but also for materials that take them into more depth into a subject, or which offers more sophisticated and wider reading choices than their school library can offer.

School and Public Library Cooperation

It should seem obvious that a high degree of cooperation between the school and the public librarian can benefit students who seek additional materials, or more hours of access through the public library. The school librarian can serve as an invaluable asset when it comes to working in conjunction with the public library and in some cases with academic college and university libraries through Interlibrary Loan and access privileges.

Be careful, however, to assume qualities regarding a library that may or may not be true. First, recognize that many organizations (public and school)

 are cutting budgets for both collections and staff. Often school or public librarians are not really librarians at all but are non-certified staff members who function, because of expectations and perceived necessity, as a librarian. The problem -- checking out books and shelving is probably the less valuable function of a certified librarian. Those tasks can be easily learned and accomplished by non-certified staff, volunteers, or even student helpers. A certified librarian is capable of so much more.

Librarians, in most instances should assess the tasks they are doing and question if it is worth the taxpayer's money to pay them to do those tasks. One librarian often told her immediate administrator, "You are paying me too much to have me spend my day doing that." But once that is said, the librarian in question had to make good on the statement. In other words, the actions/tasks that were undertaken must be of greater value than shelving and checking out books. In this librarian's situation the administrator agreed and managed to fund a full-time secretary for the library, and a part-time aide to spot the secretary during lunch times, etc. and when extra assistance was needed. In return, the administrator got a librarian who regularly collaborated with classroom teachers, co-taught reference sessions, created numerous booktalks, planned school-wide literacy events, helped teachers in all curricular areas to infuse reading and literature, and research into their classroom activities. The academic results were apparent.

Simply put, all educational personnel, if they want the benefits of a certified librarian, should rally to support a reasonable budget and sufficient support staff in a library to provide the times and means for a certified librarian to effectively collaborate with students and staff to achieve curriculum standards (goals and objectives). And then staff and administration should be able to expect collaboration, co-teaching, active literary involvement and so forth.

Secondly, don't assume that the grass is greener on the other side. Just because a library is housed in the public sector or at a local college, doesn't mean their collection is superior in specific situations. During one of my stints as a public high school librarian, one of the AP science teachers asked me to arrange a field trip to a local college's library. It was a good trip in the sense that it familiarized our students with a library environment different from the more social and informal atmosphere of our high school center. However, the science teacher also wanted his students to have extended time to explore the college's collection on the topic of black holes. He felt certain the college would give his students more academic sources regarding the topic. However, that was not true. Due to the high school library personnel's diligent efforts over the years to provide support for important topics taught in curriculum areas, our high school library's offerings in regard to black holes was, in fact, much superior when compared to the few titles available at the college library.

The trip resulted in a second learning. The science teacher, after the trip, regularly came to the library to cooperatively consult with the librarian in planning units. Together they identified available materials, brainstormed lesson activities, and planned co-taught sessions. And often the librarian provided a focused book talk, and instruction regarding specific databases to introduce the resources and research techniques appropriate for specific topics. The school librarian can (and should) be able to construct research/reading pathfinders for specific units/activities. Using these pathfinders often reinforce a session where specific databases, and resources are presented.

One of the most valuable cooperative endeavors will involve the classroom teacher and the school's librarian.

> Gregory, Jamie. (2018, July 30). Teacher Collaboration: Collaborating with You School Librarian: Ten ways to work with your highly trained colleagues in the library to enhance literacy instruction. Edutopia. (Online). https://www.edutopia.org/article/collaborating-your-school-librarian
>
> Freeman, Judy. (n.d.) Teacher Librarian Partnerships. Scholastic. (Online). https://www.scholastic.com/teachers/articles/teaching-content/teacher-librarian-partnerships/
>
> Trapp, Laura. (2020, June 22). More Ideas for Collaboration in Your School Library. Trapped Librarian. (Blog) http://trappedlibrarian.org/2020/06/more-ideas-for-collaboration-in-the-school-library/ - focused on elementary but many ideas to adapt.
>
> Merga, Margaret Kristin. (2019, February 21). Collaborating with Teacher Librarians to Support Adolescents' Literacy and Literature Learning. International Literacy Association. 63:1, July/August 2019, pgs 65-72. (Online) https://ila.onlinelibrary.wiley.com/doi/full/10.1002/jaal.958
>
> Latham, Don; Gross, Melissa; and Witte, Shelbie. (2013). Preparing Teachers and Librarians to Collaborate to Teach 21st Century Skills: Views of LIS and Education Faculty. American Association of School Librarians. 16, pgs 1-23. (Online) http://www.ala.org/aasl/slr/volume16/latham-gross-witte

The Culture of Teens and Reading

The culture of teens has evolved drastically in the past decades. Dominating the teens' cultural world in many different ways than previously. Technology has created a different world for all of us – especially teens who use technology in a seemingly effortless fashion. Many early primary learners have the knowledge of technology that is equal to their older counterparts. For example, seven-year-olds often play games such as *Fortnite*, *Madden*, or *Mindcraft* with older teens or those in their early twenties. But it seems when younger (or older) users begin to invade a technological area, teens move on to something else.

One consistency, it seems is mobile phones. Smart phones seem to have taken over teen connections to most everything they are interested in. Teens use their phones to communicate via messenger, use social media apps, exchange money via Venmo (or Apple pay), and sometimes Paypal. In 2018, the Pew Research Center reported that 95% of teens either have or have access to a smart phone, and 45% report that they use the technology "almost constantly" (Anderson & Jiang, para. 1). That same research finds that Facebook is no longer the dominant force it once was in the online environment. Today, or at least in 2018, YouTube was the most popular online platform. Instagram is slightly more popular than Snapchat, and Twitter, Tumblr, and Reddit garnered use by less than 1/3 of users between 13-17. TikTok is not listed on even the most recent polls but anecdotal observation attests to the popularity of that social media platform.

> Anderson, Monica, and Jingjing, Jiang. (2018, May 31). Teens, Social Media & Technology 2018. *Pew Research Center*. (Online) https://www.pewresearch.org/internet/2018/05/31/teens-social-media-technology-2018/

The Pew Study presents quite conclusive evidence that at this time the social media platforms most used by teens are YouTube, Instagram, and Snapchat. Lower income teens tend to use Facebook with more regularly than those from higher income groups. One trend that seems to be clear. In decades past, teens tended to primarily use one platform. Today, teens tend to spread their social media use over several platforms. Snapchat leads all platforms in regard to use, followed closely by YouTube which serves as instructional sites, entertainment, and educational sites. Teens change their car's headlight using instructions from YouTube. They check out sports heroes, and musical performers. And they make their own outrageous videos to entertain themselves and their friends. TikToc videos are gaining a significant share of the teen viewership.

Despite the mega use most teens make of social media platforms they tend to feel that their use neither has a positive or negative effect on their lives overall. Adults at times have decried the isolation, that technology has allowed to exist. Teens say, on the contrary, technology has helped them stay connected to their friends. Instead of communicating synchronously through phone conversations, texting and messenger allows communication to exist asynchronously. Skype and Zoom applications, and Facetime brings synchronous connections to be made visually and relatively easy.

Technology has changed homework and research. Where once teens would have had to make an in-person trip to a library; many now can find the information they need through databases available on the Internet via the library connection, or with articles and credible information mounted by subject matter authorities. Interviewing in-person (or via a virtual call) is much more available. All learners can attend seminars on specialty subjects via conference apps. Once meetings that required transportation, lodging, and days away from a home base can be part of a person's experience virtually, without the time commitment or money that such attendance previously demanded. Collaborative work is now very possible across the country.

This accessibility has changed how we must teach. Previously when research was mostly a function of obtaining necessary information from a traditionally published book, for the most part we could assume that the material was vetted by the experts at the publishing house, for bias, and accuracy. Now however, with the accessibility of the Internet, and on-demand printing, almost anyone can successfully disseminate their information (right or wrong, accurate or inaccurate, biased or unbiased) in a matter of minutes. And more than ever, the end user is responsible for making the decision of credibility.

The ease of publishing information (or disinformation) makes the idea of vetting authors/illustrators, and sources, all the more vital.

And technology influences our relationship with literature and reading as well. Digital books to read and audio books are more available than ever. While once we were concerned that the popularity of books through technology would mark the end of publishing as we knew it. Quite the opposite has come about. According to a survey reported by Emily Drabble for the Guardian, "Teens prefer the printed page to e-books" (Drabble, 2014, para. 1).

> Drabble, Emily. (2014, December 16). Teens Prefer the Printed Page to e-books. *The Guardian.* (Online) https://www.theguardian.com/childrens-books-site/2014/dec/16/teens-ebooks-ereaders-survey

Several more recent surveys continue to verify that many teens prefer print books although those who do read e-books tend to use file-sharing sites, or free sites to access material to read. Price and ease of access is a factor in teens' preference for print. Even teens who are technologically adept find the lack of compatibility between programs used to read books and the confusion over rights to digital copies frustrating. Can a book bought and downloaded by individuals be shared with friends and family? Can a library copy be shared? Small screens on a phone (often the most available device onto which an e-book is loaded) creates a difficult reading environment, as does certain locations where a teen might want to read a selection. Bright sunshine and most devices do not make for a comfortable reading environment.

Graphic Novels and Manga

In past decades books generated in the graphic format were all referred to as Manga – which is the written version of the Japanese Anime films. Manga has its own conventions of presentation: black and white, smaller volume size, large-eyed characters, and reads front-to-back. While Manga is still very popular with teen readers, the format itself has emerged in the Western hemisphere as a highly illustrated version with many subject areas. The term graphic novel refers more to the format than the genre or subject.

Graphic novel can refer to any book, as long as the presentation is in a graphic format. Storytelling with pictorial storyboards creates an obvious connection to movies (in Japan these animated movies are termed Anime). Titles that have become popular include The Road to Perdition, The League of Extraordinary Gentlemen, and The X-Men. However, in the last decade or more, well-known titles have been re-issued in a graphic format.

Recent examples include the many books in Rick Riordan's Percy Jackson series. Each book has now been released as a graphic novel. See Rick Riordan's website at https://www.rickriordan.co.uk/books/graphic-novels/ for more information. Laurie Halse Anderson recently worked with illustrator Emily Carroll to create a graphic novel of her award winning Speak. The graphic novel is available in English, Spanish, and French.

National Public Radio shared a list of the 100 favorite comics and graphic novels (up to and including the publication date of 2017). Don't be confused by referring to graphic novels as comics – although Gene Luen Yang refers to his books as comics so perhaps the distinction is not so important. There is a distinct difference to many, however. A graphic novel defined as an ambitious comic book misses one major component. A comic book is most often the creation of a creative group who carry a storyline forward based on a formula and have an agreed upon character profile.

At times these comic books are strung together in sequential episodes to tell a cohesive story of that character. The character and storyline belong to the publishing enterprise that publishes the novel. A graphic novel is usually the work of one or two writers who develop the character and storyline much as a conventional writer would develop a story. The critical difference between a novel/information text and a graphic novel is that in graphic novels, story and character development is shared with the reader in a graphic format similar to a storyboard format as opposed to the use of words alone.

Since 2007, the YALSA (Young Adult Library Services Association), a division of the ALA, has developed a list of "Top 10 Great Graphic Novels for Teens." A list of nominated titles is also available.

> Great Graphic Novels. (n.d.). Great Graphic Novels. Young Adult Library Services Association: A Division of the American Library Association. (Online) http://www.ala.org/yalsa/great-graphic-novels . Lists are available from 2007 to the present.

The 2020 list included a great variety of titles including: *Best Friends* by Shannon Hale, *The Faithful Spy: Dietrich Bonhoeffer and the Plot to Kill Hitler* by Jimi Hendrix, *Gender Queer: A Memoir* by Maia Kobabe, *The Life of Frederick Douglass: A Graphic Narrative of a Slave's Journey from Bondage to Freedom* by David F. Walker, *A Quick and Easy Guide to Queer and Trans Identities* by Mady G. and J.R. Zuckerberg, and *They Called Us Enemy* by George Takei, Justin Eisinger, and Steven Scott. This list demonstrates the wide variety of subjects presented as graphic novels.

In the Spotlight: Gene Luen Yang

Gene Luen Yang
In 2007, Gene Luen Yang's graphic novel, *American Born Chinese*, became the first graphic novel to be awarded the Michael L. Printz Award and the first graphic novel to be nominated for a National Book Award. Yang's website *Gene Luen Yang: Cartoonist and Teacher* at https://geneyang.com/ shares information about Yang's recent titles including his well-received *From Small Steps to Great Leaps: Dragon Hoops* (First Second, 2020) -Yang puts the spotlight on his own life, his family, and on the high school where Yang teaches.

Yes, Yang spent his early career as a computer programmer, and then taught computer science at Bishop O'Dowd High School in Oakland, California. Eventually becoming the school's Director of Information Services and at the same time he became an Eisner winner (considered the equivalent of the Oscars in the world of comics). Several of his books have been nominated for the National Book Award. In 2016 he was named the National Ambassador for Young People's Literature, by the Library of Congress and the Children's Book Council. Someday he might return to the classroom to teach younger learners, but for now in conjunction with his writing, and book tours he teaches creative writing in the Hamline University's Masters of Fine Arts in Writing for Children and Young Adults program.

Gene Luen Yang presents his view on using comics in the classroom,
Why Comics Belong in the Classroom TEDX Talk (2016, December 2).
> Available on YouTube https://youtu.be/Oz4JqAJbxj0 or from a link from the about page on his website https://geneyang.com/ (10:43 minutes).

Resources for Using Graphic Novels

A Guide to Using Graphic Novels with Children and Teens

Download a full-color 14 page guide, *A Guide to Using Graphic Novels with Children and Teens* from Scholastic publishers directly from this site at https://www.scholastic.com/content/dam/teachers/lesson-plans/18-19/Graphic-Novel-Discussion-Guide-2018.pdf

For strategies to help use graphic novels effectively – check this book out.

Brozo, William. G., Moorman, Gary, & Meyer, Carla K. (2014). *WHAM! Teaching with Graphic Novels Across the Curriculum*. Teachers College Press.

Manga and Anime

Manga is still popular and often requested by readers but in the United States the variation that we refer to as graphic novels has gained in popularity as the topics address more closely the issues and interests of a majority of teens. Anime conventions and cosplay are very popular in pop culture.

Manga is an overall term used for a variety of print materials originating in Japan. While graphic novels, in the United States, are most often printed in full color. Manga is printed in black and white. Color is reserved for very special editions. Also, the Manga is read from right-to-left as opposed to left-to-right as is the norm in Western culture. In Japan the publications are often released in a serial basis, month-by-month, or chapter-by-chapter. Magazines such as the *Weekly Shōnen Jump* is an example of such a publication. Manga is most often long running series, and are published in multiple volumes. It is important to read the series in the correct order. An example of a short series would be Naoko Takeuchi's *Sailor Moon* series which consists of only 12 volumes. A much longer series would be the over 40 volumes of *Dragon Ball* by Akira Toriyama.

Both the *Sailor Moon* series and the *Dragon Ball* series have been made into popular animated films. Those publications are published in Japan – and are Anime since they are a media version other than printed. Anime is visual (film, television) while Manga is print. Sometimes a popular Manga series is made into Anime, or popular Anima might be reinterpreted in print as Manga. In short, Anime is animation. Manga is print.

Manga, just like the Western graphic novel, is a format and contains something of interest to a broad range of readers. Manga is put in categories first by gender, then age, and then by subject. For example, within Manga there is a shojo category – shojo are manga titles marketed to young girls; shonen manga titles are marketed to young boys. So a book might be deemed to be a shojo mystery. That would indicate the mystery is intended and marketed to girls. There are many manga subjects and sub-subjects. However, there are five most popular categories, and several others including one targeted specifically for the education of elementary and high school students.

1. Gakushü – Manga intended for educational purposes
   These titles target the educational aspect of a broad range of topics, i.e. history, math, art, literature, home improvement, budgeting, folk crafting and so forth. Many are only available in Japanese but there are some that are translated into English. More discussion of this category and a bibliography on the Ohio State University Libraries website
   Itoh, Yuka. (2018, December 10). Educational manga at Ohio State Libraries. (Online)
   https://library.osu.edu/site/manga/2018/12/10/educational-manga/#more-777

2. Shonen – Manga marketed to 'tweens and teen males.
   This category is known to feature action, comedy, and often some form of coming-of-age friendships among the characters.
   Examples of Shonen titles include: Akira Toriyama's *Dragon Ball*, Koheil Horikoshi's *My Hero Academia*, and Masashi Kishimoto's *Natuto*.

3. Shojo – Manga targeted at 'tween and teen girls
   This category is more concerned with drama, emotion, and often idealized romance, as well as coming of age elements featuring a young protagonist. Covers often showcase pink, flowers, and cutesy images. The most popular or famous example of Shojo is Naoko Takeuchi's *Sailor Moon* series. The series features Usagi Tsukino, who at first is a normal 14-year-old who is reincarnated as Sailor Moon. She is charged with defending love and justice from the Moon Kingdom. Her Sailor Scouts help her defend the earth from the forces of evil.

4. Seinen – Manga targeted at adult men (18+)
   This manga is action packed with a lot of violence but of a darker and more serious nature. There is much adult content: sexual situations, graphic violence, and very mature language. In comparison to shonen titles which feature naïve characters who idealize the world with a naïve view, seinen story lines are very dark, gritty, and feature adult protagonists. Katsuhiro Otomo's *Akira* is a long running series set in a post-apocalyptic future. A title *Berserk* by Kentarō Miura is a high fantasy series with elements of European mythology.

5. Josei – Manga targeted at adult women (18+)
   This category often features very mature storylines which deal with romantic and personal relationships. Josei titles are similar to American adult romance novels and sometimes feature very graphic romantic interludes, sometimes borderline pornographic. Josei novels often feature female and male protagonists. This category is not easily recognized by its cover. And one cannot depend on annotations indicating the age of the chief protagonist to provide an idea of category. One of the most well-known examples of Josei is Yun Kouga's *Loveless* series. The chief protagonist, Ritsuka, is actually only 12-years-old but is dealing with a mysterious older man, Soubi, in her search for information about a mysterious and vicious murder.

6. Kodomomuke – Manga targeted to the very young series.
   Cute and moralistic – and fun-filled. Most Pokémon manga fit into this category.

Just as with Western literature categories often cross boundaries and deal with aghast topics. There is no compulsion to avoid gender issues, sexual encounters, and many do. It is worth noting that culturally sexual views and attitude toward the female gender is notably different in the Japanese culture. There are several online sources for Manga bibliographies, the following are useful lists to begin with:

Pagan, Amanda. (2020, November 13). Blast from the Past: Historical Fiction Manga. *New York Public Library*. (Online) https://www.nypl.org/blog/2020/11/13/blast-past-historical-fiction-manga

Brenner, Robin. (2014, April 21). Must Have: Manga for Teens 2014 Update. *No Flying No Tights*. (Online) https://noflyingnotights.com/blog/2014/04/21/must-have-manga-for-teens-2014-update/ --

NOTE: this list is from 2014 however, since the availability of manga is governed in most cases by the continuation of the series; this list is valuable in. that it provides titles and authors which can be used to check for in-print series titles available now, and if so that infers continuing popularity and new volumes.

Additional lists of books can be located using the search functions at Good Reads - https://www.goodreads.com/ and at most of the online sales sites

Ideas to Use with Teen Readers

Creating Graphic Novels to Enhance Understanding

Read this article and consider the possibilities for your class – Miller, Shveta. (2019, July 21). The Surprising Benefits of Student-Created Graphic Novels. (Blog) https://www.cultofpedagogy.com/student-graphic-novels/

Using Graphic Novels in Chemistry Class-A First Foray

Many discuss the benefits of graphic novels in the literature classroom, but graphic novels are equally as valuable in other classrooms. Graphic novels are here to stay, and the creative teacher or librarian will find a way to utilize them to enhance the learning and comprehension in their classroom. Using graphic novels in the classroom might take some tweaking of details in your plans but the only way to develop a plan is to plan and try it out.

Here are three ways one chemistry teacher used in this first foray into chemistry and graphic novels in an effort to heat up interest in the chemistry classroom, using graphic novels.

An Example: Options for the Chemistry Classroom

Involve students in a comparison of graphic and traditional texts related to the topic. Locate a graphic novel guide and a basic standard textbook used in your classroom.

A series of books by Larry Gonick is invaluable to get started. The Cartoon Guide Series is older but still in print and available in paperback. The topics included in the series include: chemistry, physics, biology, calculus, algebra, genetics, statistics, history of the United States, introduction to Economics (by Yoram Bauman), and others.

The titles used for this example from the chemistry classroom:

Gonick, Larry and Criddle, Craig. The Cartoon Guide to Chemistry. HarperCollins, 2005.

Timberlake, Karen. Chemistry: An Introduction to General, Organic, and Biological Chemistry. 13th Edition. Pearson 2017.

Students (ages 15-17) were asked to read the section from each book related to gas laws and asked for their reactions in regard to level of detail, readability, and engagement of the texts. Some of the students felt that the graphic texts were much more engaging and that the pictures helped their understanding of the content, and others felt the traditional text was easier to understand and that the traditional text explained vocabulary better. All in all, the reaction was mixed and dictates that using both the traditional and the graphic texts would benefit some students. The graphic version seemed the most beneficial to those who were not strong readers and those who tend to display characteristics present in primarily visual learners.

Share graphic biographies of leaders in the field of science. Read:

Ottaviani, Jim. Dignifying Science: Stories About Women Scientists. Ann Arbor, MI: General Tektronics Labs, 2009.

Some students were familiar with stories about Rosalind Franklin, Marie Curie, and Barbara McClintock and felt that seeing the stories dramatized in a graphic historical context added to their understanding of their lives and achievements. Others were interested in learning about Emmy Noether, Barbara McClintock, and especially Hedy Lamarr.

Final project option. Students were asked to select one chemistry concept and to read about the development of the idea, how it was discovered, and then to survey graphic novels available in the library. The assignment is to write a graphic short fiction story in first person about how an experiment they constructed led to the discovery of the chemistry concept/idea.

Ideas to Use with Teen Readers

Students Creating Graphic Novels – Book Creator

Consider using Book Creator as an application to assist students in designing student made graphic novels. The free resource allows an educator 1 free class at a time (up to 40 books can be stored) and students can work independently on their own book. The application helps with some of the design elements so students can focus on their story boarding! Paid accounts are $10 per month per teacher with discounts for 5 or more teachers. School district accounts are available by quote. Tools for Schools, Inc. (2011-2021). Book Creator. https://bookcreator.com/

Picture Books for Teens

Picture books are often designated as "E" books in libraries serving a much larger range than early primary or preschool readers/listeners. The "E" was short for easy but over time users have recognized that the heavily illustrated books are not easy reading, so the "E" morphed into being a shortened term for everybody and indeed many of those books were, but not all. Basically, picture books are illustrated narratives intended to read or share with preschool or primary-aged readers. But in recent years library patrons have come to recognize that picture books appeal to those who learn visually and those who want a quick overview of a topic.

Today it is very true that picture books by any other name are books for everyone. The growth of popularity of graphic novels has contributed to the acceptance and popularity of picture books. Picture books, as are graphic novels, are a format not a subject/genre. Within this format there are many subjects. Most of those shelved in the "E" sections of libraries would most often be fiction or folk literature.

Actually, some titles are sophisticated and beyond the scope of understanding for the very young reader – more suited to those who have some prior knowledge and are more mature as readers. Consider *Pink and Say* by Patricia Polacco (1994), a tale from the Civil War, or *Hiroshima No, Pika!* by Toshi Maruki (1980), a powerful book about the bombing of Hiroshima-these are classic picture books that are very well suited for older readers. Both of these are classic titles that contributed to the idea that even serious topics can be dealt with through picture book narratives.

Picture books with a strong curriculum narrative are, for many purposes, a short story with illustrations. There are many uses for these abbreviated stories or texts in the middle school and senior high curriculum. Musical directors planning a Madrigal dinner theater might find the exact depictions of costumes that are needed in Aliki's *Medieval Feast* (1986). Franklyn Branley's *Journey into a Black Hole* (1988) is the perfect introduction to a scholarly unit on black holes. Those readers examining Christopher Columbus's role as seen by contemporary historians will find using Jane Yolen's *Encounter* (1996) very useful. Similarly, a unit on World War II would not be complete without introducing some of the faces of the Japanese citizens who were interned during World War II in the USA-*A Place Where Sunflowers Grow* by Amy Lee-Tai and Felicia Hoshino (2006) puts a human face on the experience.

While some of the picture books are fiction titles, there are also many informational titles such as *Parrots Over Puerto Rico* by Susan L. Roth and Cindy Trumbore (2013). Books such as this title can do much to introduce basic facts, activate prior knowledge, and stimulate additional research into a specific topic. The six-page afterward, including a timeline and bibliography of authors' sources, will be a strong research resource.

The above-mentioned titles are titles that have been around for several years and exemplify the trend to picture books for older readers. The trend continues and there are many new titles being published today that have utility for sharing with teens.

Uses and a Selected List

Picture books or short stories (illustrated or not) are successfully used to:
- promote literacy across the curriculum,
- convey ideas simply,
- introduce/encourage the reading of more difficult books on the same subject,
- encourage creative writing in prose and poetry,
- promote awareness of language,
- teach artistic styles in illustrations,
- encourage the development of creativity and imagination,
- introduce a person or topic for more in-depth study,
- provide a schema for students who need background information for assisting in the comprehension of more difficult texts,
- provide models for teen parents to read to their own children,
- teach elements of literature-plotting, characterization, setting and so forth,
- provide material for reader's theater, speech class, and performance events,
- teach literary devices: foreshadowing, flashbacks, and other devices.

With creativity almost any picture book can lend itself to one of the above uses with older students. Here are a few selected picture book titles that might start you on the road to thinking. about how to use books with older readers/adults. Each title cited is followed by informal notes to suggest some curriculum uses in the classroom.

Alexander, Kwame. *The Undefeated*. illustrated by Kadir Nelson. Versify/Houghton Mifflin Harcourt, 2019.
A poetic introduction to black history in the USA, and features references to people such as Martin Luther King, Jr., Langston Hughes, Gwendolyn Brooks.
Note for use: Many bits and pieces that can inspire further research and information about those who persisted and never gave up. Who else could be included in a collective biography. Research and write additional profiles.

Alznauer, Amy. *Flying Paintings-The Zhou Brothers: A Story of Revolution and Art*. Paintings by ShanZuo Zhou and DaHuang Zhou.Candlewick Press, 2020.
From the back of their grandmother's bookstore, in China, the brothers took their paintings through China's Cultural Revolution, and through

collaboration took their art to the White House and into their galleries in Chicago, Bejing, and Kansas City, Missouri.

Note for use: Renowned artists lived through a repression of their art when they were only allowed to paint Mao. Research and discuss the suppression of thought and artist expression during China's Cultural Revolution. Compare to the suppression in pre-World War II years in Germany. Eric Carle, the author/illustrator of *the Very Hungry Caterpillar*, whose art teacher, Herr Krauss, defied the government and secretly showed Carle forbidden art from the German Expressionists and abstract artists. The art helped inspire Carle to become the artist he is today. Discuss the reasons a government would ban artistic expression.

Blackall, Sophie. *Hello Lighthouse*. Little, Brown/Hachette, 2018.
A poetic celebration of the lighthouses that guided water transportation in a past era.

Note for use: Study history and use of lighthouse, geography, mapping existing lighthouses. Pair with *Lighthouse for Kids: History, Science, and Lore with 21 Activities* (Pawprints, 2008) which brings to life the era when the was a major traffic route and lighthouses guided the traffic. Much information that provides a look at one era of the transportation timeline in the United States.

Charles, Tami. *All Because You Matter*. Illustrated by Bryan Collier. Scholastic, 2020.
Affirms the beauty of Black and brown children in a poetic love letter that nurtures self-esteem and value.

Note for use: Promotes discussion. Mentor text for writing about individuals and positive attributes.

Greenberg, Jan. *Two Brothers, Four Hands: The Artists Alberto and Diego Giacometti*. Neal Porter/Holiday House, 2019.
Biography of 20th century artists and their connection to the White House and Barack Obama. One brother a sculptor – the other a dare devil who created remarkable pieces of furniture. Both are artists and their inspiring story of dedication, to the art, and to one another.

Note for use: Explore the relationship between the siblings one noted early for success and the other less so, but talented. Locate other brothers (or sibling sets) in history that have interesting relationships – e.g. *Good Brother, Bad Brother: The Story of Edwin Booth and John Wilkes Booth* by James Cross Giblin (Clarion, 2005).

Hopkinson, Deborah. *Thanks to Frances Perkins: Fighter for Workers' Rights*. Illustrated by Kristy Caldwell. Peachtree Publishing Company, 2020. Frances Perkins witnessed the Triangle Waist Factory Fire in 1911 and later became the only female cabinet member and created the Social Security program. *Note for use*: See the Krull listing.

Krull, Kathleen. *The Only Woman in the Photo: Frances Perkins & Her New Deal*. Illustrated by Alexandra Bye. Atheneum Books for Young Readers, 2020. Perkins became an activist speaking out for suffrage,

safe workplaces, and later became the Secretary of Labor.
Note for use: Compare and contrast the emphasis each of these authors gave to Frances Perkins. What did both authors feel important to include? Compare and contrast the treatment of Perkins's life.

Loney, Andrea J. *Double Bass Blues*. Illustrated by Rudy Gutierrez. Knopf/Random House Children's Books, 2019. – Fiction focusing on determination, music and family support.
Note for use: Discuss the making of a successful person. What makes an elite athlete? Refer to the studies summarized here:
Elsevier B.V. (2018). Elite Athlete – an overview |ScienceDirect topics. https://www.sciencedirect.com/topics/psychology/elite-athlete/pdf
Are those same traits applicable to other successful individuals?

Lyon, Kelly Starling. *Going Down Home with Daddy*, illustrated by Daniel Minter. Peachtree, 2019. – a story of family celebrations and traditions.
Note for use: Inspiration for retelling personal stories of celebrations and traditions in a family or ancestorial stories.

Motum, Markus. *Curiosity: The Story of a Mars Rover*. Candlewick, 2018. Space exploration in 2012.
Note for use: Investigate and more research, science facts, roving vehicles, spacecraft.

Nelson, Vaunda Micheaux. *Let'er Buck: George Fletcher, the People's Champion*. Illustrated by Gordon C. James. Carolrhoda Books, 2019. – African American Cowboys, 1911 history,
Note for use: Research other black cowboys, for example, Bill Pickett.

Slade, Suzanne. *Swish! The Slam-Dunking Alley-Ooping, High-Flying Harlem Globetrotters.* Illustrations by Don Tate. Little Brown Books for Young Readers, 2020. – History of Globe-trotters, Black players in NBA, Wilt Chamberlain.
Note for use: More research, history of sports, individuals.

Steptoe, Javaka. *Radiant Child: The Story of Young Artist Jean-Michel Basquiat.* Little, Brown and Company, 2016. – Art, artist biography, elements of painting. *Note for use*: Investigate other artists, their technique, timelines, and well-known works.

Tate, Don. *William Still and His Freedom Stories: Father of the Underground Railroad*. Peachtree, 2020. – underground railroad, Henry "Box" Brown, Ellen and William Craft. Inspires more research and more reading of the longer accounts of Ellen and William Craft, Henry Brown, and others mentioned in the text.
Note for use: Investigate how the underground railroad impacted your state's history. For example: Iowa had an active underground railroad travel route. Begin an investigation into your state's history at National Geographic. (n.d.) Resource library: The Underground Railroad. https://www.nationalgeographic.org/maps/undergroundrailroad

The POWER of ONE BOOK

After the Fall: How Humpty Dumpty Got Back Up Again, written and illustrated by Dan Santat Roaring Book Press, 2017.

One author of a very popular picture book discovered his own connection with adults and his picture book. If you ever doubt the power of a book. Inspiration from a book.

The best birthday story ever. Santat, Don. (2019 Oct 2). 44 (The Annual Birthday Rant): The best birthday gift I ever received from a stranger. https://www.dantat.com/post/188082081547/44-the-annual-birthday-rant-the-best-birthday

Who Says Picture Books Are Just for Kids
There are plenty of books that might fit into a secondary curriculum, as mentor texts, strategies for research, introductions to a topic.
Building Background--Read carefully the passages dealing particularly with the use of picture books in the sections titled "Importance of Background Knowledge" and "Using Picture Books to Build Background" in this article: Lent, ReLeah Cossett. (2012). Chapter 2. Background knowledge: The glue that makes learning stick. From Overcoming Textbook Fatigue: 21st Century Tools to Revitalize Teaching and Learning. Alexandria, VA: ASCD. Chapter retrieved from http://bit.ly/chapter2-ASCD

> "One of the great things about books is sometimes there are some fantastic pictures."
> ~ George W. Bush (43rd President of the United States

Before you dismiss the idea of reading picture books for information (and entertainment) consider that a celebrated Jeopardy winner, James Holzhauer, actually won thousands of dollars and credits his reading of children's books for the knowledge that made him a mega-winner.

LeBlanc, Cameron. (2019 Apr 10) This Guy Used Kids' Books to Become the Biggest "Jeopardy!" Winner Ever. Fatherly.com.
https://www.fatherly.com/news/childrens-books-biggest-jeopardy-winner-james-holzhauer/

But this is the article that gave the most details about what to look for in a picture book --

Springen, Karen. (2019 Apr 30). "Jeopardy!" Star James Holzhauer on His Children's Book Strategy. *Publishers Weekly*.
https://www.publishersweekly.com/pw/by-topic/childrens/childrens-industry-news/article/79918-jeopardy-star-james-holzhauer-on-his-children-s-book-strategy.html

Using Picture Books

Biographies as Introductions

One example is information about Sir Nicholas George Winton – a World War II hero. As a young man he saved hundreds of Jewish children by spiriting them out of Germany and into England where he arranged foster homes for them.

Nicholas George Winton

Nicholas Winton – at age 29 (1938)

Nicky & Vera

In 2021, Winton's efforts to save 669 children from Nazi extermination became the subject of a picture book by Peter Sis. The book focuses on Winton and one child, six-year-old Vera Gissing who was among the many children saved. The story does not dwell on the Nazi atrocities but rather on the children and the life they left behind, and their rescuer

Sis, Peter. *Nicky & Vera: The Quiet Hero of the Holocaust and the Children He Rescued.* Norton Young Readers, 2021.

The book is marketed to young readers ages 6-9 but its story is important and is a powerful book to stimulate discussions among older elementary and secondary readers (not to mention adults who may have their own memories of learning about or living through the war years).

For more information about Winton and the book including activities to extend and use this book with older readers go to:

McElmeel, Sharron. (2021, Jan. 31). Nicky Winton - A Hero Hidden in Plain Sight. McBookwords (Blog). http://bit.ly/WWII-hiddenhero

The blog post will give additional information about Winton, Sis's book, and a longer book about Winton that can provide more details about his World War II kindertransport; and his unassuming life from that time until his death at the age of 106 in 2015. This book is one that absolutely should be read by all readers.

1. Read details about using Google doodles to stimulate curiosity about people and events, and
2. For incorporating books such as *Nicky & Vera* into history curriculum.
3. Comment on the ideas presented from: Nicky Winton - A Hero Hidden in Plain Sight. McBookwords (Blog). http://bit.ly/WWII-hiddenhero
4. The blog includes other books, novels that coordinate, concepts that can be discussed with details from the book or book's background
5. See the interview with Peter Sis as cited in the blog.

Sis, Peter. (2021) *Nicky & Vera: The Quiet Hero of the Holocaust and the Children He Rescued*. Norton Young Readers.

Picture Books: Making Connections for Readers

Unspeakable

More and more picture books are being used to highlight important, and often ignored, events in history. Have you ever heard about the Tulsa Race Massacre?

Weatherford, Carol Boston. (2021). *Unspeakable: The Tulsa Race Massacre*. Illustrations by Floyd Cooper. Carolrhoda Books.

In 1921 a white mob attacked the African American community in Tulsa's Greenwood district. For 75 years this event was sweep under the rug and omitted from news sources throughout the United States. The event is finally getting some news time after the HBO show *Watchman* was released during the summer of 2020. While the subject is a difficult one–the beauty and productivity of the Greenwood area prior to May 31, 1921 is part of the information shared in this book. But on that day more than 300 African Americans were killed; and more than 8,000 more were displaced. A stretch of businesses in the Greenwood area was referred to as the Black Wall Street. A mob of two thousand, upset about a young white man's transgression (supposedly) of assaulting a white woman, gathered at the jail where the man was being held, and then the mob stormed the Greenwood section. Completely destroying the thriving community. Floyd Cooper's grandfather had been part of the Greenwood Community.

Use Carol Boston Weatherford's book *Unspeakable: The Tulsa Race Massacre* as a companion to the fiction title that uses the massacre as a historical backdrop - *Dreamland Burning* by Jennifer Latham (Little, Brown Books for Young Readers, 2017). Latham's book weaves together the story of two affluent mixed-race teenagers, one in the present (Rowan) and one who lived in Tulsa in 1921 (Will). This book deals with racism, past and present, but offers hope.

Ladybird Johnson – The First Lady

Introductory Readings:
Maurer, Tracy Nelson. *Lady Bird Johnson, That's Who!: The Story of a Cleaner and Greener America.* Illustrated by Ginnie Hsu. Henry Holt and Co, 2021.
Appelt, Kathi. *Miss Lady Bird's Wildflowers: How a First Lady Changed America*. Illustrated by Joy Fisher Hein. HarperCollins, 2005.

In-depth Reading:

Sweig, Julia. Lady Bird Johnson: Hiding in Plain Sight. Random House, 2021.

Claudia Alta "Lady Bird" Johnson is often lauded for her efforts to beautify the landscape across America but she was much more than that one initiative. She was Lyndon B. Johnson's political partner – his secret weapon. Sweig's book illuminates her real impact on Johnson's Presidential years and reveals their true partnership.

Discuss: The contributions of Lyndon B. Johnson to our emerging cultural changes, especially in the area of civil rights and human rights, and the Vietnam War; the contributions of Lady Bird Johnson and her impact on environmental initiatives (including but beyond beautification and floral plantings), feminism, and political strategies (including the stance on the Vietnam War).

Dispelling Myths about Women in All Cultural Corners

Reid, Megan. (2021). *Maryam's Magic: The Story of Mathematician Maryam Mirzakhani*. Illustrated by Aaliya Jaleel. In Iran, Maryam loved to read, mathematics was boring until she discovered geometry. Geometry opened a new world to her and brought her to love numbers and shapes and the stories told through equations.

She became a trailblazing mathematician. She made history by becoming the first woman, and Iranian, to win the Fields Medal, mathematics' highest award. Seque the story of Maryam Mirzakhani into a discussion of other women who are breaking barriers in all areas of stereotypic categories.

> For more great picture books about women in science go to amightygirl.com. For a list:
> *Science Is for Girls: 25 New children's Books About Girls and Women in Science* go to https://www.amightygirl.com/blog?p=32798

Yasmin, Seema, and Azim, Fahmida. *Muslim Women are Everything: Stereotype-Shattering Stories of Courage, Inspiration, nd Adventure.* Harper Design, 2020.
Muslim women are often portrayed as weak and sheltered. This book reveals the many ways that Muslim women express themselves and achieves in, among other endeavors: the arts, business, science, and politics.

Skeers, Linda. *Women Who Dared: 52 Stories of Fearless Daredevils, Adventurers, and Rebels*. Illustrated by Livi Gosling. Sourcebooks Explore, 2017. Meet amazing, daring, and ingenious women such as: Annie Edson Taylor – the first woman to go over Niagara Falls in a barrel, Valentina Tereshkova, the first woman to fly in space, and the first professional female stunt person, Helen Gibson.

Primary & Secondary Research -- Cubs in a Tub

Candance Fleming wrote a picture book biography of Helen Martini, *Cubs in the Tub; The True Story of the Bronx Zoos First Woman Zookeeper* (Neal Porter, 2020).

Read the article about the illustrator and the research she did to create the illustrations. Downing, Julie. (2020 May 12). The Power of Primary Sources: Walking the line between facts and fiction. Retrieved from https://bit.ly/downing-cubsinatub

Discuss the difference between primary and secondary sources and how that impacts real research.

An outstanding example of research that goes beyond writing all you know about the topic but instead answers specific questions needed for the article or writing that is to be done. In this case Julie Downing researched to find answers for creating accurate illustrations. To illustrate this book, Julie Downing sought to answer specific questions. Where did Helen Martini live? Not just where in terms of address but actually "where"? Was it a small apartment? Large? Third floor? What kind of car would have been used during this time period? Julie Downing talks about the research she did to create accurate illustrations for this biography (Nonfiction) in a blog entry. A very interesting read.

Listen to a reading by Julie Downing at Stimola Live:

Stimola Literary Studio. (2020, May 26). *Cubs in the Tube with Julie Downing.* https://youtu.be/RBc2fQiznY4 . Downing also discusses much of the information that she shares in the blog post cited above.

Little Known Heroes

Picture book biographies often highlight people and events that have been dismissed in the mainstream history accounts. Dr. Martin Couney is one such person. Most of us take the existence of incubators to care for premature babies for granted but they were not always used. In fact Dr. Couney and his Coney Island experiment was among the first.

Author Marissa Moss, introduces "an incredible-but-true story of a doctor who used a Coney Island exhibit to care for premature babies for decades (including his own daughter) until hospitals accepted the use of incubators." Dr. Martin Couney saved the lives of many babies at the 1937 New York World's Fair with his incubators. The exhibit saved 6,500 babies from 1903 to 1943.

Moss, Marissa. *Boardwalk Babies*. Illustrated by April Chu. Creston Books, 2021. ISBN: 9781939547668

Meet Don Tate & Picture Biographies

Don Tate is an author/illustrator with many books to his credit. He is introduced very well in this 3.24 minute YouTube video:

Vaughn, Robbie. (2021, February 19). *An Illustrated Lesson.* https://youtu.be/k5wM_wre1RU

Finding More Picture books

A selected list of picture books worth a look – make your own connections to curriculum, novels, books of information.

Spillett-Sumner, Tasha. (2021). *I Sang You Down From the Stars*. Illustrated by Michaela Goade. Little, Brown. The author, Inniniwak (Cree) and Trinidadian writer reaches into her Native heritage to share this story of a mother's love for her infant. Illustrated by 2021 Caldecott artist Michaela Goade, a Tlingit artist, and illustrator of the award-winning *We Are Water Protectors*.

Giardino, Alexandria. (2021). *Me + Tree*. Illustrated by Anna Balbusso and Elena Balbusso. Creative Editions. A tree stump sits in the middle of an old dead stump. A young girl comes by and brings the stump alive in her imagination and shows the power of friendship and being loved.

Sidman, Joyce. (2021). *Hello, Earth! Poems to Our Planet*. Illustrated by Miren Asianin Lora. Eerdmans Books for Young Readers. A poetic conversation between a curious person and the planet – from the first concept of a tiny rock hurling through space.

McGinty, Alice B. (2019). *The Girl Who Named Pluto: The Story of Venetia Burney*. Illustrated by Elizabeth Haidle. PenguinRandomHouse. ISBN: 9781524768317. Venetia Katharine Douglas Burney was only 11 years old and living in England when she first suggested the name Pluto to the man, Clyde Tombaugh, who discovered the planet in 1930. Author's note provides additional information. Story is based on the actual events and the life of Venetia Burney Phair. Note: National Pluto day is February 17.

Metcalf, Lindsay H. (2020). *Beatrix Potter, Scientist (She Made History)*. Illustrated by Junyi Wu. Albert Whitman. ISBN: 9780807551752. Most readers know Potter for her charming stories of Peter Rabbit, Benjamin Bunny, and other creatures in the woods, but feel realize that she was a true scientist. She studied the anatomy of her pets, and created detailed scientific drawings. This is the story of her scientific endeavors.

Sorell, Traci. (2021). *Classified: The Secret Career of Mary Golda Ross, Cherokee Aerospace Engineer*. Illustrated by Natasha Donovan. Millbrook Press. ISBN: 9781541579149. This picture book biography gives Mary Golda Ross her rightful place in history and highlights the life and work of Cherokee aerospace engineer. A world leader and innovator who loved puzzling out math equations and sought loftier goals.

Walker, Sandra Neil. *Between the Lines: How Ernie Barnes Went from the Football Field to the Art Gallery.* Simon & Schuster, 2018. ISBN: 9781481443876. Inspiration, spirit, and of an American original who pursued his dream first on the football field and then ultimately to be recognized as one of the most important artists of his times. Compare Walker's book to another title about Ernie Barnes by Don Tate,

Tate, Don. *Pigskins to Paintbrushes: The Story of Football Playing Artist Ernie Barnes.* Abrams Books for Young Readers, 2021.

Ideas to Use with Teen Readers

Read a picture book and share one new fact that you learned. What fun that would be! Of course, even more fun would be becoming that million-dollar winner on Jeopardy!

"'What is the use of a book,' thought Alice, 'without pictures or conversations?'"
~ Lewis Carroll (1832-1898)

Adult Books and the Teen Reader

Interest and maturity of readers varies greatly among all age groups. And many books span the interest of readers from upper elementary to adulthood. Generally, one can gauge the interest in the book based on the age of the chief protagonists. But there are many exceptions. For example, when the first Harry Potter book, by J.K. Rowling was released in England many adults took up the book and began to read the series. However, not wanting to be seen reading a book originally intended for youth, on public transportation, the older readers covered the book jacket. This spurred the publisher to issue an edition with a more adult cover so that the book would appeal to even more readers. The history of the covers is interesting and attests to the fact that when allowed readers will make their own choices and age designation or the publishers suggested age makes little difference. You can see the Harry Potter covers here:

The Visual Rhetoric of the Harry Potter Books: UK Covers vs. US Covers. (Online) https://visualrhetoricofharrypotter.weebly.com/uk-covers-vs-us-covers.html

Alex Award

Margaret A. Edwards was one of the first librarians to focus on services to young adults. She worked for many years at the Enoch Pratt library in Baltimore and her work inspired many other librarians to provide young adults with services, books, and programs that met their needs and interest. The ALEX award is sponsored by the Margaret A. Edwards Trust and is named in her honor – her nickname was Alex (short for Alexander). The Margaret A. Edwards Award is also named after her.

The Young Adult Library Services Association (YALSA) selects ten titles each year of adult books they consider of particular interest to teen readers. Their list is worth reviewing to see if any of the titles would be of interest to teens in your area.

Titles on the 2021 ALEX list

- *Black Sun* by Rebecca Roanhouse
- *The House in the Cerulean Sea* by TJ Klune
- *The Impossible First: From Fire to Ice – Crossing Antarctica Alone* by Colin O'Brady
- *Kent State: Four Dead in Ohio* by Derf Backderf
- *The Kids are Gonna Ask* by Gretchen Anthony
- *The Only Good Indians* by Stephen Graham
- *Plain Bad Heroines* by Emily M. Danforth
- *Riot Baby* by Tochi Onyebuchi
- *Solutions and Other Problems* by Allie Brosh
- *We Ride Upon Sticks* by Quan Barry.

Titles on the 2020 ALEX list

- *A Boy and His Dog at the End of the World* by C. A. Fletcher
- *Do You Dream of Terra-Two?* by Temi Oh
- *Dominicana* by Angie Cruz
- *Gender Queer: A Memoir* by Maia Kobabe
- *High School* by Sara Quin and Tegan Quin
- *In Waves* by AJ Dungo.
- *Middlegame* by Seanan McGuire
- *The Nickel Boys* by Colson Whitehead
- *Red, White & Royal Blue* by Casey McQuiston
- *The Swallows* by Lisa Lutz

Each year there are numerous books nominated for the ALEX award and only the top 10 are designated for inclusion on the ALEX list. However, there are other interesting titles nominated each year. The Young Adult Library Services Association (YALSA) division of the American Library Association (ALA) annually publishes the ALEX list as well as those titles nominated in any one year. Those lists along with the ALEX winners for years past can be accessed at the official site: http://www.ala.org/yalsa/alex-awards The available list goes back to 2010 when the association began to publish the official nominations list.

Popular Best-Selling List

Looking at *USA Today's* list of bestselling books there are several titles that will appeal to teen readers – links to reviews of each of these books are available at the USA Today news site at:

USA Today. (2020 Dec 14). *The Best Books of 2020: What USA Today's Critics Loved Reading*. https://www.usatoday.com/picture-gallery/entertainment/books/2020/02/19/best-books-2020-what-usa-todays-critics-loved-reading/4531064002/

- *The Cold Millions* by Jess Walter
- *Leave the World Behind* by Rumaan Alam
- *White Ivy* by Susie Yang
- *Just Like You* by Nick Hornby
- *A Brotherhood Betrayed: The Man Behind the Rise and Fall of Murder, Inc.* by Michael Cannell
- *Transcendent Kingdom* by Yaa Gyasi
- *What Are You Going Through* by Sigrid Nunez
- *Vesper Flights* by Helen Macdonald
- *Punching the Air* by Ibi Zoboi and Yusef Salaam
- *The Death of Vivek Oji* by Akwaeke Emezi
- *Luster: A Novel* by Raven Leilani
- *Wandering in Strange Lands: A Daughter of the Great Migration Reclaims Her Roots* by Morgan Jerkins
- *Utopia Avenue* by David Mitchell
- *The End of Her* by Shari Lapena
- *Memorial Drive: A Daughter's Memoir* by Natasha Trethewey
- *Home Before Dark* by Riley Sager
- *Florence Adler Swims Forever* by Rachel Beanland
- *A Beautiful Foolish Endeavor* by Hank Green
- *The Vanishing Half* by Brit Bennett
- *Dead Reckoning: The Story of How Johnny Mitchell and His Fighter Pilots Took on Admiral Yamamoto and Avenged Pearl Harbor* by Dick Lehr
- *A Burning* by Megha Majumdar
- *All My Mother's Lovers* by Ilana Masad
- *Big Summer* by Jennifer Weiner
- *Enemy of All Mankind* by Steven Johnson

- *Southern Book Club's Guide to Slaying Vampires: A Novel* by Grady Hendrix
- *Days of Distraction: A Novel* by Alexandra Chang
- The Mirror & The Light by Hilary Mantel
- The Night Watchman by Louise Erdrich
- Oona Out of Order by Margarita Montimore
- Eight Perfect Murders by Peter Swanson
- *The Mercies* by Kiran Millwood Hargrove
- The Adventurer's Son by Roman Dial
- *Weather* by Jenny Offill
- *Franklin & Washington: The Founding Partnership* by Edward J. Larson
- *The Truants* by Kate Weinberg
- *Parable of the Sower* by Octavia E. Butlers (created as a graphic novel by Damian Duffy and John Jennings)
- *The Age of Illusions: How America Squandered its Cold War Victory* by Andrew Bacevich
- *Zed* by Joanna Kavenna
- House on Endless Waters by Emuna Elon

New Adult (NA) Fiction

In 2009, St. Martin's Press coined the phrase when they established a New Adult Contest for "...fiction similar to YA that can be published and marketed as adult-a sort of an 'older YA' or 'new adult'." Soon other publishers were publishing in this category as well. Generally, the new adult field has been intended for the 18-30-year-old. The books focus on YA topics (but feature older characters): self-worth, coming of age, sexuality, depression, suicide, drug/alcohol abuse, family issues, bullying, etc. But additional topics are also in the new adult titles – topics of interest to those moving from a school/teen environment to post teen years/school years era: post-high school friendships, military enlistment, financial independence, living arrangements, employment concerns, fear of failure, and so forth. The perspective across all topics shifts from the YA focus of popularity and acceptance to a more adult focus of success and survival. The New Adult category seeks to bridge the gap between Young Adult and Adult titles. The chief protagonists are most often, between the ages of 18 and 25, but can be as old as 30.

Good Reads an interactive web bibliography searchable by category, has a category searchable by the term, "new adult." A recent search yielded more than 9000 titles. Note that "new adult" is not a genre or subject per se but is a category of book based on the audience intended. Young Adult, children's and so forth are also categories not genres.

Interestingly many of the new books entering this New Adult category seem to be written more by women than men, and in general seem to appeal directly to females. Despite that there are new books being offered that are historical fiction, fractured fairy tales, and slice of life tales of sibling interaction. A few of the very recent titles are listed below and will provide a brief look into the type of books that are in this category. These books reach into the young adult category.

A Few Titles

- Axelrod, Aio. *The Girl with Stars in Her Eyes*. Sourcebooks Casablanca, 2021. ISBN: 978-1492698760. The first in a proposed series about the Lillys. A story of musicians and coming of age. A story where one note can mean the end of a dream or the beginning of one. Antonia "Toni" Bennette has heard all the jokes before – and she is almost famous; but someday she may be.
- Green, Amy Lynn. *Things We Didn't Say*. Bethany House, 2020. ISBN: 9780764237164. Intersection between faith and fiction. Witty banter. A historical fiction collection from the World War II Homefront. Johanna is sent back to her Minnesota home to serve as a German translator for a German war camp. True stories from the home front. Forgiveness and justice prevail.
- Green, Amy Lynn. *The Lines Between US*. Bethany House, 2021. ISBN: 9780764237164. Smokejumpers and the Triple Nickels. Conscientious objectors during WWII, Gordon Hooper and Jack Armitage have begun volunteering as smokejumpers, serving their country by parachuting into dangerous wildfires in an effort to contain devastation. But the danger doesn't add up. The number of fires escalates in early 1945. When Jack is injured, his sister Dorie (a member of the Women's Army Corps) enters the story determined to find out what is going on. Gordon and Dorie with much different views on the war, find common ground to work together to find out what has gone on. And all find out what the Triple Nickels are all about.
- Murphy, Jill. *If the Shoe Fits*. Disney Press, 2021. ISBN: 9781368053372. A contemporary Cinderella story featuring a plus-sized shoe designer who finds herself a last-minute contestant on a reality dating show "Before Midnight." As the first and only body positive contestant she attracts a lot of interest (and haters) and trust issues with the rest of the contestants. Cindy finds herself falling in love with Prince Charming, but dare she hope? A delightful contemporary take on a favorite fairytale written by a popular young adult novelist — author of *Dumplin* (2015) and *Pumpkin* (2021)/
- Fisher, Suzanne Woods. *At Lighthouse Point*. Revell, 2021. ISBN: Book three in the Three Sister's Island Series. A father notices that his three adult daughters are growing distant from one another, so he buys them an island. This series of books provide an interesting perspective on sibling order and the impact that has on one's personality development. *On a Summer Tide* (Book #1) and *On a Coastal Breeze* (Book #2) are the first two books in the series.

Contemporary Literature for Teens – Fiction

Robert Cormier and S.E. (Susan Eloise) Hinton are often credited with developing the Young Adult Literature (formerly adolescent literature) category. This focus began with contemporary realistic fiction and enveloped subject groups designated as problem novels, school stories, humor, and so forth – anything that dealt with the life of a teenager. Once established more edgy topics began to be incorporated into the narratives. Authors dealt with mental illness, sex trafficking, rape, and other very angst topics. Both lighter topics and those more serious and edgy topics existed in the offerings. And then the lives of teens began to bring a focus to a more worldwide view and more diversity.

Books for young adults minimize the existence of parents, and when they do appear in a book's plot, the parent is shown in a more balanced light - supportive but not controlling of the teens' lives. Often today topics are surrounded by ethnic and cultural identity considerations. Contemporary realistic fiction encompasses a wide range of topics and issues.

Major Subject Groups in Contemporary Realistic Fiction

Family stories – family values are the focus, with family relationships as a strong component of these stories – divorce, sibling rivalry, and so forth. All the Days Past, All the Days to Come by Mildred D. Taylor (Viking, 2020) is a classic example of family stories. This book ends the story of the Logan family first introduced with Roll of Thunder Hear My Cry, forty years ago. The strong characters from this family saga are now flung far and wide but the family is still dealing with seismic social movements, and relationships impacted by events outside their family.

Coming-of-Age – Relationships with peers, puberty, sex, and dealing with transitioning into adulthood. Girl Crushed by Katie Heaney (Knopf, 2020) deals with Quinn's break-up with her best friend right before their senior year and how she struggles to deal with moving on. A classic YA novel about love, hope and uncertainty.

Problem Novels – Teen life is complicated and the problems in current novels have gotten more intense. Rape, cutting, mental illness, teen pregnancy are all part of the discussion of problems teens face. Authors of note in this sector include: Laurie Halse Anderson, Patricia McCormick, and Ilsa Madden-Mills. The Hate U Give by Angie Thomas (Balzer + Bray, 2017), On the Come Up (Balzer + Bray, 2019) and her more recent Concrete Rose (Balzer + Bray, 2021) all deal with making choices in the face of difficult circumstances.

Romance -- Generally focuses on the love life of two persons – female to male, male to male, female to female. Often light-hearted and optimistic but recent romantic novels often deal with the serious complications that surface with same-sex relationships. The focus on LGBTQ category has put a new focus and level of awareness on teen book dealing with romance.

Mystery and Suspense -- detective fiction which seeks to solve a crime. The distinction between mystery and suspense is predicated on who knew what when.

In suspense the reader knows, early on, who the culprit is but the plot advancement creates suspense by creating situations where the reader is in anticipation for others to learn what they already know. A mystery maintains the secrecy of the culprit for both the reader and the characters within the story being told. Red herrings, plot twists, and cliffhangers are utilized in both mystery and suspense tales. Those who solve the mystery are predominately white. Any type of diversity seems to be missing in a majority of these tales.

Historical fiction – Historical events and people populate these books that can serve to flesh out the emotions and details that were part of a historical era. However, authors do not have to rely on exact quotes or actions taken during these times but rather only include those events and actions that are realistic for the period. For example, in Catherine, Called Birdy by Karen Cushman (HarperCollins, 1994) Cushman describes a medieval meal. Whether or not that meal took place or not is not known – probably not. But the description of the actions of the characters at that meal are as accurate as she could make it. Cushman researched medieval manners by finding a book of the times describing proper behavior at banquets. So historically the information is correct in terms of description but time and place and actual event, no. In a Nonfiction book the event would have had to have actually occurred.

Sports – Focuses on some aspect of the sports world. Most are dominated by teens who are involved in amateur sports. There are far fewer sports books featuring female protagonists. Roller Girl by Victoria Jamieson (Dial, 2015) was a break-through title with a female protagonist. Kwame Alexander also broke barriers when his award-winning verse novel, Crossover by Kwame Alexander (Newbery Award in 2015. This is a area where there are far more male protagonists than female. Informational books on sports are even more popular.

Adventure – These books are often categorized in other categories as they include other elements such as fantasy (Harry Potter), Dystopian and Utopian narratives (Hunger Games series), other such as Pax by Sara Pennypacker which is an adventure story involving a dog as a main character.

Science Fiction – These are novels that are speculative and imagined but could occur in the scientific world, although not yet part of our everyday life. It's a look into the future with futuristic elements that are possible according to the science we know at the present day.

- Dystopian novels – take place in societies deemed worse than the one in which we live.
- Utopian novels – takes place in societies deemed better than the one in which we live.

Science Fantasy – Speculative novels that share imaginary characters in imaginary universes. These titles often incorporate mythology, folklore and elements of magic. Popular titles here include the classic Alice in Wonderland tales and books such as the Harry Potter series. Fantasy involves making magic and the supernatural the main plot element, theme, or setting, fantasy worlds do not rely on the science principals as science fiction does. Nothing about the elements in science fantasy depend on science itself. Authors are free to create the fantasy world as a civilization with characters created from the whole cloth of their imagination. The author makes the rules, and apply those rules to the plot, characters, and setting. There are infinite possibilities, goals and connections as imaginary. Fantasy is filled with fantastical beasts, wizards and dark forces. Fantasy is where all things are possible without regard to science or reality of any type.

There are some common standard themes utilized in the world of fantasy:

- Quest – characters seek a prize, a secret, something elusive and which demands effort and secrets to achieve or obtain.
- Good vs. Evil – the classic element that is present in folk literature as well as fantasy
- Time Travel - forward or backward
- Animal societies
- Utopias (societies better than ours) and Dystopias (societies worse than ours)

Seldom is any one title a pure form of one subject or another. For example, a book dealing with sports might well have a romantic component to it that would, in some reader's eyes deem the title a book of romance, while the reader more interested in the sports angle would see it as a YA sports title.

Other Literary Subjects

In addition to the subjects above these are others that are commonplace:

Literary Fiction -- Written for literary merit, literary fiction is often political criticism, social commentary or reflections about humanity. Most of these books are character driven rather than plot driven.

Horror -- These are meant to repulse and scare through themes of death, demons, evil spirits, and after life. The story line engages with fears of scary things, such as, ghosts, werewolves, witches, monsters, demons, mythical creatures.

Western -- Plot driven tales of the American Old West. The tales are often told from the perspective of the settlers or the white settler. The narrator tells the story of settlers and outlaws. Stories of Black Cowboys have pretty much been ignored and the perspective of the Native American is for the most part absent.

Authors to Watch

- Alexander, Kwame
- Anderson, Laurie Halse
- Block, Francesca Lia
- Brande, Robin
- Burgess, Melvin
- Caletti, Deb
- Chokshi, Roshani
- Clayton, Dhonielle
- Cohn, Rachel
- Colbert, Brandy
- Dessen, Sarah
- Flinn, Alex
- Giles, Gail
- Green, John
- Going, K.L.
- Hesse, Karen
- Hopkins, Ellen
- Johnson, Maureen
- Jones, Patrick
- King, A. S.
- Klass, David
- Koertge, Ron
- Korman, Gordon
- Levithan, David
- Lee, Mackenzi
- Lockhart, E.
- Lynch, Chris
- Lu, Marie
- Maas, Sarah J.
- Menon, Sandhya
- Ness, Patrick
- Oliver, Lauren
- Rainfield, Cheryl
- Reynolds, Jason
- Rowell, Rainbow
- Sanchez, Alex
- Scott, Elizabeth
- Silvera, Adam
- Stone, Nic
- Telgemeire, Raina
- Thomas, Angie
- Trueman, Terry
- Wittlinger, Ellen
- Wolff, Virginia Euwer
- Yoon, Nicola

In the Spotlight: Angie Thomas

Angie Thomas

The Hate U Give (2017)
On the Come Up (2019)
Concrete Rose (2021)

Angie Thomas Website
https://angiethomas.com/

    Angie Thomas became a writer to watch when she was the inaugural winner of the Walter Dean Myers Grant in 2015, an award presented by WeNeedDiverseBooks. Her debut novel, *The Hate U Give* (2017) became a #1 New York Times bestseller and the basis for a 2018 American drama film from Fox 2000 pictures. Her most recent book, *Concrete Rose* (2021) is a prequel to *The Hate U Give* (2017).

    Thomas is a native of Jackson, Mississippi where she still lives. As a very young child she witnessed a shoot-out, and her family lived just blocks from where Medgar Evers was assassinated. She was a teen rapper before earning a BFA in creative writing from Belhaven University in Jackson. The shootings of Oscar Grant, Trayvon Martin, Tamir Rice, Michael Brown, and Sandra Bland had a major impact on the writing of her first novel. Thomas's professors encouraged her to use her unique experiences to give voice to those who had been silenced.

Books by Angie Thomas

The Hate U Give -- The book follows the struggles of 16-year-old American girl, Starr Carter, living in a predominantly black neighborhood but who attends a prestigious private (and predominantly white) school. Starr observes her friend Khali's murder when stopped by an officer during a traffic stop. Starr's family has inner-connections to a feared crime gang in her neighborhood – and the struggle is real.

Thomas 's second book, *On the Come Up* (2019) is the story of sixteen-year-old Bri who wants to be one of the greatest rappers ever. Inspired by her own early days as a rapper, Thomas writes a compelling saga of Brianna Jackson who seeks to honor her father (who died 8 years previous) who was an underground hip hop legend. But Bri has other battles as well. Her adored Aunt is drug dealer, and her mother is a crack addict and though she has been clean for 8 years, a relapse is always on the edge. Bri's grandmother does not feel that Jay is a fit mother for either Brianna or her brother Trey. The family situation is toxic, and the home's refrigerator is often empty. The situation, though fuels Bri's passion for rap and her talent shows through.

Concrete Rose, a prequel to *The Hate U Give*, Thomas revisits her neighborhood, Garden Heights seventeen years before the events that take place in *The Hate U Give*. The story focuses on Maverick, Starr Carter's father, who was part of the King Lords but offered a chance to go straight. But one cannot just walk away. This is the story of Maverick finding his way in the midst of dope, going to school, being a father – and his attempts to amount to something.

Poetry and Full-Length Works in Verse

Poetry has always been a form that many have avoided. The offerings were romanticized and somewhat stilted writings that readers of all ages tended to avoid. Then along came Jack Prelutsky and Shel Silverstein. Their poems, and books of poetry, popularized contemporary humorous light-hearted verses that entertained readers. The poems particularly appealed to middle school readers. The poems were short, funny, and engaging to read. Those readers who learned to enjoy those poems they began to look for more poets who wrote in a similar fashion. Poets such as:

- Paul B. Janeczko
- Jason Reynolds
- Nikki Grimes,
- Sharon G. Flake
- Naomi Shihab Nye
- Joyce Sidman
- Nikki Giovanni
- Sonya Sones
- Marilyn Nelson.

In addition to poetry written for young readers authors, some authors began to create narratives in verse and to prepare interesting stories about many subjects and wrote the tales in verse form rather than prose. Now there are also informational texts that are beginning to be written in verse, e.g. biographies, general history.

Verse Novels in the Classroom

One of the first verse novels to gain recognition was *Out of the* Dust by Karen Hesse (Scholastic, 1997) which won the Newbery Award in 1998. Hesse's book recounts the struggles and desperation that existed during the Depression. The recognition for Hesse's book brought on a deluge of verse novels and the contemporary category began to be very popular and evoke many powerful narratives using the richness of verse. Within the verse novel are many subjects. Paul B. Janeczko gave readers a historical piece with Worlds Afire.

Verse "novels" range from historical pieces such as Paul B. Janeczko's *Worlds Afire* (Candlewick, 2004) which recounts the historical 1944 Hartford circus fire. There are powerful biographies (not novels but rather informational verse texts) such as Marilyn Nelson's *Carver: A Life in Poems* (Front Street, 2001), Nelson's *A Wreath for Emmett Till* (Houghton Mifflin, 2005). Tanya Lee Stone wrote a widely successful teen problem/romance novel, *A Bad Boy Can Be Good for a Girl* (Wendy Lamb, 2006). And now Kwame Alexander has brought the verse novel into another exciting era-this time with a sports focus that clearly hooks in readers who gravitate toward books with action, and sports. Verse novels retain a narrative structure much as a prose novel does. There are changing perspectives and episodic events. Narratives are often multiple and provide various perspective. Verse novels can attract the reader who enjoys the no frills narrative, and the sparse but rich description of event unfolding. Kwame Alexander has brought a full focus to the verse novel with his first book, *Crossover* (Houghton Mifflin, 2014).

Prose & Poetry Connections

Using poetry as the lure to bring readers to longer books of poetry, to traditional fiction, or to suggest research topics is often a successful venture. After reading Dudley Randall's "The Ballad of Birmingham," a poem about the church bombing in that city during the civil rights movement, Christopher Paul Curtis changed the destination in *The Watsons Go to Birmingham–1963 from Florida to Birmingham* (Delacorte, 1995). The book earned a Newbery honor and a Coretta Scott King honor award. Randall's poem might be just the piece to introduce Curtis's book.

There are many connections from verse novels to collections of poetry, to prose novels, and other rhythmic writings such a rap verse. Already comfortable with verse, a rapper is often searching for alternative formats of poetry. Capitalize on this connection by suggesting poems as a source for performance works. Establish a forum for an afternoon of poetry readings/raps.

Poetry Blasts, Jams, and Slams

A Poetry Blast could become a popular forum for sharing poetry, a forum for performance, and encourage reading of all types. Marilyn Singer surveyed several of her poet friends to get their suggestions connecting young readers to poetry. Read this article from 2010 – it's still so relevant.

Marilyn Singer's suggestions and ideas for establishing a Poetry Blast. Her post: Singer, Marilyn. (2004) A Blast of Poetry. Marilynsinger.net (Online) https://marilynsinger.net/a-blast-of-poetry/

On May 12, 2009, First Lady Michelle Obama and the President hosted the first "Poetry Jam" at the White House. Several YouTube videos have been posted showing some of the poets from 2009 through several years of the poetry jams. At that time President Obama said the poetry jam was a chance to, "celebrate the power of words and music to help us appreciate beauty, but also to understand pain" (Lundberg, 2009, para 1).

Lundberg, John. (2009, June 17). The Blog: Poetry Jam at the White House. *Huffington Post.* (Online) https://www.huffpost.com/entry/poetry-jam-at-the-white-h_b_204012

> Poetry gives us the chance to "celebrate the power of words and music to help us appreciate beauty, but also to understand pain."
> ~ President Barack Hussein Obama, 2009

In the Spotlight: Kwame Alexander

Kwame Alexander

Kwame Alexander. http://www.kwamealexander.com

Kwame Alexander is known as a poet, educator, and a bestselling author. His father was a publisher and his mother an English teacher but as a very young boy he had any books surrounding him. He read everything he could get his hands on: Eric Carle (remember *The Very Hungry Caterpillar*), Lee Bennett Hopkins (a poet and anthologist extraordinaire), and Eloise Greenfield. But by fourth or fifth grade he hated books, he hated being told to read something he wasn't interested in reading. What he was interested in was playing sports – football and basketball.

Finally, he got back into books by reading *The Greatest: My Own Story*, an autobiography by Muhammed Ali (Random House, 1975). But it wasn't until he was studying medicine at Virginia Tech and writing poetry as a hobby that he began to think about writing seriously. Nikki Giovanni was very supportive. He started his own publishing company and published ten volumes of poetry and two picture books before coming to the idea of sports-themed novels written in verse. That book brought him to the forefront of writing for sports interested teens. *The Crossover* was named the Newbery Award winner in 2015. Alexander has published many popular titles novels, picture books, -- popular books for all readers – with verse novels Alexander has found his niche.

Selected Books by Kwame Alexander

- Playbook: 52 Rules to Aim, Shoot, and Score in this Game Called Life (Houghton Mifflin Harcourt, 2017)
- *Booked* (Houghton Mifflin Harcourt, 2016)
- *Crossover* (Houghton Mifflin Harcourt, 2014)
- *Rebound* (Houghton Mifflin Harcourt, 2018)
- *Undefeated* (Houghton Mifflin Harcourt, 2018)
- *Solo* (Houghton Mifflin Harcourt, 2017)
- *Swing*, with Mary Rand Hess (Blink, 2018)

Opportunities for Community Service in Literacy – World-Wide Poetry and Literacy

Literacy Empowerment Action Project (LEAP) —Kwame is the co-founder of the Literacy Empowerment Action Project (LEAP) that built the Barbara E. Alexander Memorial Library and Timber Nkwanta Health Post in the eastern region of Ghana, in the Village of Konko. His work there is ongoing. The work helps to raise up the children and young adults in Ghana. Learn more about the initiative on the organization's website at https://leapglobal.org/. The organization welcomes others who can get involved as a charitable opportunity to support literacy in a global environment.

Ethiopia Reads and Ready, Set, Go Books—Another initiative with literacy in Africa that is worthwhile, and seeks involvement by those who wish to have an impact across the world is Ethiopia Reads (https://www.ethiopiareads.org/), this is an initiative that was co-founded by Jane Kurtz (http://www.janekurtz.com/). Currently she has stepped back as a member of the board and she spearheads an initiative to write and publish early reading books for children in Ethiopia. Jane is now a member of the advisory board for Ready, Set, Go books which are a literacy project of Open Hearts, Big Dreams (https://openheartsbigdreams.org/) that work with Ethiopia Reads and other organizations to get books into the hands of young readers.

Mysteries and Suspense

The standard elements in a young adult mystery novel include an interesting setting, characters that readers care about, a personal problem for the main character, and a compelling mystery-all tied together with good writing that brings together the solution to the personal problem with the solution to the mystery. The trend that has been developing for the past decade is toward stronger (and more sophisticated) female protagonists and less cozy pivotal incidents. Murders are commonplace in many mysteries and the action is becoming more and more chilling.

Mysteries for the younger reader were traditionally built around such incidents as lost lunch money, a stolen bike, and mysterious happenings- cozy events that provided a mystery but not a lot of heart-pounding suspense. Even the mysterious happenings were later explained away by natural events. But times began to change. Mysteries that once included *cozy* incidents are now laced with murders, drugs, and real villains. Young adult protagonists were once pitted most often against those of their own age; but now they often find themselves confronting real adult criminals.

Young adult detective novels focus on the activities of the young adult in solving the crime. Adult police and detectives are tolerated as support personnel, but it is the young adult protagonist that is responsible for uncovering the important clues and weaving them together to uncover the villain.

Personal problems are woven through the weft of the mystery novel. Actions are often fueled by the jealousy of one character for another. A mystery moves into the suspense category when the reader of the story knows the identity of the culprit long before the characters in the story do. Suspense is built by placing the main character in situations where that character is vulnerable.

Suspense is achieved by information control: What you know. What the reader knows. What the characters know.
~ Tom Clancy

Authors of mystery and suspense tales, as with mainstream novels, find themselves mirroring the changing society and drawing more and more on events that are occurring around them. And some writers reach back into their lives to revisit events from their past. In April 1990, when Alane Ferguson accepted the Edgar Allan Poe Award from the Mystery Writers of America for her 1989 title *Show Me the Evidence* (Avon) she did so in the name of her very best friend, Savannah. Savannah had been brutally raped and murdered several years before. Her friend's murder and the subsequent investigation marked Ferguson's mystery writing for young adults. Through the experience surrounding her friend's murder Ferguson said that she 'became both fascinated and repelled by the law." She had to testified at Savannah's murderer's trial and describes her observation, "I remember staring at the hands of her killer, which at the time were folded harmlessly in his lap and thinking how bizarrely civilized we'd all become . . .. All of my mystery books have their genesis in the loss of my friend." Two years later the shadows of Ferguson's memories of that experience show up in *Overkill* (Bradbury, 1992).

Ferguson's *Show Me the Evidence* is a gripping tale of the experiences of two 17-year-olds caught in the middle of an investigation into the deaths of three infants/toddlers who are at first thought to have died of SIDS, but later as the police link all the deaths to Janaan, the mystery begins. The novel deals with solving the death of the babies. When the police exhumed the bodies, the police find the graves empty. Lauren, and Janaan prove themselves to be innovative thinkers in a tightly drawn whodunit that touches on the exotic when the girls unravel the mystery and identify the culprit. The children had been drugged into a zombie state and retrieved only to be sold on the black market to unsuspecting couples. The tale had been inspired by a report on 20/20 in buried, and then years later reappeared among the living. It seems there is a poison extracted from Haiti's native puffer fish that could cause a death sleep, much like Juliet experienced in Shakespeare's famous play. Most SIDS babies are autopsied and embalmed before burial but then Ferguson discovered that some religious denominations bury their dead by sundown. These two discoveries made the plot envisioned by Ferguson, plausible and it became her award-winning debut novel.

But her second book, *Overkill*, drew on her experiences in dealing with her best friend's murder. Ferguson's mystery writing career began with research and her own personal experience to write compelling novels. She wrote more than thirty books, some of them with her mother Gloria Skurzynski – The Mysteries in Our National Parks series.

Lois Duncan, for many years was a perennial favorite of young adult readers. She drew on her interest in psychic phenomena as a popular element in her novels which were more suspense than mystery. However, her writing came squarely into the realm of a true-life mystery after her book *Don't Look Behind You* (Dell, 1989). The heroine, April was based on Duncan's eighteen-year-old daughter, Kait. One month after that book was released, Kait was murdered in a case that has never been solved. Many of the facts surrounding the murder that were uncovered-mirror incidents, bit and pieces that had previously been written into the plot of *Don't Look Behind You*. Both the fictional April and Duncan's daughter Kait were chased down by a hit man in a Camero. Mike Gallagher, a real-life investigative reporter that worked on Kait's murder case, shared his name with a boyfriend from a previous book

(*Summer of Fear*). Duncan details all the eerie coincidences in *Who Killed My Daughter?* (Delacorte, 1992). Lois Duncan passed away in 2016 with the case still unsolved. Her website is still up, seemingly untouched since 2016 at https://loisduncan.arquettes.com/. For years before her death, Lois Duncan had sought help from psychics to solve her daughter's murder. Those efforts were unsuccessful. But her life account of her daughter's murder and the efforts to solve the crime still haunt me – some thirty years later. That's what a good book does to you.

Joan Lowery Nixon was a long-time standout in the field of mystery writing for young adults, often uses the technique of pushing a young adult into a sudden crisis that leads directly into involvement in a murder. Her plots involved bodies discovered in a pool, séance that results in a murder, and a protagonist who is in a coma for four years, and when she wakes up finds herself as the only witness to an unsolved murder.

Among the early mystery writers are: Joan Lowery Nixon, Mary Downing Hahn, Keith Robertson, Scott Corbett, Alane Ferguson, Lois Duncan, Mary Higgins Clark, and Phyllis Reynolds Naylor.

- While murders once populated the majority of mystery books, today's mysteries focus on other problems as well: kidnappings, lost families, espionage, hiding family secrets, involvement with the mafia, strange and devious events, home burglaries, and many other common events.
- Mysteries primarily focus on the "whodunit" aspect of a crime. Clues are revealed, sometimes false clues (red herrings), and in the end all is revealed.
- Suspense titles reveal, to the reader, the culprit of the crime and the suspense builds around the interaction the unsuspecting characters have with the villain.
- Most spy novels are thrillers in which the hero must stop some major act and save the world. Spy novels are impacted by current politics as villains have changed from Nazis, to KGB, to Al-Qaeda style terrorists, and most recently domestic terrorists, and political sabotage.
- Supernatural and horror novels often play on the psychological elements of human nature. Supernatural fiction accepts the presence of witches, vampires, werewolves, zombies, and other supernatural creatures, but not always as evil monsters.

Many authors have published single mystery or suspense stories, but several authors have published series. Or at least authors have included reoccurring characters in. their tales. Adult novelists often build a following by featuring a specific detective in their books. This is sometimes common in young adult novels as well, e.g. Charlotte Holmes, Elizabeth Parrot.

At the turn of the century, vampires, witches, and werewolves were popular characters in a new breed of horror. When, in 2008, Stephenie Meyer infused a bit of romance into the mix, the books rose to great popularity increasing with each of the four books in Meyer's *Twilight Saga*. The Twilight series focuses on Edward (a vampire), Jacob (a werewolf), and what Bella's sacrifice will bring. The line between mystery/horror or plain fantasy is thin. The very popular movies based on the *Twilight* books helped the popularity of the books to peak.

In the early 2000s, spies found their way into teen fiction. Alex Rider, a teenage British Spy, battles evil terrorists in a series authored by Anthony Horowitz. The first book, *Stormbreaker* (2000), premiered as a movie in 2006. The 9th and last title in the series, *Scorpia Rising,* was published in 2011. The book series sold more than 12 million copies. F.T. Bradley has followed with more spy thrillers, a very popular series *Double Vision* (2012) featuring Lincoln Baker. The first in the series, *Double Vision* is a page-turner that will have readers engrossed in Baker's James Bond type action-packed adventure. Lincoln Baker's adventures continue in the second book, *Code Name 711* (2013). Following the immense success of the initial spy books, many other mystery writers have joined the lexicon of young adult mystery writers.

These are some mystery writers to watch

- Karitzer, Naomi
- Mather, Adriana
- Ribay, Randy
- Simmons, Kristen
- Thomas, Leah
- Bowman, Erin
- Dawn, Sasha
- Hill, Will
- Suma, Nova Ren
- Summers, Courtney

In the Spotlight: Nancy Werlin

Nancy Werlin

Nancy Werlin. http://www.nancywerlin.com

Nancy Werlin's first novel was *Are You Alone on Purpose* (1995) but she really made her mark in the world of YA lit when her suspense thriller *The Killer's Cousin* won the Edgar Award, and the next novel, *Locked Inside*, was named an Edgar finalist.

New editions of *The Killer's Cousin*, *Locked Inside*, and *Black Mirror* were independently published in 2021.

Werlin's writing is not limited to mystery and suspense. She has written several fantasy titles and her 2021 title is a realistic fiction title that has Zoe Rosenthal taking one more fling at fandom and cosplay before planning her future with her perfect boyfriend, Simon. But will her final fling be enough and what does the future hold? *Zoe Rosenthal Is Not Lawful Good* (Candlewick, 2021)

Edgar Allan Poe Award

For an update of the winners of the annual Edgars award go to the Internet site at: http://theedgars.com/awards/category-list-best-young-adult/

The Edgar Allan Poe Awards are generally awarded in April of each year. Categories include a Best Juvenile and a Best Young Adult category.

In 2021 (published in 2020) these are the short-list of nominees:

The Companion by Katie Alender (G.P. Putnam's Sons)
The Inheritance Games by Jennifer Lynn Barnes (Little, Brown)
They Went Left by Monica Hesse (Little, Brown)
Silence of Bones by June Hur (Feiwel & Friends)
The Cousins by Karen M. McManus (Delacorte Press)

Information about all the winners and future year's nominees are available at http://www.theedgars.com/

Winners – the past decade
- 2020 Naomi Kritzer's *Catfishing on CatNet*
- 2019 Courtney Summers's *Sadie*
- 2018 Jason Reynolds's *Long Way Down*
- 2017 Monica Hesse's *Girl in the Blue Coat*
- 2016 Mindy McGinnis's *A Madness So Discreet*
- 2015 James Klise's *The Art of Secrets*
- 2014 Annabel Pitcher's *Ketchup Clouds*
- 2013 Elizabeth Wein's *Code Name Verity*
- 2012 Dandi Daley Mackall's *The Silence of Murder*
- 2011 Charlie Price's *The Interrogation of Gabriel James*

Today's young adult demands that the mystery include a crime -a significant crime. Often that crime is a murder or the threat of murder lurking in the background. Other crimes that are included in mysteries include high-stakes drug trafficking, kidnapping, or a mysterious family secret that threatens the well-being of the family or community. While the characters in the well-written mystery must be someone readers will care about, the clues and the puzzle are the significant elements of the novel. Readers care more about the plot's puzzle which must be a complicated weaving of suspicion, clues, motives, and red herrings. The puzzle must be center stage at all times. Bits of background information must be woven throughout the novel as the story progresses. The first choice of most teen readers are those novels hat immediately grab their attention and keep it until the end of the book. Good mysteries do this from the very beginning to the very end.

Folklore /Mythology

Folklore is the umbrella term that encompasses various forms of folk literature. The oral folklore, including those tales now in written form, are tales that have been shared for generations in the oral tradition. Basically, traditional folklore has no author (although some have been attributed to specific collectors, such as the Grimm Brothers and Charles Perrault who collected tales from the common people in their regions.). Retellers did not originate the stories but rather collected and wrote the tales down in a written form so they have endured through the decades. As the stories have been retold over and over again various details have changed and embellished or simplified depending on the reteller. The Grimm version of some tales tend to be much more gruesome than versions of the same/similar tale collected by Perrault. The tales told by Hans Christian Andersen mimics some of the same motifs and themes as the traditional folk literature but Andersen created the tales from his own imagination, so they are not folklore in the traditional sense but are considered fiction or at best literary folk literature.

Literary folklore is also the term for those stories created by contemporary authors that closely mimic the motifs and themes of traditional tales – often dubbed fractured folktales, or contemporary folklore. These tales follow traditional motifs but with some new characters or twisted details applied to setting, characters and details of the plot.

Most of the folklore collections read by young adults do not differ from those that elementary readers or adults read – the editions seem to be universally enjoyed. However young adult writers have created some great fiction titles based on the folklore usually shared in short stories, anthologies, collections, or in picture books. The author has taken the core story and added details, and enhanced the plot with supporting events and ideas to create a book length tale mirroring the motif, theme, and story line of the traditional folk literature. Many of the novels based on the folklore have developed into series, and enter the world of fantasy with magic, princesses, and the traditional hero saving the day.

One notable example is the New Adult novel written by Jill Murphy. *If the Shoe Fits* (Disney Press, 2021) is a contemporary tale incorporating motifs from the traditional Cinderella tale and infused into a reality dating show, After Midnight. The author is a successful young adult author whose popular title, *Dumplin'* (HarperCollins, 2015) is the basis for a Netflix movie starring Jennifer Aniston, Danielle Macdonald, and Dove Cameron, as well as a soundtrack from Dolly Parton!

More Subjects (Genres or Categories)

What many refer to as genres are really subjects. For example, sports books are really a subcategory of contemporary fiction, or perhaps historical fiction depending on who or what is the focus of the sports. And then there are sports books that are informational books.

Basically, there are three genres in literature: prose, poetry, drama. Beyond that we are dealing with subject matter. Many subjects are commonly referred to as sub-genres but they are really the subject. There are prose titles that are fiction or Nonfiction; and within each of these there are romances, or historical, biographical, focused on sports etc. Same with poetry. There can be romantic poetry, biographical writings, and so forth. Sports? What is Casey at the Bat? Poetry? Sports?

Most of us can easily discuss the subject of a book. The Dewey Decimal system categorizes books based on subject – not genres as other than poetry or drama the books are all prose. There are fiction books and Nonfiction books that deal with history. There are science books that are fictional (and sometimes goes beyond science and into fantasy). There are history books that deal strictly in facts and are informational books (but still prose) dealing with history, and then there are prose titles that weave historical facts throughout the story but along the way authors make up dialogue or events (even if the events could have happened) and while those books share history, they are fiction. Books of history information and history fiction are generally prose.

So, in short – we have poetry, prose, and drama. In all three categories we have true and fictionalized (even if only some of the information is made up, it's fiction). Beyond that we have subjects. Books are written about all types of subjects. When librarians say they are genrefying their libraries they really are saying we are arranging our libraries by subject. Some libraries are only genrefying their fiction section while leaving the Dewey Decimal classification system in place for nonfiction titles. I can't get too excited about the idea of genrefying a library. I think the library catalog can use the subject lines to categorize the books and print out a list and locations. What I can't figure out is how I have to think like the librarian that genrefies the collection. For example, a book about the artist Grant Wood that discusses his art alongside his evolution as an artist, and which uses plates of his art to illustrate his artistic growth. So, is this a biography or a book of art? Where do I look? I just want to know where it is without guessing so I will need to look in the catalog anyway.

Kwame Alexander's *Crossover* (HMH, 2014) is a book of basketball, and has a romantic element, and it is a story of sibling relationships, and all told in verse. So what is it? A sports book? A romance book? Family dynamics? Poetry? To be able to browse to find it, I would need to be able to duplicate the thinking of the person who genrefied the collection. So back to the catalog – I need to find the location.

By sectioning books by subject (genres) rather than by author as traditionally done, we have begun to label student readers. No one needs to be privy to the type of reading or browsing a student chooses. Browsing in the LGBTQ section or the Romance section, for example, leaves readers open to comments and oversight. When all of these books are intermixed and accessible by author or catalog search, readers are free to choose titles more anonymously and without comment from fellow library patrons.

GLBTQ Literature for Teens - The History

Books for Gay, Lesbian, Bisexual, Transgender, and Questioning teens (GLBTQ) encompass all the genres but include a plot or a subplot that includes protagonists that belong to the GLBTQ community or focuses on concerns of specific interest to GLBTQ readers. The history of GLBTQ titles have basically paralleled the history of the YA category in general. In the late 1960s and early 1970s there were few novels published with gay and lesbian themes: John Donovan's *I'll Get There. It Better Be Worth the Trip* (1969), Isabelle Holland's *The Man without a Face* (1970), Sandra Scoppettone's *Trying Hard to Hear You* (1974), Rosa Guy's *Ruby* (1976), and Mary W. Sullivan's *What's This About, Pete?* (1976).

The books written in this category (not a separate genre as GLBTQ books should encompass all types of books, e.g. poetry, prose, and drama, but feature characters who represent the GLBTQ community) have steadily increased over time. GLBTQ literature still seems to be dominated by male characters in white middle-class settings, change is coming as young adult literature has begun to feature more diversity.

A writer that has emerged as notable in this demographic is Alex Sanchez. As a Mexican immigrant, Sanchez, has infused a level of diversity in the category and has become a very popular author of books that deal directly with topics of importance to GLBTQ teens. *Boyfriends with Girlfriends* (Simon & Schuster, 2011) is a romantic comedy featuring two pairs of teens (bisexual, gay, lesbian, and straight). Sanchez's 2020 title, *You Brought Me the Ocean* is a graphic novel which features Jake Hyde who is dealing with his father's death, his crush on the swim team captain, and his hesitation to come out to his mom, and to his best friend.

David Levithan's book *Boy Meets Boy* (2003), a light-hearted tale that introduced a world where characters not only know they are gay by kindergarten, but their homosexuality is accepted, the cheerleaders ride Harleys, and the quarterback is also the homecoming queen.

In this decade Alex Sanchez, Brent Hartinger, Julie Peters, David Leviathan, and Brian Sloan consistently publish novels that show a diverse range of quality GLBTQ literature.

In the Spotlight: Alex Gino

Alex Gino

An activist for rights for all people Alex Gino (they/their) has long been involved in organizations and causes that promote recognizing all as equal persons. With their debut novel Gino brings to the forefront some of the most engaging narratives in the young adult category. In *George*, Gino's debut novel, the chief protagonist is seen as a boy by others, but she knows she's not a boy. She knows she is a girl. And others come to learn who she really is when she decides that she wants to be Charlotte in the middle-school play of *Charlotte's Web*. It is only at the end that George becomes a deadname. It is a very insight portrayal of a transgender teen coming to terms with gender identification. A Stonewall Award Winner.

In their second novel, *Rick*, Gino writes of a middle school boy who has never questioned who he is, much as others seem to have it figured out. When Rick goes to middle school he has the opportunity to be part of the Rainbow Spectrum club and to meet Melissa, who seems to have her life together.

Gino's third novel *You Don't Know Everything Jilly P!* does not deal specifically with GLBTQ issues, but rather approaches the issue of social justice. Jilly's sister, Emma, is born deaf. Jilly realizes that she and Emma will be treated differently because of the hearing issue; but both of them recognize that each of them-as white females, will be treated differently from their Black cousins.

Don't miss this interview with Alex Gino as published in *The Guardian*

Hansen, John. (2015, September 9). Interview: Alex Gino "I knew I was different as a kid." (Online) https://www.theguardian.com/childrens-books-site/2015/sep/09/alex-gino-george-transgender-protagonist-interview

How to Feature GLBTQ books

In days past librarians and teachers alike segregated and labeled GLBTQ books into a separate section so that their patrons could easily locate them. The impact is that the books did not get read by those who truly needed them but did not have the confidence to browse in that section and fully disclose their interest in the topic.

Far better to make sure the GLBTQ designation is indicated on the library record so that a key search could locate specific titles. (All the more reason to teach catalog and location skills as part of library instruction). Readers who seek to confirm their own identity will need these books to help them deal with their own thoughts and ideas. Straight teens who have no concerns regarding themselves need to read these books to help them understand their friends. All readers need to see others, unlike themselves, in all books read. GLBTQ characters no exception. We need diversity of all types and it is just not readers in one specific category that needs the books showing the character in their own demographics. All readers need to see and develop empathy and understanding regarding the struggles and successes others experience

Diversity Concerns

Diversity is a concept that all educators have heard and have embraced. There is probably not one educator who does not have some concern for how various ethnic and minority groups are portrayed in literature.

At this time Hispanic and Latino Americans are the largest ethnic minority at approximately 18% of the population. African Americans are the second largest racial minority with approximately 14% of the population. This has major implications for the books we select and the literature we recommend to young learners. In many people's minds, the term *multicultural* translates into African American, but the term means much more than just one race. Diversity is a more accurate term as it encompasses more than just racial concerns but ethnic and cultural groups as well. Asian and Hispanic cultures, and an increasing amount of attention is now being paid to Native Americans and cultural and religious minorities.

Ashley Bryan, a noted African American author and illustrator, once wrote an article for the Children's Book Council in which he discussed the emergence of literature that acknowledged minority cultures. In that article, Bryan said, "Children can now see their images in illustrated books and in stories of their people. They make a direct connection to these pictures and stories." (Ashley Bryan: Discovering Ethnicity Through Children's

Books. *CBC Magazine: The Children's Book Council.* 2006.) While images of many cultures are being shown in picture books and middle-grade books and young adult novels are including a diversity of characters in greater numbers, those images and portrayals are often unflattering or deemed stereotypic by the groups portrayed. For example, visit Debbie Reese's blog, *American Indians in Children's Literature,* htttp://americanindiansinchildrensliterature.blogspot.com -- discusses many aspects of the portrayal of Native American Indians in books for young readers. Reese is a tribally enrolled at the Nambe Pueblo in northern New Mexico and is an outspoken advocate for accurate portrayal of all Native Americans in books.

Interestingly, it seems that most young adult novelists assume that readers view all characters as white and tend to identify only those characters of an ethnic or cultural background that is not white and European in origin. One author that does not do that is Christopher Paul Curtis; he assumes his characters are Black and identifies characters as white, when appropriate. In Cynthia Leitich Smith's *Rain is Not My Indian Name,* readers might assume that Rain's best friend, Galen, is Native American. If a reader does assume that, they will be surprised in the middle of the novel.

Both teachers and librarians should be aware of the growing number of multi-racial teens in our society that do not identify with a particular racial or ethnic background but consider themselves just plain American. The most famous example, of course, is Tiger Woods. Many cultures would like to claim him as their own, but he has generally refused to identify with one group or another. On the other hand, Barack Obama is generally identified as African American, but his mother was white, a native of Kansas. Adults need not pressure teens into choosing a cultural or ethnic background either in conversation with them or in the books recommended for them to read. While all readers like to see their own faces and situations mirrored in books, others who do not share the same heritage must find windows to other cultures and ethnic groups. Mirrors and windows must be available - but let the reader decide which view they wish to have. As in other situations, choice is the key element in building readers.

In the field of children and teen literature circles, there is a fierce debate about who should be able to write and illustrate about a particular culture. Is it acceptable? Is the story credible if a non-African American writes a story where the chief protagonist is African American? Can a non-Native American write of growing up in an Indian boarding school? Can a Native American who was raised off the reservation, and in an urban area write about life on a reservation and attending an Indian boarding school? Can a Christian writer write of teenagers growing up in a Jewish household? In a *School Library Journal* article (Anderson, Laurie Halse. "The Writing of Fever 1793." *School Library Journal.* May 2001. Volume 47, p 44.) Laurie Halse Anderson said, "In some ways, writing historical fiction is like writing outside of one's culture. The author must be scrupulous about detail and motivation, sensitive to cultural (and time) differences, wary of interpretation, and conscious of the reader's background and ability." Anderson is correct about historical fiction and in regard to authors who write outside of their culture. Authors who do write outside of their culture must be absolutely scrupulous about details, show extreme sensitivity to the cultural nuances and interpretations, and always remain conscious of the perspective of those about whom they write. Some would argue, however, that someone writing outside of their own culture simply do not understand that culture well enough to know what nuances they are missing.

A new term being used recently refers to "intercultural literacy." Watch for this term and how it interplays with information about multicultural and diverse literacy.

Resources for Understanding and Keeping Up with Multicultural Concerns

> The Brown Bookshelf: United in Story. (Online) https://thebrownbookshelf.com/ -- focuses on books for younger readers but many mentor texts and books that should stimulate research to acquaint older readers with diverse people whose contributions are often overlooked.
> Cooperative Children's Book Center (CCBC). CCBC Diversity Statistics (WEB) https://ccbc.education.wisc.edu/literature-resources/ccbc-diversity-statistics/
> Debbie Reese's American Indians in Children's Literature Blog at: http://americanindiansinchildrensliterature.blogspot.com/ -Debbie Reese (Nambe Pueblo) provides critical thoughts on children's and young adult literature
> Jewish Book Council. Booklists and more featuring Jewish topics. (Online) https://www.jewishbookcouncil.org/books/search
> McElmeel, Sharron L. "Good Intentions Are Not Enough." Library Media Connection, Nov/Dec 2004, Vol. 23 Issue 3, p28. (WEB) http://www.mcelmeel.com/author/otherwritings/articles/goodintentions.html
> We Need Diverse Books (WNDB) - A non-profit and a grassroots organization that advocates essential changes in the publishing industry. (Online) https://diversebooks.org/. Find great new books and authors/illustrators here.

Publishers to Watch

> Lee & Low Publishers -- Lee & Low Books is the largest multicultural children's book publisher in the United States. https://www.leeandlow.com/
> Cinco Puntos Press -- With roots on the U.S./Mexico border, Cinco Puntos Press publishes great books which make a difference in the way you see the world. https://cincopuntos.com/
> Simon & Schuster/Denene Miller Books – publishes African American authors/illustrators for all ages.
> Disney-Hyperion/Rick Riordan Presents – publishes middle grade authors from underrepresented cultures and backgrounds who tell stories inspired by mythology and folklore of their own culture.

Since Winter of 2021 HarperCollins Children's Books launches Heartdrum, A New Native Focused Imprint; Heartdrum offers stories from Native creators, drawing on their lived experiences, and with an emphasis on the present and future of Indian Country and on the strength of young Native heroes. Cynthia Leitich Smith (Muscogee Creek) is a lead in this imprint. She is a well-known author whose work is showcased on her personal website @ https://cynthialeitichsmith.com/

Teaching Tolerance

Much of what we label as diverse literature is anything but. Books that deal with Black History and focus only on slavery, and the trauma and struggle of civil rights perpetuate that the only history of Blacks is the history of trauma. Black history is so much more. It's creativity, its life just as other cultures and races know it. The books shared throughout the years of a student's education should encompass all phases of history. The same is true of other cultures. Native American tales seem always to center on the history of the Westward Movement. Chiefs defending their homeland, war bonnets, teepees, and life in past centuries. While all of those phases of history are very important, we must not relegate the history of Native Americans to war bonnets and face paint.

Coshandra Dillard says it very clearly in an essay she wrote for Black history month. Read this article and then think about the books you share with students. Are the books dealing with the stereotypical topics generally associated with the history of these cultures or are people of color actually part of stories and informational texts that have nothing to do with trauma and struggle.

Dillard, Coshandra. (2020, January 29). Black History Month: Teaching the Complete History. *Teaching Tolerance.* https://www.tolerance.org/magazine/black-history-month-teaching-the-complete-history

Do you think of diversity only from a white European perspective? To a Native American diversity is viewed from a different vantage point. Same with Black Americans, or Asian Americans. We should be careful not to assume that diverse means "other." All readers should be given the opportunity to read books that provide mirrors and other books that provide windows to other views.

Dr. Seuss and Other Classics to Re-evaluate

In March of 2021, Dr. Seuss Enterprises announced that six titles in its backlist would no longer be published. The titles include: *And To Think I Saw It on Mulberry Street*; *If I Ran the Zoo*; *McElligot's Pool*; *On Beyond Zebra!*, *Scrambled Eggs Super!*, and *The Cat's Quizzer*.

Politicians, librarians, parents – everyone seemed to have an opinion and many I suspect, that had never read the books in question. But there were some very reasoned responses. And the responses actually resonant regarding many other titles, e.g. *The Outsiders* by S.E. Hinton, and The Little House Series by Laura Ingalls Wilder. Read some of these articles and make your own decision.

    Yorio, Kara. (2021, March 19). School Librarians Must Lead the Ongoing Conversation About Problematic Titles and Library Collections. School Library Journal (digital). http://bit.ly/3rbn934

Reese maintains a website (a blog) at In this article, Ryan Tahmaseb, director library services at the Meadowbrook School in Weston, Massachusetts is quoted as saying, "It is reading, re-evaluating, and weeding when deemed necessary. Libraries are not archives" (Para 7). He goes on to say, "Whenever a book diminishes human beings through harmful stereotypes or racist language or imagery, that book has no business being on a school library bookshelf."

American Indians in Children's Literature (Blog)

Debbie Reese regularly comments on books that represent in some way American Indians. She comments on books for young adults as well as books for younger readers. Accessing the site can provide comments about many books – search the keywords and archival posts by using the "find" function once you get to the blog's home page.

    Debbie Reese's site (a blog) http://americanindiansinchildrensliterature.blogspot.com/ is absolutely the most comprehensive look at books that include any references to American Indians – and some of the titles with negative images/texts are surprises. For example, don't miss her discussion of The Outsiders by S.E. Hinton -- https://americanindiansinchildrensliterature.blogspot.com/2020/10/anti-indigenous-content-in-s-e-hintons.html

    Reese also discusses Kate diCamillo's Because of Winn-Dixie and diCamillo's decision to revise a scene in her book where a librarian recommends Gone with the Wind. The change is made to use a recommendation for David Copperfield in its place. The details can be found on Reese's blog at: https://americanindiansinchildrensliterature.blogspot.com/2021/03/gone-with-wind-is-no-longer-in.html

    Reese, Debbie. (2021, March 5). Revised and Withdrawn-A log of children's books that have been revised or withdrawn. https://americanindiansinchildrensliterature.blogspot.com/p/revisions-to.html

    Reese, Debbie. (2018, February 25). An Open Letter About Sherman Alexie. https://americanindiansinchildrensliterature.blogspot.com/2018/02/an-open-letter-about-sherman-alexie.html

Comments about Classic Books from Others

Several authors have commented about the lack of sensitivity in classic titles. Among those articles are these:

Welsh, Lara. (2019, May 14). 10 classic children's books that haven't aged well. Insider. https://www.insider.com/classic-childrens-books-that-havent-aged-well-2019-5   The article includes the following titles:

- *If I Ran the Zoo* by Dr. Seuss (This is one of the titles ultimately declared out-of-print).
- *The Cat in the Hat* by Dr. Seuss (This book has not yet been withdrawn from future printings).
- Little House (series) by Laura Ingalls Wilder
- The Indian in the Cupboard by Lynn Reid Banks
- *Peter Pan* by J.M. Barrie
- Pippi in the South Seas by Astrid Lindgren
- The Story of Doctor Doolittle by Hugh Lofting
- *Charlie and the Chocolate Factory* by Roald Dahl (revised edition still has objections)
- *The Secret Garden* by Frances Hodgson Burnett
- *The Giving Tree* by Shel Silverstein

In an article from the Whatcom County (Washington state) Library lists "Children's Literature with Negative Portrayals and Stereotypes for Curriculum. https://wcls.bibliocommons.com/list/share/606377252/606389837
Titles listed include:
- If I Ran the Zoo by Dr. Seuss
- Charlie and the Chocolate Factory by Roald Dahl
- *Googles* by Ezra Jack Keats
- The Adventures of Huckleberry Finn by Mark Twain
- *A Fine Dessert* by Emily Jenkins
- The Indian in the Cupboard by Lynne Reid Banks
- *Alvin Ho* by Lenore Look
- Tintin in America by Herge
- The Five Chinese Brothers by Claire Hutchet Bishop
- The Story About Ping by Marjorie Flack
- Tikki Tikki Tembo by Arlene Mosel
- Eight cousins: Or, the Aunt-Hill by Louisa May Alcott
- *Skippyjon Jones* by Judith Byron Schachner

Censorship Issues & Banning Books

Censorship vs selection. Library use vs materials taught in the classroom. Educators, administrators, and librarians serve students as *in loco parentis,* that is for the time the student is in attendance educators are the *parents* of the children and teens under their direction. As such efforts are made to keep students safe from harm. Schools are generally designated as drug and alcohol-free zones, firearms on campuses are forbidden, visitors are asked to register, ill students are asked to follow protocols for avoiding exposure to other students. And schools regularly put filters on Internet connectivity to lessen exposure to pornography, predators, and blatant propaganda produced by both large corporations and terrorists.

The concern comes when opinions of what is appropriate and what is not differs among those selecting, monitoring, or using material with students. Sometimes discussions come into conflict with the principles of free speech or the supposed right of teenagers to consume any types of information they wish. Both teachers and librarians, according to the courts, must take into consideration the standards of their communities for such things as decency and teen rights to controversial or pornographic information. For the most part, objections to information in our society center on foul language, politics, or sexual messages, and schools tend to respond to the wishes of parents in their communities. To do so, schools generally set up policy statements approved by a board of education laying out a defensible position with respect to controversial materials.

Schools, in general, must operate within the scope of established policies and procedures. Specifically, policies and procedures should also guide the activities of the library media collection program and the selection and use of materials in the classroom. Selection policy and considerations for library collections will vary somewhat from the policy for identifying materials to "teach" in the classroom, but many of the same considerations are important.

Policies address the ideals and generalities, and the procedure statement explains how those policies should be implemented, e.g. the daily activities that are necessary to meet the ideals and generalities. In most cases the policy and procedure documents are separate publications-the policy statement for general distribution and publication while the procedure statements are internal documents meant to be the working guidelines for the organization or library/classroom. Having a board-approved selection policy (and procedures that support the implementation of policy) may help avert concerns with book censors, copyright infringement, and collection bias.

Libraries should have a clear selection policy but, should also have a de-selection/acquisition policy, a policy on gift acceptance, and a reconsideration policy. The procedure accompanying the reconsideration policy will be extremely important, as those citizens asking for the reconsideration of an item in your library/classroom should have a clear understanding of how to make a request that a title be reconsidered. Generally, a form will be necessary to assist citizens in making a formal request.

Schools should ALWAYS have a formal reconsideration committee/procedure to facilitate the orderly requests for library books and classroom materials to be reconsidered in terms of appropriateness. The American Library Association has some excellent suggestions in their Tools, Publications & Resources section on their organization's website. Create a form for official requests for reconsideration so the questions/standards remain the same for all requests.

    American Library Association. (2021) Formal Reconsideration. (Online) http://www.ala.org/tools/challengesupport/selectionpolicytoolkit/formalreconsideration

Public libraries will generally have different policies than school libraries in areas of controversy. Public libraries are more diverse and serve the entire community. Public libraries typically have more diverse collections and defend them in the words of one public librarian: "We have something that will offend everyone." Public libraries are freer to do this because they are free of the burden of *in loco parentis*. Teachers, school librarians, and public librarians should engage in a discussion of controversial materials, their defense or reconsideration, and what constitutes ways to protect young people while encouraging them to learn how to live and work in a free society.

The Right Information at the Right Time

An increasing discussion is the prevention of access to resources on the Internet and other social media platforms based on the fear that young people will use these tools as gateways to dangerous materials. Some have said that this constitutes a new frontier in intellectual freedom. Some are now realizing that whatever is banned at school is most often available to many at home so the most important thing we can do is to TEACH responsible use of the technology and teach learners how to distinguish between credible information and that information that is unreliable and opinion rather than fact. Whatever is banned at school, that turns out to be legitimate in terms of education and learning is also forbidden to those who do not have the same access at home as some of their classmates. Thereby widening the information gap between the haves and the have nots.

ALA, Intellectual Freedom, and Banned Book Week

The American Library Association (ALA) and its members are fierce defenders of the right of citizens to choose their own reading material. Their site provides many resources for those librarians and educators facing challenges to materials that they have deemed as appropriate to their clientele. Visit their site at http://www.ala.org

The ALA has an Office of Intellectual Freedom that is charged with implementing the goals embodied in the organization's Library Bill of Rights online at http://www.ala.org/advocacy/intfreedom/librarybill. Each year the ALA sponsors Banned Book Week to highlight the rights of readers. Resources and suggestions for celebrating the freedom to read are included on the Banned Books Week pages at: http://www.ala.org/advocacy/bbooks

A Few Common-Sense Suggestions for Controversial Materials

1. Always provide alternatives and choice.
2. Provide alternatives for teens whose parents/guardian ask that their teen is not required to read, view, or listen to classroom/library materials.
3. Erase circulation records immediately when materials are returned to library collections.
4. Alert teens that search histories of the Internet are easily recovered by snoopers of any kind.
5. Teach teens to deal with uncomfortable situations in cyberspace, including behavior in chat rooms, giving out personal information, getting involved in scams, and avoiding predators.
6. All teens will encounter messages with which they are uncomfortable. Teach them to click out or notify adults of the problems they encounter.

Many books have been challenged over the years and surprisingly the challenges actually show the trend regarding where society is at, in regard to certain mores and topics in the current culture. Do keep in mind that *challenged* does not strictly translate into banned. Books can be challenged but the challenge not reaffirmed and not banned but kept on the shelves or in the classroom.

Top Challenged Books
Top 10 Most Frequently Challenged Books of 2012

1. Captain Underpants (series), by Dav Pilkey.
   Reasons: Offensive language, unsuited for age group
2. *The Absolutely True Diary of a Part-Time Indian*, by Sherman Alexie.
   Reasons: Offensive language, racism, sexually explicit, unsuited for age group
3. *Thirteen Reasons Why*, by Jay Asher.
   Reasons: Drugs/alcohol/smoking, sexually explicit, suicide, unsuited for age group
4. *Fifty Shades of Grey*, by E. L. James.
   Reasons: Offensive language, sexually explicit
5. *And Tango Makes Three*, by Peter Parnell and Justin Richardson.
   Reasons: Homosexuality, unsuited for age group
6. *The Kite Runner*, by Khaled Hosseini.
   Reasons: Homosexuality, offensive language, religious viewpoint, sexually explicit
7. *Looking for Alaska*, by John Green.
   Reasons: Offensive language, sexually explicit, unsuited for age group
8. Scary Stories (series), by Alvin Schwartz
   Reasons: Unsuited for age group, violence
9. *The Glass Castle*, by Jeanette Walls
   Reasons: Offensive language, sexually explicit
10. *Beloved*, by Toni Morrison
    Reasons: Sexually explicit, religious viewpoint, violence

Top 10 Most Frequently Challenged Books of 2019

By 2019 the list of the ten top challenged titles still included *And Tango Makes Three* by Peter Parnell and Justin Richardson. However, other titles on the 2012 list had moved off to make room for other titles. It's interesting to note that eight of the ten titles in 2019 are on the list for their references to LGBTQIA content.

1. *George* by Alex Gino
    Reasons: LGBTQIA+ content and a transgender character; because schools and libraries should not "put books in a child's hand that require discussion"; sexual references; conflicting with a religious viewpoint and "traditional family structure."
2. *Beyond Magenta: Transgender Teens Speak Out* by Susan Kuklin
   Reasons: LGBTQIA+ content, sexually explicit and biased
3. *A Day in the Life of Marlon Bundo* by Jill Twiss, illustrated by EG Keller
   Reasons: LGBTQIA+ content and political viewpoints, "designed to pollute the morals of its readers," and for not including a content warning
4. *Sex is a Funny Word* by Cory Silverberg, illustrated by Fiona Smyth
   Reasons: LGBTQIA+ content; for discussing gender identity and sex education; title and illustrations were "inappropriate"
5. *Prince & Knight* by Daniel Haack, illustrated by Stevie Lewis
   Reasons: featuring a gay marriage and LGBTQIA+ content; for being "a deliberate attempt to indoctrinate young children"
6. *I Am Jazz* by Jessica Herthel and Jazz Jennings, illustrated by Shelagh McNicholas
   Reasons: LGBTQIA+ content, for a transgender character, topic that is "sensitive, controversial, and politically charged"
7. *The Handmaid's Tale* by Margaret Atwood
   Reasons: profanity and for "vulgarity and sexual overtones"
8. *Drama* written and illustrated by Raina Telgemeier
   Reasons: LGBTQIA+ content; goes against "family values/morals"
9. Harry Potter series by J. K. Rowling
   Reasons: referring to magic and witchcraft, for containing actual curses and spells, and for characters that use "nefarious means" to attain goals
10. *And Tango Makes Three* by Peter Parnell and Justin Richardson illustrated by Henry Cole
    Reason: LGBTQIA+ content

Lists for Other Years

Lists for several years are available on the ALA' website at http://www.ala.org/advocacy/bbooks/frequentlychallengedbooks/top10   The website tells us that the lists, "are only a snapshot of book challenges. Surveys indicate that 82-97% of book challenges – documented requests to remove materials from schools or libraries – remain unreported and receive no media."

Authors – Often Challenged

Some authors are often challenged, although any one of their books are not listed in the book list of most challenged books. These authors are those whose collective works were among those that were challenged most frequently in 2012.

- Dav Pilkey
- Sherman Alexie
- Jay Asher
- E.L. James
- Ellen Hopkins
- Jimmy Santiago Baca
- Patricia Polacco
- John Green
- Luis Alberto Urrea
- Alvin Schwartz
- Dagberto Glib

Some of these authors were great surprises to some – such as Patricia Polacco. She writes and illustrates magnificent picture books – all with a life's lesson or several that readers can take away. None seem didactic to the casual reader. Dav Pilkey uses a lot of 2nd grade humor, poop words, and shows underwear-exactly the things that make the books so humorous to primary aged readers but nothing that offends most readers. John Green writes YA books and does use a lot of profanity – more than some would endorse but nothing that most teens are not used to hearing in everyday situations. And Alvin Schwartz–yes his books are scary stories just right for sharing around a campfire or on the night ghosts and goblins inhabit the night. Guess they scared too many readers.

An extensive banned book face book group is very interesting and valuable. Banned Books Week had a live event with Alex Gino, the author of *George*. The live Zoom event is available at (2020, September 30) Alex Gino Live with Banned Books Week. https://www.facebook.com/bannedbooksweek/videos/2787501158197649

Alex Gino (they/their) has some very important comments about selection of books for young readers and why books should not be restricted by anyone but the reader. Don't miss what they have to say.

Filters in the Classroom

When the Internet first came to schools, Internet filters was (and maybe in some school districts) a controversial topic. Most filtering companies are driven by religious or ideological considerations and the filters are either managed automatically by analytics or by keywords that were generated manually according to some dictates prescribed by the filtering company. It is rather standard that many social media platforms are blocked using the school servers. Facebook is blocked. YouTube is blocked, Snapchat, and other platforms are as well. What many have found is that a lot of students have their own ways and means of accessing the Internet and other social media platforms. And while the school bans some sites/platforms students who have their own devices or Internet access find their way to access whatever information they need or want. Many school personnel are now recognizing that restrictions put less advantaged learners at a disadvantage. Their more privileged classmates have access to devices and service that allows them to have an advantage that is not available to their less privileged classmates. And while the discussion of who and why certain sites and locations are blocked is an important one it is much less crucial to many students, but it creates a very restrictive environment for many others. This topic should not be ignored. For more information about filtering check these articles:

An Atlantic article recount the situation: "The Children's Internet Protection Act (CIPA) specifically requires schools and libraries to block or filter Internet access to pictures and material that are "obscene, child pornography, or harmful to minors" on computers that are used by students under 17 years of age. The fundamental question has been how schools are interpreting the law-and whether districts are acting in the best interests of children or simply functioning as online overlords" (Anderson, 2016, para 4).

    Anderson, Melinda D. (2016, April 26). Education: How Internet Filtering Hurts Kids. Atlantic. https://www.theatlantic.com/education/archive/2016/04/internet-filtering-hurts-kids/479907/

    Starr, Linda. (2003). Filtering Software: The Educator's Speak Out. *Education World.* https://www.educationworld.com/a_tech/tech155.shtml

Chapter II – Finding Books

This section is a selective bibliography with very brief annotations for each book. The most authoritative information about publisher, and original copyright dates for each book is available at the Library of Congress's catalog site.

http://catalog.loc.gov

Searching using the quick search function will be the quickest but might not identify the specific title you want. However, the advanced search can pinpoint specific editions/titles more closely.

Sales sites such as http://amazon.com and https://www.barnesandnoble.com/ are useful sites to confirm if a book is still available for purchase, or general status. Most useful is their frequent preview function which allows readers to view a couple pages online. This is most useful for picture books but for novels and so forth the verso of the title page is often visible and that does contain the correct bibliographic information for a specific edition. Often a publisher's official website will have "assets" available for specific books. Assets often include high resolution pictures of the author and the book jacket – excellent for creating an author bulletin board. Other assets may include study guides for a specific book, a link to a first chapter audio or the text of a selection from the book, and links to related information, or the author's website. And of course, many authors have their own official webpage that will provide a plethora of information related to the author and their books. The sites will most often have links to study guides or narratives about the inspiration or back story about their books.

Publishers

The Largest Trade and Educational Publishers

- Penguin Random House (PRH) https://www.penguinrandomhouse.com/
  Includes imprints: Random House; Penguin; Knopf Doubleday; Crown Publishing; Viking Press
- Hatchette Livre – United States/Canada publishing
  https://www.hachette.com/en/a-threefold-business/publishing/usa-canada/
  Includes imprints: Grand Central Publishing; Little, Brown and Company; Mulholland Books
- HarperCollins Publishers https://www.harpercollins.com/
  Includes imprints: Avon Romance; Harlequin Enterprises; Harper; William Morrow
- Macmillan Publishers https://macmillan.com/
  Includes imprints: Farrar, Straus and Giroux (FSG); Picador; Thomas Dunne Books; Macmillan
- Simon & Schuster   https://www.simonandschuster.com/
  Includes imprints: Simon & Schuster; Howard Books; Scribner; Touchstone

- McGraw-Hill Education https://www.mheducation.com/
  Includes imprints: Glencoe/McGraw-Hill; Macmillan/McGraw-Hill, McGraw-Hill Higher Education
- Houghton Mifflin Harcourt https://www.hmhco.com/
- Includes imprints: Clarion; Graphia; John Joseph Adams Books; Sandpiper
- Pearson Education   https://www.pearson.com/en-us.html
  Includes imprints: Adobe Press; Heinemann; Prentice Hall; Wharton Publishing
- Scholastic https://www.scholastic.com/home
  Includes imprints: Arthur A. Levine; Klutz Press, Orchard Books, Scholastic
- Cengage Learning. https://www.cengage.com/
  Includes imprints: Chilton, Education to Go; Gale; National Geographic Learning

Other Publishers

- Springer Nature. https://www.springernature.com/gp
  Includes imprints: BioMed Central; Nature Research; Palgrave Macmillan
- Wiley (formerly John Wiley & Sons). https://www.wiley.com/en-us
  Includes imprints: Bloomberg Press, Capstone Hungry Minds, Wiley-Blackwell
- Oxford University Press https://www.oup.com.au/
  Includes imprints: Clarendon Press
- Kodansha   https://kodansha.us/
  Includes imprints: Kobunsha Company; Kodansha USA; Ichijinsha
- Shueisha https://www.shueisha.co.jp/english/ (Note: Site says all sites are in Japanese only. However, when you access the inner pages some are initially in English and those that are not will bring up a small pop-up that asks Google to translate.
  Includes imprints: Hakusensha, Shueisha Creative, Shueisha English Edition
- Bonner Books. https://bonnierbooks.com/
  Includes imprints: Blink; 535; Autumn Publishing; Hot Key Books; Piccadilly Press

The Bibliographies

Included in this list are award winners, young reader favorites, and new releases by popular authors. This is a list selected by the author and editors as the best new books for the years covered. The list includes graphic novels, fiction, Nonfiction (information books) including poetry and biography, and picture books that have utility of use with young adult readers.

We select from recently published lists, and award books, and books that we particularly enjoy or see a potential for an appreciative audience. In selecting books for your classroom or library you must be aware of your community, needs and wants of your patrons, and the elements that make for good literature. Balancing the availability by subject, perspective, images conveyed, diversity, and so forth is of great importance. In the following list Fiction, Nonfiction and GN (graphic novels) are used.

Books * Books * Books

Afro. *Laid Back Camp*. Illus. by the author. Yen Press, 2018.
V.1. ISBN: 9780316517782; V.2. ISBN: 9780316517829; V.3. ISBN: 9780316517850.
Rin loves to go camping, with or without her new friend, Nadeshiko - eating cup ramen and enjoying the view from their campsite. GN -Fiction

Ahmed, Saladin. *Miles Morales, Vol. 2: Bring on the Bad Guys.* Art by Alitha E. Martinez, Vanesa R. Del Ray, and Javier Garrón. Marvel Comics, 2020. ISBN: 9781302914790. Miles leaves behind his superheroing until he realizes his city needs him. GN -Fiction

Ahmed, Saladin. *Miles Morales: Straight Out of Brooklyn.* Art by Javier Garron. Marvel Comics, 2019. ISBN: 978-1302914783. The villain Rhino and Miles team up to save abducted children. But at school he is a bad egg. GN -Fiction

Ahmed, Saladin. *Ms. Marvel, Volume 1: Destined.* Art by Minkyu Jung. Marvel. ISBN: 978-1302918293; *Ms. Marvel, vol. 2: Stormranger.* Art by Minkyu Jung, Joey Vazquez. Marvel Comics, 2020. ISBN: 9781302918309. Ms. Marvel must fight Deathbringer (twice) and save the alien planet, Saffa, from the Beast Legions; and later runs into a bad guy which cuts her break is cut short. GN -Fiction

Ahmed, Samira. *Internment.* Little, Brown, 2019. ISBN: 9780316522694. In a situation much as the American internment of Japanese citizens during World War II, seventeen-year-old Layla and her family, Muslim citizens, are interned in camps. With help from a guard Layla builds a resistance movement inside the camp. Fiction

Aldridge, Ethan M. *Estranged*. Illus. by the author. Harper Collins, 2018. ISBN: 9780062653871. The Human Childe, taken as a baby, encounters numerous dangers in an effort to save the fay kingdom. GN -Fiction

Alexander, Kwame. *The Crossover: Graphic Novel*. Art by Dawud Anyabwile. Houghton Mifflin Harcourt, 2019. ISBN: 978-1328575494. Twins Josh and Jordan (JB) have basketball and stardom in their blood. When JB gets a girlfriend, Josh feels left out and they begin to drift apart. GN -Fiction

Ali, S.K. *Love from A to Z*. Simon & Schuster/Salaam Reads, 2019. ISBN: 9781534442726. A spring break visit to Doha, Qatar brings Zayneb and Adam together – both fascinated with marvels and oddities. Fiction

Ali, S.K. and Saeed, Aisha, editors. *Once Upon an Eid: Stories of Hope and Joy by 15 Muslim Voices*. Illustrated by Sara Alfageeh. Amulet Books, 2020. ISBN: 9781419740831. An Own Voices collection of Eid celebrations throughout the Muslim world. Eid is celebrated twice a year and literally means a festival or feast in Arabic. Fiction

Alkaf, Hanna. *The Weight of Our Sky*. Simon & Simon & Schuster/Margaret K. McElderry, 2019. ISBN: 9781534404403. Rosalie and Amanda are both getting threats, and both are dating Carter Shaw. Do these two events have anything to do with one another and who is responsible for the threats. An intense thriller. Fiction

Allen, Carrie. *Michigan vs. the Boys*. Kids Can/KCP Loft, 2019. ISBN: 9781525301483. After her high school cuts girls' hockey – she tries out for the boys' team. There will be more challenges than Michigan anticipates in order for her to play the game she loves. Fiction

Allen, Sarah. *What Stars Are Made Of*. FSG Books for Young Readers, 2020. ISBN: 9780374313197. Turner syndrome is a chromosomal disorder that impacts Libby's development. Her situation heightens her interest in science and is intent on winning a science contest in order to use the prize money to help support her pregnant sister's family. Fiction

Allison, John. *Giant Days* (series) Art by Max Sarin and Liz Fleming, Julia Madrigal. *Giant Days: Early Registration*. Boom! Box, 2018. ISBN: 978-1684152650; V.6, 2017. ISBN: 9781684150281; V. 7, 2018. ISBN: 9781684151318; V.8, 2018. ISBN: 9781684152070; Vol. 9-10. Art by Max Sarin, Julia Madrigal, 2019. ISBN: 978-1684153107. ISBN: 978-1684153718. *Vol. 12-14*. BOOM! Box / BOOM! Studios, 2020. ISBN: 9781684154845. ISBN: 9781684155422. ISBN: 9781684156054. Esther, Daisy, and Susan all met as college freshmen. Solving mysteries bring a challenge to Esther, Susan, and Daisy. Vol. 14 brings an end to the series, when the three women graduate from college. GN -Fiction

Amado, Elisa. *Manuelito*. Art by Abraham Urias. Annick Press, 2019. ISBN: 978-1773212661. Thirteen-year-old Manuelito is in a tiny village in the Guatemalan countryside and the armed civil patrol are a constant threat to his life. GN -Fiction

Amano, Hugh. *Let's Make Ramen! A Comic Book Cookbook*. Art by Sarah Becan. Ten Speed Press, 2019. ISBN: 978-0399581991. A comic book cookbook with accessible ramen recipes for the home cook. Accessible and fun. GN -Nonfiction

Anashin. *Satoko and Nada*. Art by the author. *Vol. 1*. Seven Seas Entertainment, 2018. ISBN: 978-1626929098. *Vol. 2*. Seven Seas Entertainment, 2019. ISBN: 978-1626929852. Satoko is from Japan and Nada is from Saudi Arabia. Satoko and Nada are college students and roommates attending school in America. Told as short one-page vignettes, Satoko and Nada get to know each other's cultures through food, religion, and custom; leading to a great friendship. GN -Fiction

Anashin. *Waiting for Spring*. Illus. by the author. Kodansha Comics, V.3, 2017. ISBN: 9781632365187; V.4, 2018. ISBN: 9781632365859; V.5, 2018. ISBN: 9781632365866; V.6, 2018. ISBN: 9781632365873; V.7, 2018. ISBN: 9781632366313; V.8, 2018. ISBN: 9781632366900. Mitsuki was determined to have a high school experience full of friends, but she never expected to fall love with the star of the boys' basketball team, Towa. But … an old childhood friend challenges Towa as a rival for Mitsuki's affection. GN -Fiction

Andersen, Sarah. *Fangs*. Andrews McMeel Publishing, 2020. ISBN: 9781524860677. A love story between a vampire and a werewolf. GN -Fiction

Andersen, Sarah. *Herding Cats: A Sarah's Scribbles Collection*. Illus. by the author. Andrews McMeel Publishing, 2018. ISBN: 9781449489786. Sarah's tasks and life as a creative person is dealt with online harassment. GN -Nonfiction

Anderson, Laurie Halse. *Speak: The Graphic Novel*. Illus. by Emily Carroll. Farrar Straus Giroux, 2018. ISBN: 9780374300289. Melinda is sexual assaulted at a party and calls the cops. Her classmates shun her and Melinda must learn how to deal with the fall-out. GN -Fiction

Anderson, M. T. *The Daughters of Ys*. Art by Jo Rioux. First Second / Macmillan, 2020. ISBN: 9781626728783. After the death of their father Princesses Rozenn and Dahut turn to different lives. While one leaves the luxury of city life behind, the other utilizes magic to help her city. GN -Fiction

Andrews, A. *A Quick & Easy Guide to Sex & Disability*. Limerence Press/Oni Press, 2020. ISBN: 9781620106945. Sexual education resources for disabled individuals which dispelling myths about disabled bodies. Self-love and communication. GN -Nonfiction

Andrews, Ryan. *This Was Our Pact*. Art by the author. First Second, 2019. ISBN: 9781626720534. Following the paper lanterns (during the Autumn Equinox Festival) is a tradition, but this year, Ben, his buddies, and tagalong Nathaniel vow to follow them to the end- not turning back and not looking back. GN - Fiction

Aoki, Spica. *Kaiju Girl Caramelise, vol. 2*. Yen Press, 2019. ISBN: 9781975359461. Kuroe Akaishi's must suppress her feelings or give up her human-size. She must keep her giant kaiju secret, secret. GN-Fiction

Aoki, Spica. *Kaiju Girl Caramelise, Volume 1*. Yen Press, 2019. ISBN: 9781975357054. Faced with a crush, Kuroe Akaishi turns into a Godzilla-like creature. GN-Fiction

Arakawa, Hiromu. *Silver Spoon*. Illus. by the author, 2018.Yen Press, V.1. ISBN: 9780316416191; V.2. ISBN: 9781975326197; V.3. ISBN: 9781975327460; V.4. ISBN: 9781975327590. Yuugo Hachiken has always been a great student. Yuugo decides to enroll in Ooezo Agricultural High School for an easy journey through high school. But Yuugo did not count on waking up at 5AM to do chores, raise piglets and learn to ride a horse. GN -Fiction

Arnold, Marie. *The Year I Flew Away*. Versify, 2021. ISBN: 9780358272755. Lola StVil writing under a pseudonym mirrors her own immigrant story with that of Gabrielle. Gabrielle comes to America to live with her uncle, aunt and cousins, leaving her parents behind in Haiti. The winter cold, the challenges of negotiating relationships in schools, and adjusting to cultural changes. Her pet Rat, Rocky, helps her through the hurdles. Fiction

Ashiya, Kuniichi. *What the Font?! – A Manga Guide to Western Typeface*. Seven Seas Entertainment, 2020. ISBN: 9781645056393. A strange adventure as Marusu takes over for a missing logo designer. He is helped by anthropomorphic fonts. GN -Fiction

Ayala, Vita. *Submerged*. Art by Lisa Sterle. Vault Comics, 2019. ISBN: 978-1939424426. Her whole Life, Elysia Puente has been cleaning up the messes her younger brother, Angel, now on one of the stormiest nights of the year, Elysia descends into a flooded subway station in a quest to find her brother. GN -Fiction

Backerf, Deft. *Kent State: Four Dead in Ohio*. Abrams ComicsArts / Abrams Books, 2020. ISBN: 9781419734847. May 4, 1970, the confrontation between Kent State students and the National Guard troop sent to squash a trucker strike. GN -Nonfiction

Badger, Darcie Little. *Elatsoe*. Illustrated by Rovina Cai. Levine Querido, 2020. ISBN: 9781646140053. Ellie seeks answers about her cousins death and uses her Lipan Apache family's ability to call spirits back to life, and uncover her town's evil past, in order to identify and bring the murderer to justice. Fiction

Bagieu, Pénélope. *Brazen: Rebel Ladies Who Rocked the World*. Illus. by the author, 2018. First Second. ISBN: 978626728691. Brief portraits of women in various countries and cultures who revolutionized the world around them, and the image of women. GN -Nonfiction

Barnes, Rodney. *Quincredible, Volume 1: Quest to Be the Best!* Art by Selina Espiritu. Lion Forge, 2019. ISBN: 9781549302824. Just trying to fit in, Quin discovers a secret superpower: invulnerability. Will that power help save his family and his New Orleans community. GN -Fiction

Barry, Lynda. *Making Comics.* Drawn & Quarterly, 2019. ISBN: 9781770463691. Cartoonist and professor, Barry invites readers into her classroom- creative joy and freedom found through drawing. GN -Nonfiction

Bascomb, Neal. The Racers: How an Outcast Driver, an American Heiress, and a Legendary Car Challenged Hitler's Best. Scholastic Focus, 2020. ISBN: 9781338277418. Published by Houghton Mifflin Harcourt, 2020 with the title: Faster: How a Jewish Driver, An American Heiress, and a Legendary Car Beat Hitler's Best. ISBN: 9781328489876. Covers are different but both tell the story of an outcast Jewish race car driver, Rene Dreyfus - banned by Hitler and Mussolini, who teamed up with Lucy Schell an adventurous American, and a Jewish, down on his luck car manufacturer, Charles Weiffenbach to take on Hitler and his quest to dominate the Grand Prix. In the end, Hitler attempted to erase the account of this remarkable race from history. Nonfiction.

Behar, Ruth. *Letters from Cuba.* Nancy Paulsen Books, 2020. ISBN: 9780525516477. Esther's life as a Jewish refugee, in 1930s Cuba is punctuated by her work as a seamstress - work that will help pay for her family to escape in Poland. Fiction

Bellaire, Jordie. *Buffy the Vampire Slayer: Volume 1, High School Is Hell.* Art by Dan Mora, Raul Angulo. Boom! Studios, 2019. ISBN: 978-1684153572, 2020), Vol. 2, ISBN: 9781684154821. Vol. 3, ISBN: 9781684155347. Buffy Summers, a new high school, slaying demons, and making friends in (2019; and later Buffy must save Xander and stop Druscilla and Spike from creating more havoc. GN -Fiction

Bendis , Brian Michael, and Walker, David F. *Naomi: Season One* . Art by Jamal Campbell. Wonder Comics / DC Comics, 2019. ISBN: 9781401294953. Once Superman comes through her small town, Naomi, feels a bond and seeks her own family origins. GN -Fiction

Bendis, Brian Michael. *Young Justice. Vol. 1: Gemworld.* Art by Patrick Gleason and John Timms. *Vol. 2: Lost in the Multiverse.* Art by John Timms, Andrea Lima Araujo, and Nick Derington. Wonder Comics / DC Comics, 2020. ISBN: 9781401292539, ISBN: 9781779500380. Some new faces and an old favorite in this multiple dimensional action-packed, humorous superhero series. GN -Fiction

Berry, Julie. *Lovely War*. Viking, 2019. ISBN: 9780451469939. Aphrodite sets out to provide justification for her infidelity. And cites as proof – the tale of couples that she brought together during World War I. A love story that will make a difference. Fiction

Billet, Julia. *Catherine's War*. Art by Claire Fauvel. HarperAlley/HarperCollins, 2020. ISBN: 9780062915597. Based on a true World War II survival story - Rachel Cohen, must change her identity. And as Catherine she uses her camera to capture her experiences. A Batchelder Honor book. GN -Fiction

Blankman, Anne. *The Blackbird Girls*. Viking Books for Young Readers, 2020. ISBN: 9781984837356. Sometimes it takes life circumstances to bring foes together. In the aftermath of the Chernobyl nuclear disaster, two girls find companionship where there was adversity. Fiction

Blas, Terry. *Hotel Dare*. Art by Claudia Aguirre. Boom! Studios, 2019. ISBN: 978-1684152056. Three teenage siblings, Olive, Darwyn, and Charlotte, are sent to their estranged grandmother's guestless hotel in Mexico. The visit goes to bizarre when they are transported through portals to strange worlds. GN - Fiction

Blumenthal, Karen. *Jane Against the World: Roe v. Wade and the Fight for Reproductive Rights*. Roaring Brook Press, 2020. ISBN: 9781626721654. A history of birth control and abortion, from ancient times to Roe v. Wade, and exposes the misogyny, racism, and classism that has been inherent in the fight for more than a century. Information/Nonfiction

Bond, Shelly. *Femme Magnifique: 50 Magnificent Women Who Changed the World*. Art by various. Black Crown. 2018. ISBN: 978-1684053209. Four-page summaries of each of 50 women. GN -Nonfiction

Bonde, Jessica Bab. *We'll Soon Be Home Again.* Art by Peter Bergting and Kathryn Renta. Dark Horse Books. 2020. ISBN: 9781506715490. Follows six survivors of the Holocaust-from childhood/teen years. First-person testimonies. GN -Nonfiction

Bongiovanni, Archie, and Jimerson, Tristan. *A Quick and Easy Guide to They/Them Pronouns*. Illus. by Archie Bongiovanni. 2018. Limerence Press, ISBN: 9781620104996. Archie, a genderqueer comic artist, and Tristan, a cisgender male writer, team up to explain the challenges faced by gender non-conforming. GN -Nonfiction

Bradley, Kimberly Brubaker. *Fighting Words*. Dial, 2020. ISBN: 9781984815682. Only their sisterhood helps sisters Della and Suki move forward after years of abuse from their mother's boyfriend. Newbery Honor Book. Fiction

Brosgol, Vera. *Be Prepared*. Illus. by the author. First Second, 2018. ISBN: 9781626724457. Vera heads to Russian Heritage Camp with the school's the "popular girls" at school. At Russian Heritage Camp, Vera thinks she's finally found a place where she might fit in, but camp isn't at all what she expected. Will she survive a summer filled with girl drama, shifting camp alliances and an outhouse from hell? GN -Fiction

Brown, Don. *Fever Year: The Killer Flu of 1918*. Art by the author. Houghton Mifflin Harcourt. 2019. ISBN: 978-0544837409. The story of the Spanish Influenza pandemic of 1918. GN -Nonfiction

Brown, Don. *The Unwanted: Stories of the Syrian Refugees*. Illus. by the author. 2018. Houghton Mifflin Harcourt, ISBN: 9781328810151. A description of the political and social implications of the Syrian refugee crisis. GN -Nonfiction

Brown, Echo. *Black Girl Unlimited: The Remarkable Story of a Teenage Wizard*. Macmillan, 2020. ISBN: Based on much of her own life, Echo Brown writes a tale that intertwines poverty, sexual violence, depression, racism, and sexism in a not to be missed coming of age tale. Fiction.

Brown, Lisa. *The Phantom Twin*. First Second / Macmillan, 2020. ISBN: 9781626729247. Isabel is left alone after separation surgery does not go as expected for Isabel and Jane, cojoined twins aka the Extraordinary Peabody Sisters. What will life be like for Isabel? GN -Fiction

Brown, Monica, 2020. *Sharuko: El Arqueólogo Peruano/Peruvian Archaeologist Julio C. Tello*. Illustrated by Elisa Chavarri. Lee & Low/Children's Book Press. ISBN: 9780892394234. The biography of Julio C. Tello, from his childhood to becoming an accomplished archaeologist in Peru's indigenous history. Book is bilingual. Belpré Youth Illustrator Honor Book. Fiction

Bruchac, Joseph. *One Real American: The Life of Ely S. Parker, Seneca Sachem and Civil War General*. Abrams, 2020. ISBN: 9781419746574. A long-overlooked historical figure – Ely Parker was with Ulysses S. Grant during most of the Civil War. Later he was the Commissioner of Indian Affairs, during Grant's presidency. Primary documents provide an incredibly interesting account. Information/Nonfiction

Bryant, Jen. *Above the Rim: How Elgin Baylor Changed Basketball*. Illustrated by Frank Morrison. Harry N. Abrams, 2020. ISBN: 9781419741081. Basketball legend Elgin Baylor's 1959 protest against racial injustice – activism = change. Information/Nonfiction

Buhrman-Deever, Susannah. *If You Take Away the Otter*. Illustrated by Matthew Trueman. Candlewick Press, 2020. ISBN: 9780763689346. Prose and research connect the protection of the sea otters with the preservation of the kelp forests. Information/Nonfiction Bo

Butler, George. *Drawn Across Borders: True Stories of Human Migration.* Candlewick Studio, 2021. ISBN: 9781536217759. Sketches by the author archiving the stories and images of over a decade of migrants and refugees in the Middle East, Europe, Africa, and Asia. Human stories - flights from poverty, war, disaster, and the unknown. Introduce this book with a picture book story of a young Lebanese boy forced to flee from his home in the face of war. He is able to return but at a cost. *The Three Lucys* by Hayan Charara, illustrations by Sara Kahn. Lee & Low, 2016. Nonfiction.

Caletti, Deb. *Girl, Unframed.* Simon and Schuster, 2021. ISBN: 9781534426979. Sydney Reilly is headed to San Francisco to be with her mother, Lila Shore - a film star, but Shore is involved with the dangerous Jake. And then Sydney learns a terrible truth.

Calin, Cassandra. *I Left the House Today.* Andrews McMeel Publishing. 2020. ISBN: 9781524855574. Everyday life and humorous meditations on beauty, stress, and relationships. GN -Nonfiction

Callender, Kacen. *King and the Dragonflies.* Scholastic, Inc. , 2020. ISBN: 9781338129335. Believing his brother has been reincarnated as a dragonfly, King begins to deal with his grief over his brother's death, there is another question that he must deal with – both his and his friend, Sandy's sexuality. Fiction

Cameron, Sophie. *Last Bus to Everland.* Roaring Brook, 2019. ISBN: 9781250149930. Always compared to his overachieving brother, and his star destined sister, Brody feels inferior until he is introduced to "Everland," by Nico. Brody can choose to live in the real world or in a world of fantasy. Which will it be? Fiction

Carey, Mike. *The Highest House: Book One.* Art by Peter Gross. IDW Publishing, 2018. ISBN: 978-1684053544. A high fantasy story about a young boy Moth, sold into slavery. Surviving in the highest house brings him to Obsidian who leads him on a journey of self-discovery and survival. GN -Fiction

Castellucci, Cecil. *The Plain Janes* . Art by Jim Rugg. Little, Brown Books for Young Readers / Little, Brown and Company, 2020. ISBN: 9780316522724. Four best friends at a suburban school, all named Jane discover the real value of their activist art. GN -Fiction

Chii. *The Bride Was a Boy*. Illus. by the author. Seven Seas, 2018. ISBN: 9781626928886. Chii's autobiographical account transitioning and finding love in Japan as a trans individuals. GN -Nonfiction

Chin, Jason. *Your Place in the Universe.* Illustrated by Jason Chin. Neal Porter Books, 2020. ISBN: 9780823446230. An exploration of scale, size, and distance to the far reaches of the observable universe. Fiction

Chmakova, Svetlana. *Crush*. Illustrated by Svetlana Chmakova. JY, 2018. ISBN: 9780316363242. Friendship drama, a crush, Jorge Ruiz and Jazmine must learn to negotiate both emotions. (Book 3 of Berrybrook Middle School series). GN -Fiction

Chu, Amy. *Sea Sirens: A Trot & Cap'n Bill Adventure*. Art by Janet K. Lee. Viking Books for Young Readers, 2019. ISBN: 978-0451480170. A Vietnames American surfer girl, Trot, and her cranky one-eyed cat are sucked into the magic of an underground kingdom and find themselves in the middle of a deep-sea battle. GN -Fiction

Chuperco, Rin. *The Never Tilting World*. HarperTeen, 2019. ISBN: 9780062821799. The world cracks open and one side has perpetual day while the other side is perpetually nighttime. Twin goddesses are trapped on opposite sides of the world and each go on a journey to discover what has really happened. Fiction

Cisneros, Ernesto. *Efrén Divided*. Harper/Quill Tree, 2020. ISBN: 9780062881687. Efrén is a seventh grader – and he faces an awesome responsibility. His mother has been deported to Mexico and he is the only one who can bring his mother home from across the border. Belpré Children's Author Award Book. Fiction

Clayton, Dhonielle, et.al. Blackout. Quill Tree Books, 2020. ISBN: 9780063088092. Authors that contribute to this collection include: Dhonielle Clayton Tiffany D. Jackson, Nic Stone, Angie Thomas, Ashley Woodfolk, and Nicola Yoon. Six love stories. Fiction

Colbert, Brandy. *The Revolution of Birdie Randolph*. Little, Brown, 2019. ISBN: 9780316448567. Dove's problems just begin when she begins to date a boy from juvie – and her parents are so against the situation. During that same time her aunt comes home from rehab. Dove is conflicted. Fiction

Colbert, Brandy. *The Only Black Girls in Town*. Little, Brown Books for Young Readers, 2020. ISBN: 9780316456388. Alberta and Edie come from two different worlds. Dynamics are changed when the two girls discover a collection of hidden journals – journals that hold secrets to the past. Fiction

Colfer, Eoin, and Donkin, Andrew. *Illegal*. Illus. by Giovanni Rigano, 2018. Sourcebooks Jabberwocky, ISBN: 9781492662143. Left behind in Ghana by his older sister, and his brother, Ebo finds himself in a struggle to survive. GN -Fiction

Collins, Suzanne. *The Ballad of Songbirds and Snakes*. Scholastic Australia, 2020. ISBN: 9781743836811. Prequel to Collins's *Hunger Games*— eighteen-year-old Coriolanus Snow is looking toward the tenth annual Hunger Games. The success of the House of Snow rests squarely on the shoulders of Coriolanus, but there are obstacles, inside and outside of the arena.

Cooper, Candy J., and Aronson, Marc. *Poisoned Water: How the Citizens of Flint, Michigan, Fought for Their Lives and Warned the Nation*. Bloomsbury Children's Books, 2020. ISBN: 9781547602322. The 2014 dangerous water and fight for the safety of the citizens of Flint, Michigan. Information/Nonfiction

Copeland, Cynthia L. *Cub*. Algonquin Young Readers / Workman Publishing. 2020. ISBN: 9781616208486. Experiences of a cub reporter and her changing perspective on her town, community, and the world. GN -Nonfiction

Corrina, Heather. *Wait, What?: A Comic Book Guide to Relationships, Bodies, and Growing Up*. Art by Isabella Rotman. Limerence Press / Oni Press. 2019. ISBN: 9781620106594. Changing bodies, relationships, and what it means to grow up. GN -Nonfiction

Craft, Jerry. *Class Act*. Quill Tree Books / HarperCollins, 2020. ISBN: 9780062885500. Companion to *New Kid*. spotlights Jordan's friend Drew during 8th grade at Riverdale Academy Day School, as one of the only students of color. GN -Fiction

Craft, Jerry. *New Kid*. Art by the author. HarperCollins Publishers, 2019. ISBN: 978-0062691194. Jordan Banks starts a new school and finds himself torn between his neighborhood in Washington Heights and the posh environment of Riverdale Academy Day School. GN -Fiction

Crewes, Eleanor. *The Times I Knew I Was Gay*. Scribner / Simon & Schuster. 2020. ISBN: 9781982147105. Autobiographical tale of growing up gay and realizing who she was. GN -Nonfiction

Cuevas, Adrianna. *The Total Eclipse of Nestor Lopez*. Farrar, Staurs Giroux, 2020. ISBN: 9780374313609) When his town is threatened by a witch who is able to transform into animals, Nestor realizes that he must use his secret ability to communicate with animals to save them from a tule vieja. Belpré Children's Author Honor Book. Fiction

Curato, Mike. *Flamer*. Henry Holt & Co. / Macmillan, 2020. ISBN: 9781250756145. At camp during his last high school summer, Aiden must figure out his crush on his tent mate. GN -Fiction

Curlee, Lynn. The Great Nijinsky: God of Dance. Charlesbridge Teen, 2019. ISBN: 9781580898003. The life of the prodigal dancer Vaslav Nijinsky an unconventional personality who rose to stardom and then succumbed to mental illness. A frank account of Nijinsky's struggles. Information/Nonfiction

Dahliwal, Aminder. *Woman World*. Art by the author. Drawn and Quarterly, 2018. ISBN: 978-1770463356. The future is female-literally-unified under the flag of "Beyonce's Thighs," led by their cheerfully nudist mayor Gaia who has all-consuming knowledge about men. GN -Fiction

Dandro, Travis. *King of King Court*. Art by the author. Drawn and Quarterly. 2019. ISBN: 978-1770463592. Growing up with a drug-addicted birth father, alcoholic step-dad, and overwhelmed mother-tension, finding refuge. GN - Nonfiction

Dass, Sarah. *Where the Rhythm Takes You.* Balzer+Bray, 2021. ISBN 9780063018525. Seventeen-year-old Reyna's mother has died, her best friend, Aiden, has left Tobago to pursue his musical dreams. Even her father has left emotionally — leaving Reyna to run the family's seaside resort. Reyna feels as if she has been abandoned and now in purgatory. Until Aiden returns as a VIP resort desk. Fiction

Davis, Charlotte Nicole. *The Good Luck Girls.* Tor Teen, 2019. ISBN: 9781250299703. Girls in Arketta are sold and at age 16 prostituted. The first time Clementine is raped, results in a murder– and Clementine's escape but will she and her squad remain free and survive. Fiction

Davis, Kenneth C. *Strongman: The Rise of Five Dictators and the Fall of Democracy.* Henry Holt and Co, 2020. BYR. ISBN: 978-1250205643. The dictatorships of Mussolini, Hitler, Stalin, Mao, & Hussein are examined. Davis' offers a timely warning about the need to protect democracy. Information/Nonfiction

Dayton, Arwen Elys. *Stronger, Faster, and More Beautiful.* Delacorte, 2018. ISBN: 9780525580959. Body and genetic modifications progress to even more darkness and advance through six short stories. Fiction

de Radigués, Max *Simon & Louise.* Art by the author. Conundrum Press, 2019. ISBN: 978-1772620351. Simon is not content to accept that Louise's dad has forbidden his relationship with Louise. In an effort to win her back, Simon sets out to hitchhike to their summer vacation home. GN -Fiction

Deaver, Mason.. *I Wish You All the Best.* Scholastic/Push, 2019. ISBN: 9781338306125. Ben's parents cannot accept that they are nonbinary. They are taken in by their estranged sister. Anxiety and depression follow, as they deal with the family dynamics, a new city, and falling in love. Fiction

Deonn, Tracy. *Legendborn.* Margaret K. McElderry Books, 2020. ISBN: 9781534441606. Bree Matthews, a sixteen-year-old Black whiz kid must face her battle with grief in this intense fantasy braiding together Arthurian adventure with southern Black culture – a story full of magic, romance, and mystery. Fiction

DeWoskin, Rachel. *Someday We Will Fly.* Viking. ISBN: 9780670014965, 2019. During WWII, 15-year-old Lillia must leave her mother behind and flees with her father and baby sister. They are Jewish refugees who settle in Shanghai, China – which is occupied by Japan. A 2020 Sydney Taylor Gold Medal winner. Fiction

Diaz, Alexandra. *Santiago's Road Home.* Paula Wiseman Books, 2020. ISBN: 9781534446236. Santiago is used to being on his own, but when he attempts to cross the Mexican border into the United States, he is detained by ICE. His treatment in the detention camp is not what he envisioned America to be. Fiction

Diaz, Natasha. *Color Me In.* Delacorte, 2019. ISBN: 9780525578239. Caught between her divorcing parents and their two divergent cultures. Neveah Levitz's mother is Jamaican African American; her father is a Jew. Who is Neveah? Fiction

Doller, Trish. *Start Here*. Simon & Schuster/Simon Pulse, 2019. ISBN: 9781481479912. Willa, Taylor, and Finley are planning a sailing trip from Ohio to Key West. But Finley dies of leukemia. And Willa and Taylor are estranged but have a compulsion to take the trip in Finley's honor. How will that happen? Fiction

Donne, Evette. *Lifting as We Climb: Black Women's Battle for the Ballot Box*. Viking Books for Young Readers, 2020. ISBN: 9780451481542. The work of Black suffragists, their views of white suffragists, and the hypocrisies that were in the movement. Information/Nonfiction

Donnelly, Jennifer. *Stepsister*. Scholastic, 2019. ISBN: 9781338268461. In a fractured rewriting of the Cinderella tale, one of the stepsisters makes her own fate and must find lost pieces of her heart. Fiction

Dorkin, Evan. *Blackwood*. Art by Veronica Fish, Andy Fish. Dark Horse, 2018. ISBN: 978-1506707426. Blackwood College teens must save the world when they encounter supernatural happenings. GN -Fiction

Doyle, Moïra Fowley. *All the Bad Apples*. Penguin/Kathy Dawson, 2019. ISBN: 9780525552741. When Deena's sister dies Deena must face coming out on her own. But clues come about that suggest her sister may still be alive – Deena must find the truth and deal with the family curse. Fiction

Dunbar, Helene. *We Are Lost and Found*. Sourcebooks/Fire, 2019. ISBN: 9781492681045. Set in 1980s New York City, Michael just wants to do is fall in love. Fiction

Dungo, AJ. *In Waves*. Art by the author. Nobrow, 2019. ISBN: 978-1910620632. Dungo explores the history of surfing (his passion) side-by-side with his resilient girlfriend Kristin 's history of recovery and relapse, from bone cancer. GN -Nonfiction

Elliott, David. *Voices: The Final Hours of Joan of Arc*. HMH, 2019. ISBN: 9781328987594. Concrete poetry and Joan of Arc's story are blended in this sparse verse that portrays Joan as an empowered person. Fiction

Elliott, Zetta. *A Place Inside of Me: A Poem to Heal the Heart*. Illustrated by Noa Denmon. Farrar, Straus and Giroux, 2020. ISBN: 978- 037430741. Poetry: A Black child's year-long emotions from joy to sorrow and anger as he deals with a shooting and moved from to hope and love. Caldecott Honor Book. Information/Nonfiction

Elliott, Zetta. *Say Her Name (poems to Empower*. Little Brown Books for Young Readers, 2020. ISBN: 9781368045247. Forty-nine poems in tribute to victims of police brutality and the activists of the Black Lives Matter movement. Information/Nonfiction

Elston, Ashley. *The Lying Woods*. Disney/Hyperion, 2018. ISBN: 9781368014786. Owen's privileged life at a prestigious boarding school comes crashing down when his father disappears with his client's money. Now Owen Foster must return home and he must live among the clients his father cheated. Fiction

Emezi, Akwaeke.. *Pet*. Random/Make Me a World, 2019. ISBN: 9780525647072. There are no monsters in Pet's world, or so she thought until she sees a monster and she seeks to uncover the secrets and protect those in her world from any harm. A 2020 Top 10 Rainbow List selection. Fiction

England, M.K. *The Disasters*. HarperTeen, 2018. ISBN: 9780062657671. Faced with having been framed for a terrorist attack on the academy that expelled him, Nax must find out who actually did engage in the attack, in order to clear himself. Fiction

Erskine, Kathryn. *Lily's Promise*. Quilt Tree Books, 2021. ISBN: 9780063058156. Yes, as her father was dying Lily promised him that she would speak up – five times – but now that she must go to public school it will be even more difficult. When Lily and her new friends are bullied by Ryan and his group of mean group. She knows that now is the time. She must draw up the courage – and with friendship and speaking out she will find a way. Fiction.

Ewing, Eve L. *Ironheart, vol. 2: Ten Rings.* Art by Luciano Vecchio. Marvel Comics, 2020. ISBN: 9781302915094. A zombie invasion must be stopped and Ironheart, aka Riri Williams, finds herself in unlikely alliances with Wasp and later with Princess Shuri despite their personality differences. GN -Fiction

Ewing, Eve L. *Ironheart, Volume 1: Those with Courage.* Art by Kevin Libranda, Luciano Vecchio, Matt Milla. Marvel Comics, 2019. ISBN: 978-1302915087. When someone she knows go missing in Chicago, Ironheart (Riri Williams) sets out to take down a secret, villainous organization. GN -Fiction

Fauel, Claire. *Phoolan Devi, Rebel Queen.* NBM Publishing. 2020. ISBN: 9781681122519. Based on the autobiography of *I, Phoolan Devi.* Sold as a child bride, raped, and her ascension through the ranks of a gang of bandits. GN -Nonfiction

Fawkes, Glynnis. *Charlotte Bronte Before Jane Eyre.* Art by the author. Disney Hyperion. 2019. ISBN: 978-1368023290. Biography of Charlotte Bronte from age five (when her mother died) to the publication of Jane Eyre. GN -Nonfiction

Feder, Tyler. *Dancing at the Pity Party: A Dead Mom Graphic Memoir.* Dial Books for Young Readers / Penguin Random House. 2020. ISBN: 9780525553021. When Feder is 19, his mother died of cancer. This is his story of loss and grief – both humorous and serious. GN -Nonfiction

Fleming, Candace, 2020. *Honeybee: The Busy Life of Apis Mellifera.* Illustrated by Eric Rohmann. Neal Porter Books/Holiday House. ISBN: 978--8234-4285. An intimate view of the life of the honeybee. Information/Nonfiction

Fleming, Candace, 2020. *The Rise & Fall of Charles Lindbergh.* Schwartz and Wade. ISBN: 9780525646549. A new look at one of the most complicated icons in America's history. He was a scientist, an aviator, a Naz sympathizer, a believer in eugenics, and sadly a father who tragically lost his son in 1932 when he was kidnapped and murdered. Information/Nonfiction

Fletcher, Brenden. *Isola, Volume 1*. Art by Karl Kerschl, MSASSYK. Image Comics, 2018. ISBN: 978-1534309227. A queen and her guard travel to far away Isola in the hopes of removing a curse. Their journey brings danger and a quest for survival. GN -Fiction

Fletcher, Brenden. *Motor Crush, Volume 2*. Illus. by Cameron Stewart and Babs Tarr, 2018. Image Comics, ISBN: 9781534305519. In an instant, Domino Swift finds that she has traveled two years into the future – and changes that involve the love of her life, and her father who is now working for a mob boss. GN -Fiction

Flowers, Ebony. *Hot Comb*. Drawn and Quarterly, 2019. ISBN: 978-1770463486. Short stories exploring identity, race, and class. GN -Fiction

Foley, Jessie Ann. (2019. *Sorry for Your Loss*. HarperTeen. ISBN: 9780062571915. When Pup, the youngest of eight children in a loud but loving family gains unexpected success as a photographer, he begins to examine his friendships, his role in the family, and the death of his brother through a new lens. Fiction

Fowley, Moira. *All the Bad Apples*. Penguin/Kathy Dawson, 2019. ISBN: 9780525552741. After Deena's seventeenth birthday, she's forced to reconcile her own coming=out with the death of her sister. But there are clues that suggest her sister might still be alive. Now it's up to Deena to uncover the truth and break an age-old family curse of "bad apples." Fiction

Frank, Anne, and Folman, Ari. *Anne Frank's Diary: The Graphic Adaptation*. Illus. by David Polonsky. 2018. Pantheon. ISBN: 9781101871799. Graphic edition of Anne Frank's diary detailing her years of hiding with her family in Amsterdam during World War II. GN -Nonfiction

Franklin, Tee. *Bingo Love*. Illus. by Jenn St-Onge, 2018. Image Comics, ISBN: 9781534307506. After their love was denied for almost 50 years, Hazel and Mari now married, realize that their love has survived – but to accept it now, the two of them must end their marriages. GN -Fiction

Frick, Kit. *All Eyes on Us*. Simon & Schuster/Margaret K. McElderry, 2019. ISBN: 9781534404403. Rosalie and Amanda are both dating Carter Shaw, an heir to a fortune. Anonymous threats bring them together to end the terror. Fiction

Fukuda, Andrew, 2020. *This Light Between Us: A Novel of World War II*. Tor Teen. ISBN: 9781250192387. Pen pals for 10 years, Japanese American Alex Maki and French Jewish girl Charlie Lévy share a coming-of-age story and fantastical romance amidst historically accurate - and heartbreaking - injustice. Fiction

Fumino, Yuki. *I Hear the Sunspot: Theory of Happiness*. Illustrated by Yuki Fumino. One Peace Books, 2018. ISBN: 9781944937416. Brought together by Taichi's need for Kohei to take notes for him in class; the two friends find their relationship strained over events during spring break. Is there a future for Kohei in Taichi's life? GN -Fiction

G. Mady. *A Quick and Easy Guide to Queer and Trans Identities*. Art by Mady G., J.R. Zuckerberg. Limerence Press. 2019. ISBN: 978-1620105863. An educational guide to queer and trans identities: and terms associated with those identities. GN -Nonfiction

Gansworth, Eric. *Apple (skin to the core)*. Levine Querido, 2020. ISBN: 9781646140138. A verse memoir that interweaves personal experience, family stories, traditions, and culture. A Beatles theme is woven throughout the text. Information/Nonfiction

Garcia, Kami. *Teen Titans: Beast Boy*. Art by Gabriel Picolo. DC Comics, 2020. ISBN: 9781401287191. After throwing away the supplements to keep him from growing so fast, his sudden growth turns Gar into Beast Boy. And his crush begins to notice him. GN -Fiction

Garcia, Kami. *Teen Titans: Raven*. Art by Gabriel Picolo. DC Comics, 2019. ISBN: 978-1401286231. When Raven's foster mom dies, Raven is taken in by her mom's sister and daughter. Strange supernatural things begin to occur, and then there is prom night when all will come out. GN -Fiction

Gardner, Whitney. *Fake Blood*. Illustrated by Whitney Gardner. Simon & Schuster, 2018. ISBN: 9781481495561. Middle schooler, AJ wants Nia to pay attention to him – and knows that she loves vampires. What AJ doesn't know that Nia is a vampire slayer. Will they even have a life together? GN -Fiction

Garrett, Camryn. *Full Disclosure*. Knopf, 2019. ISBN: 9781984829955. Simone has tested positive for HIV. The stigma makes life difficult and she transfers schools; but the secret follows her. And when she begins to get nasty notes, she must decide whether she reveals her secret or keep running. Fiction

Gay, Roxanne, and Oliver, Tracy Lynne. *The Sacrifice of Darkness*. Art by Rebecca Kirby. Archaia / BOOM! Studios, 2020. ISBN: 9781684156245. Joshua suffers the fallout of his father's deeds, and the repercussions to his community. Finding a way to break the cycle begins with him. GN -Fiction

Gendry-Kim, Keum Suk. *Grass*. Art by the author. Drawn and Quarterly. 2019. ISBN: 978-1770463622. The story of Lee Ok-sun, a Korean woman born into poverty and kidnapped off the street but forced into sexual slavery by the Japanese military during World War II. At the end of the war, she was an outcast and entered an abusive marriage that kept her in China for five decades before she was able to return to Korea to claim her identity. GN -Nonfiction

Gharib, Malaka. *I Was Their American Dream: a Graphic Memoir*. Art by the author. Clarkson Potter. 2019. ISBN: 978-0525575115. Malaka details her life of being the "perfect Filipino kid" growing up in Cerritos, California. GN -Nonfiction

Giles, Lamar. *Spin*. Scholastic, 2019. ISBN: 9781338219210. Although estranged from their friend, Paris Second, when she is murdered, the two friends, Fuse and Kya must figure out who has killed her – or be killed themselves. Fiction

Gill, Joel Christian. *Fights: One Boy's Triumph Over Violence*. Oni Press. 2020. ISBN: 9781549303357. From childhood to young adulthood, in a single parent household -Black, broke, and surrounded by uncertainty. GN -Nonfiction

Gill, Joel Christian. *Strange Fruit, Volume II: More Uncelebrated Narratives from Black History*. Illus. by the author. 2018. Fulcrum Publishing, ISBN: 9781938486579. Eight stories from early African American History- uncelebrated heroes or events. GN -Nonfiction

Gillman, Melanie. *Stage Dreams*. Art by the author. Graphic Universe, 2019. ISBN: 978-1541572843. In New Mexico Territory, 1861, Grace is fleeing inscription into the Confederate Army when the coach she's riding is attacked by the notorious outlaw Ghost Hawk. GN -Fiction

Girner, Sebastian. *Scales & Scoundrels, Volume 1: Into the Dragon's Maw*. By Sebastian Girner. Illustrate by Galaad, 2018. Image Comics, ISBN: 9781534304826. Treasure hunter Luvandra sets off on a quest for gold and adventure with her rag tag group of misfits. GN -Fiction

Glasgow, Kathleen. *How to Make Friends with the Dark*. Delacorte, 2019. ISBN: 9781101934753. Tiger has never known who her father is. and doesn't' have any relatives. After her mother dies of an aneurysm. Tiger Tolliver must find a way to "make friends with the dark." Fiction

Gong, Chloe. *These Violent Delights*. Simon and Schuster, 2021. ISBN: 9781534457690. A Romeo and Juliet retelling from 1920 Shanghai. Includes rival gangs, with a blood feud, and a monster in the shadows and in the depths of the Huangpu River.

Goslee, S.J, 2019. *How Not to Ask A Boy to Prom.* Roaring Brook. ISBN: 9781626724013. Nolan is set-up by his sister to invite his crush with a "promposal" but things do not go as expected. So Nolan is left with a fake date – but somehow that begins to make sense. Fiction

Grace, Sina. *Ghosted in L.A., vol. 1.* Art by Siobhan Keenan. BOOM! Box / BOOM! Studios, 2020. ISBN: 9781684155057. Daphne has moved to Los Angeles because her boyfriend is there – but he dumps her and she ends up in a mansion with ghosts. Soon they are a family. GN -Fiction

Grant, Brea. *Mary: The Adventures of Mary Shelley's Great-Great-Great-Great-Great-Granddaughter.* Art by Yishan Li. Six Foot Press, 2020. ISBN: 9781644420294. An untypical goth teen, Mary Shelley is determined to be on her own and use her newly discovered power of monster healing. GN -Fiction

Gray, Claudia. *Star Wars Lost Stars, Volume 1.* Illus. by Yusaku Komiyama. Yen Press, 2018. ISBN: 9781975326531. Set in the Star Wars universe, Thane Kyrell and Ciena Ree seek better lives but when one stays with the Empire and the other joins the rebellion, the close friends become enemies. GN -Fiction

Greentea, Vera. *Grimoire Noir.* Art by Yana Bogatch. First Second, 2019. ISBN: 978-1626725980. Bucky Orson's little sister has gone missing, and Bucky must find her-all the girls where they live all have magic and all have secrets. GN -Fiction

Gudsnuk, Kristen. *Making Friends.* Illustrate by Kristen Gudsnuk, 2018. Graphix, $24.99 ISBN: 9781338139228. Seventh grade is different for Dany, a new school, and no friends. So, she created a few new friends of her own using her great aunt's drawing book. GN -Fiction

Gulledge., Laura Lee. *The Dark Matter of Mona Starr.* Amulet Books / Abrams Books, 2020. ISBN: 9781419742002. Mona is overcome with depression and anxiety when her best friend moves. Can she change all of that? GN -Fiction

Ha, Robin. *Almost American Girl.* Balzer + Bray, 2020. ISBN: 9780062685094. A fourteen-year-old South Korean teen, Chuna, ends up in Alabama with her mother and her new step-father. Chuna finds solace in her art. Information/Nonfiction

Ha, Robin. *Almost American Girl.* Balzer + Bray/HarperCollins, 2020. ISBN: 9780062685094. –Ha's faces challenges while leaving South Korea to America. GN -Nonfiction

Hale, Shannon. *Best Friends.* Art by LeUyen Pham. First Second, 2019. ISBN: 978-1250317469. Heading into sixth grade Shannon knows that stepping away from her best friend, Jen, might be the only way for her to be true to herself. GN -Nonfiction

Harari, Yuval Noah. *Sapiens: A Graphic History, vol. 1: The Birth of Humankind.* Art by David Vandermeulen and Daniel Casanave. Harper Perennial / HarperCollins, 2020. ISBN: 9780063051331. Adaptation of Harari's *Sapiens* outlines the evolution of humankind. GN -Nonfiction

Hardman, Gabriel. *Green Lantern: Earth One, Volume 1*. Illustrated by Gabriel Hardman, 2018. DC Comics, ISBN: 9781401241865. A former astronaut-turned-space miner for hire Hal Jordan and how he becomes the Green Lantern with the help of the few remaining Guardians. GN -Fiction

Harrell, Rob. *Wink: Surviving Middle School with One Eye Open.* Illustrated by the Rob Harrell. Dial, 2020. ISBN: 9781984815149. Ross deals with his cancer diagnosis and with navigating middle school – all with humor. Fiction

Hasak-Lowy, Todd. *We Are Power: How Non-Violent Activism Changes the World.* Abrams, 2020. ISBN: 978-1419741111. A look at nonviolent activism and information about Gandhi, MLK, Chavez and includes lesser-known events and details. Information/Nonfiction

Hawkins, Rachel. *Her Royal Highness*. Putnam, 2019. ISBN: 9781524738266. When her relationship with who she thinks is her girlfriend goes south, Millie splits and to attend an exclusive boarding school. There she meets a Scottish princess – and discovers a new love interest. Fiction

Heiligman, Deborah. Torpedoed: The True Story of the World War II Sinking of "The Children's Ship." Henry Holt, 2019. ISBN: 9781627795548. During the early days of World War II, 200 passengers (many children) were on the ship, *City of Benares,* when it was torpedoed off the coast of Britain This is the story of the efforts to save the passengers. Information/Nonfiction

Henderson, Joe. *Skyward*. Art by Lee Garbett. Vol. 2*, Here There Be Dragonflies*. ISBN: 978-1534308817. Vol. 3, *Fix the World*. ISBN: 978-1534312432. Image Comics, 2019. (Collection of all 15 issues of the series; *Skyward* [2021] ISBN: 978-1534316997.) Willa's mother died the day gravity changed on earth. Twenty years later, Willa and everyone else on Earth has adapted to their low-gravity world but Willa is on the run and must find a way to survive the dangers that are there. GN -Fiction

Hendrix, John. *The Faithful Spy: Dietrich Bonhoeffer and the Plot to Kill Hitler*. Art by the author. Abrams Comic Arts, 2018. ISBN: 978-1419728389. In 1930s Germany, pastor and theologian Dietrich Bonhoeffer joins his fellow German conspirators in a plot to kill Hitler. GN -Nonfiction

Hicks, Faith Erin. *The Nameless City,* Volume 3*: The Divided Earth*. Illus. by the author, 2018. First Second, ISBN: 9781626721616. With war on the front – Rat and Kai must infiltrate the palace, steal the weapon's secret code to return the city to its indigenous people. GN -Fiction

Higashimura, Akiko. *Blank Canvas: My So-Called Artist's Journey*. Art by the author. 2019. *Vol. 1.* Seven Seas Entertainment. ISBN: 978-1642750690. *Vol. 2.* Seven Seas Entertainment. ISBN: 978-1642750706. An autobiographical tale of the author's journey as an artist. GN -Nonfiction

Higuera, Donna Barba. *Lupe Wong Won't Dance*. Levine Querido, 2020. ISBN: 9781646140039. Lupe takes up the cause against square dancing in order to prevent the dance from keeping her from meeting pitching idol and fellow Mexinese/Chinacan, Fu Li Hernandez, Belpré Children's Author Honor Book. Fiction

Hinds, Gareth. *The Iliad*. Candlewick Press, 2019. ISBN: 978-0763681135. An epic poem-a classic war story during the Trojan War. GN -Poetry

Hopkinson, Deborah, 2020. *We Had to Be Brave: Escaping the Nazis on the Kinderstransport*. Scholastic Focus. ISBN: 978-1338255720. Details the rise of Hitler to power and the situation that caused hundreds of families to be split apart as parents attempted desperately to save their children. The true stories of Jewish children and how they fled Nazi Germany on the Kindertransport. Information/Nonfiction

Howard, Abby. *The Last Halloween: Children.* Iron Circus Comics, 2020. ISBN: 9781945820663. Ten-year-old Mona flees her monster-filled home but is still surrounded by monsters who will destroy all humans. GN -Fiction

Hughes, Kiku. *Displacement.* First Second / Macmillan, 2020. ISBN: 9781250193537. A young Japanese-American teen time travels to the internment camps of the 1940s. GN -Fiction

Humprhies, Sam. *Blackbird, Volume 1*. Art by Jen Bartel. Image Comics, 2019. ISBN: 978-1534312593. After surviving an earthquake Nina grows up convinced of the shadowy magical people in the world of Paragons. GN -Fiction

Husted, Ursula. Murray. *A Cat Story.* Quill Tree Books / HarperCollins, 2020. ISBN: 9780062932051. A story of friendship and loyalty. GN -Fiction

Ifueko, Jordan. *Raybearer.* Amulet Books, 2020. ISBN: 9781419739828. Tarisai must obey her mother's wish to kill the emperor's son, made at her birth, but the situation changes when she becomes part of the prince's council and his best friend. Fiction

Ireland, Justina. *Ophie's Ghosts.* Balzer+Bray, 2021. ISBN: 9780062915894. Ophelia used to live in Georgia but … a cruel act in November 1922 took her father and her family's home. It was also that day in November that she found out that she can see ghosts. Now she is with her mom in Pittsburgh with relatives – and working for the wealthy Caruther's family where the ghosts of Daffodil Manor have more secrets to share than Ophie may want to hear. Fiction.

Ishikawa, Yugo. *Wonderland*. Art by the author. *Vol. 1*, 2018. ISBN: 978-1626929081; *Vol. 2*, 2019. ISBN: 978-1626929982; *Vol. 3*. ISBN: 978-1642751277. Seven Seas Entertainment, 2019. One morning Yukko and her family shrink in size; her tiny parents are murdered (by her cat) and the rest of the story is mired in mystery and intrigue. GN -Fiction

Ishizuka, Chihiro. *Flying Witch*. Illus. by the author, 2018. Vertical Comics, V.3. ISBN: 9781945054112; V.4. ISBN: 9781945054129; V.5. ISBN: 9781945054679; V.6. ISBN: 9781947194045. The series continues to follow the sweet and gentle witch in training, Makoto, as she enjoys country life and honing her craft. GN -Fiction

Ito, Junji. *Frankenstein: Junji Ito Story Collection*. Viz Media, 2018. ISBN: 978-1974703760. A retelling of the Mary Shelley classic, Frankenstein. Includes stories about lonely high schooler Oshikiri in his haunted house and tales of horror. GN -Fiction

James, Anna. *Pages & Co.: The Bookwanders*. Philomel, 2019. ISBN: 9781984837127. Even since she was a baby, her mother has been missing and 11-year-old Tilly Pages has spent hours of every day in her grandparents' bookshop. One day she discovers she can bookwander – actually follow characters into their stories. New adventures await her and possibly answers about her mother's whereabouts. Fiction

Jamieson, Victoria, and Mohamed, Omar, 2020. *When Stars are Scattered*. Illustrated by Victoria Jamieson. Dial. ISBN: 9780525553908. Two brothers growing up as orphan refugees at a refugee camp in Kenya. Fiction

Jarrow, Gail. *The Poison Eaters: Fighting Danger and Fraud in Our Food and Drugs*. Calkins Creek, 2019. ISBN: 9781629794389. Prior to the work of Dr. Harvey Washington Wiley identified extremely harmful additives that food companies routinely added to food. These additives included substances normally used now in embalming fluid, cleaning supplies, and so forth: formaldehyde, borax, salicylic acid. Wiley is known as the father of the food and drug administration (FDA. Information/Nonfiction

Jarrow, Gail. *Blood and Germs: The Civil War Battle Against Wounds and Disease*. Calkins Creek, 2020. ISBN: 9781684371761. The Civil War is often called the deadliest war in U.S. history but is also responsible for many medical advances. Information/Nonfiction

Jenkins, Paul. *Beyonders, Volume 1: The Mapmakers*. By Paul Jenkins. Art by Wesley St.Claire. Aftershock, 2019. ISBN: 978-1949028065. High school senior Jacob Tate is obsessed with puzzles and conspiracy theories. GN -Fiction

Jenkins, Tommy. *Drawing the Vote: An Illustrated Guide to Voting in America.* Art by Kati Lacker. Abrams ComicsArts / Abrams Books, 2020. ISBN: 978-1419739989. History of voting in the United States. Explores the 13th and 19th amendment as well as the dark side of voting. GN -Nonfiction

Johnson, Leah. *Rise to the Sun.* Scholastic Press, 2021. ISBN: 9781338662238. Two girls: Toni (grieving her father), and Olivia (a square peg in a round hole) seek a chance to find their place. Three days and a life-changing music festival just may be more than they could imagine.

Junti, Ito. *Smashed: Junji Ito Story Collection.* Art by Ito Junti. VIZ Media, 2019. ISBN: 978-1421598468. Junji Ito, the Japanese master or horror, shares thirteen terrifying tales. GN -Fiction

Jusay, Jeremy. *The Strange Ones.* Gallery 13 / Simon & Schuster, 2020. ISBN: 9781982101121. A chance meeting leads Anjeline and Franck into an epic friendship (1990s. GN -Fiction

Kaito. *Blue Flag.* Vol. 1-5, VIZ Media, 2020. ISBN: 9781974713011. ISBN: 9781974713028. ISBN: 9781974713035. ISBN: 9781974713042. ISBN: 9781974713059. An unexpected love quadrangle forms when Taichi agrees to help Futaba pursue her crush, Toma, while friend Mami looks on. GN -Fiction

Kallab, Samya. *Escape from Syria.* Illus. by Jackie Roche, 2017. Firefly Books, ISBN: 9781770859821. Amina and her family's story of escape from the civil war in Syria. The plight of Syria refugees, and their eventual settling in Canada is a compelling story. GN -Fiction

Kamatani, Yuhki. *Our Dreams at Dusk.* Art by the author, 2019. *Vol. 1.* Seven Seas. ISBN: 978-1642750607. *Vol. 2.* Seven Seas. ISBN: 978-1642750607.*Vol. 3.* Seven Seas. $12.99. ISBN: 978-1642750621. Tasuku's has been outed just before meeting a mysterious woman who helps him find his place in the world? GN -Fiction

Kamatani. Yuhki. *Our Dreams at Dusk: Shimanami Tasogare, Vol. 4.* Seven Seas Entertainment, 2019. ISBN: 9781642750638. Enigmatic Tchaiko's story ends when Saki's secret is revealed, and the *Our Dreams at Dusk* series completes. GN -Fiction

Kaufman, Amie, and Kristoff, Jay, 2019. *Aurora Burning.* Knopf. ISBN: 9781524720926. The Misfits, Squad 312 are back. The galaxy is in danger from an ancient evil and the power is about to be unleashed. Fiction

Kaufman, Amie, and Kristoff, Jay, 2020. *Aurora Rising.* Knopf. ISBN: 9781524720964. A group of misfits in 2380, get their first mission; and are set to uncover Aurora's secret – her new, mysterious powers after 200 years. Fiction

Kaye, Julia. *Super Late Bloomer: My Early Days in Transition*. Illus. by the author. 2018. Andrews McMeel Publishing, ISBN: 9781449489625. A personal journey of acceptance as a trans individual. GN -Nonfiction

Keller, Tae. *When You Trap a Tiger*. By Tae Keller. Random House Children's Books, 2020. ISBN: 9781524715700. A fanciful tale of a magic tiger who negotiates with Lily to save her sick grandmother if a return of stolen stories can be made. Newbery Medal Book. Fiction

Kelly, Erin Entrada. *We Dream of Space*. Illustrated by the author and Celia Krampien. Greenwillow, 2020. ISBN: 9780062747303. A coming-of-age story during the era preceding the days before the Space Shuttle Challenger disaster. The Thomas siblings must deal with middle school and their fractured family. Newbery Honor Book. Fiction

Kemmerer, Brigid. *A Curse So Dark and Lonely.* The Cursebreaker Series: Book 1. Bloomsbury, 2019. ISBN: 9781681195087. Harper is taken illegally to Emberfall, where she can hopefully free Prince Rhen, from the curse that causes him to relive a year of his life, over and over again. *A Heart So Fierce and Broken* - The Cursebreaker Series: Book 2 (2020); *A Vow So Bold and Deadly* - The Cursebreaker Series: Book 3 (2021. Fiction

Kemmerer, Brigid. *Call It What You Want*. Bloomsbury, 2019. ISBN: 9781681198095. Both Rob and Megan have their struggles. Rob's dad is incapacitated after a suicide attempt because of his own embezzlement. Megan is known as a cheater. Both need a friend. Fiction

Kendall, Mikki. *Amazons, Abolitionists, and Activists: A Graphic History of Women's Fight for Their Rights*. Art by A. D'Amico. Ten Speed Press/Penguin Random House. 2019. ISBN: 9780399581793. Historical account of women and activism including progressive movements, i.e. abolition, labor, and LGBTQ+ rights. GN -Nonfiction

Kindt, Matt. Dept. H, Volume 3. Illus. by the author and Sharlene Kindt, 2018. Dark Horse, ISBN: 9781616559915. Mia continues to search for her father's killer miles below the ocean surface. As the answers to her questions about his death draw nearer, her chances for survival are sinking lower. GN -Fiction

King, A.S. *Dig*. Dutton, 2019. ISBN: 9781101994917. The five grandchildren of Marla and Gottfried dig through their lives-lives spawned by the origins of the dysfunctional family. All while dealing with elements of racism, white power, privilege, and class. The 2020 Michael L. Printz Award winner. Similar style/structure to *Crawl through It* (2015. Fiction

Kobabe, Maia. *Gender Queer: A Memoir.* Art by Maia Kobabe. Lion Forge. 2019. ISBN: 978-1549304002. Genderqueer author and artist Maia Kobabe explores gender, sexuality, sex, relationships, and family side-by-side; and addresses her own experiences of bullying, clothing, haircuts, coming out and finding community. GN -Nonfiction

Kobayashi, Kina. *Nameless Asterism.* Illus. by the author, 2018. Seven Seas, V.1 ISBN: 9781626927445; V.2 ISBN: 9781626927452. Since the day they met, Shiratori is secretly in love with Washio, but both are part of an inseparable friendship with Kotooka. What will become of the threes long-time friendship – and friendship survive alongside love? GN -Fiction

Konigsberg, Bill. *The Music of What Happens.* Scholastic/Arthur A. Levine, 2019. ISBN: 9781338215502. Two gay teens, Max and Jordan are operating a food truck; and together they learn through "the music of what happens." A 2020 Top 10 Rainbow List selection. Fiction

Korman, Gordon. *War Stories.* Scholastic, 2020. ISBN: 9781338290202. Trevor loves war-based video games and he loves his great-grandfather, Jacob. When the two of them retrace Jacob's heroic training and eventual liberation of a French Village during World War II secrets are revealed that impacts the importance of true valor.

Krajewski. Thomas, and Muro, Jennifer. *Primer.* Art by Gretel Lusky. DC Comics, 2020. ISBN: 9781401296575. Ashley's father is in prison, and she is in a foster home when she discovers her foster mom is working on an experiment. What she finds out turns her into a superhero with unique powers. GN -Fiction

Kristensen, Charlot. *What We Don't Talk About.* Avery Hill Publishing, 2020. ISBN: 9781910395554. During her visit to Adam's family home, Farai is met with blatant bigotry and racism. With no support from Adam, Farai must find a way to define herself and face their behavior. GN -Fiction

Krosoczka, Jarrett. *Hey, Kiddo: How I Lost My Mother, Found My Father, and Dealt with Family Addiction.* By Jarrett Krosoczka. Illus. by the author. 2018. Graphix, ISBN: 9780545902472. A memoir-raised by grandparents and finding art while dealing with family addiction and absenteeism. GN -Nonfiction

Krug, Nora. *Belonging: A German Reckons With History and Home.* Illus. by the author. Scribner, 2018. ISBN: 9781476796628. Understanding his German roots and her familial ties to the Nazi party during WWII leads her to a genealogical journey. GN -Nonfiction

Kubo, Mitsurou. *Again!!.* Illus. by the author. V.1. Kodansha Comics, ISBN: 9781632366450; V. 2, ISBN: 9781632366467; V.3., 2018. ISBN: 9781632366474; V. 4., ISBN: 9781632366481; V.5., ISBN: 9781632366498. In high school, Kinishrio is known as a troublemaker. But he gets a chance to do-over after he falls downstairs and wakes up three years later. GN -Fiction

Kuhn, Sarah. *I Love You So Mochi*. Scholastic, 2019. ISBN: 9781338302882. Spring break in Japan with her estranged grandparents seems to be an opportunity for self-discovery. The trip ends up with love and a creative endeavor – much to the disapproval of her mother. Fiction

Kui, Ryoko. *Seven Little Sons of the Dragon: A Collection of Seven Stories.* Yen Press, 2019. ISBN: 9781975359614. Seven fantastical tales. GN -Fiction

Kuwabara, Taku. *Drifting Dragons Vol. 1-5*. Kodansha Comics / Kodansha USA, 2019. ISBN: 9781632368904; 2020. ISBN: 9781632369451, ISBN: 9781632369512. ISBN: 9781632369529. Historical fantasy and cooking manga and dragons. GN -Fiction

Lai, Thanhhà. *Butterfly Yellow*. Harper, 2019. ISBN: 9780062229212. In order to find her little brother, Linh, Hang embarks on a very dangerous journey traveling from Vietnam to Amarillo, Texas. But all does not go well – Linh does not seem to remember Hang. Fiction

Larson, Hope. *All Summer Long*. Illustrated by Hope Larson. Farrar, Straus and Giroux , 2018. ISBN: 9780374304850. In this coming-of-age story, thirteen-year-old Bina missed her best friend Austin when he goes off to soccer camp. When he returns, the two must find out what friendship, true friendship really means. GN -Fiction

Larson, Hope. *All Together Now* by Hope Larson. Farrar, Straus & Giroux Books for Young Readers / Macmillan, 2020. ISBN: 9780374313654. Following *All Summer Long*, Brina's journey continues (*All Summer Long)* as she tries to figure out who she is and where she fits in the world. GN -Fiction

Larson, Hope. *Goldie Vance, Volume 4*. Illus. by Elle Power, 2018. BOOM! Studios, ISBN: 9781684151400. Marigold "Goldie" Vance lives at a Florida resort with her dad and sets out to solve the mystery of the power outages affecting their town. GN -Fiction

LaValle, Victor. *Victor LaValle's Destroyer*. Illus. by Dietrich Smith and Joana Lafuente, 2018. Boom! Studios, ISBN: 9781684150557. Two scientists find Dr. Baker conducting experiments in an effort to bring back her twelve-year-old son who was shot by the police, and the Destroyer, Frankenstein's monster, is wreaking havoc – that's when both the world of Mary Shelley's Frankenstein and the present collide. GN -Fiction

Lê, Minh. *Heavy Vinyl, vol. 2: Y2K-O!*. Art by Nina Vakueva. BOOM! Box / BOOM! Studios, 2020. $14.99. ISBN: 978168415495. The Heavy Vinyl crew returns in volume 2! to save the (digital) world from Y2K-'90s nostalgia series. GN -Fiction

Lê, Minh. *Green Lantern: Legacy.* Art by Andie Tong. DC Zoom / DC Comics, 2020. ISBN: 9781401283551. Tai Pham puts a lot of faith in someone that isn't who he seems to be. GN -Fiction

Lee, Dami. *Be Everything at Once: Tales of a Cartoonist Lady Person*. Illus. by the author. 2018. Chronicle Books, ISBN: 9781452167657. Quirky and relatable, Dami's struggle of trying to fit in growing up and transitioning into adulthood. GN -Nonfiction

Lee, Harper, and Fordham, Fred. *To Kill a Mockingbird: A Graphic Novel*. Illus. by Fred Fordham, 2018. Harper, ISBN: 9780062798183. A graphic adaptation of the classic story of race and class in the South. GN -Fiction

Lee, Julie, 2020. *Brother's Keeper*. Holiday. ISBN: 9780823444946. Sora and her family become separated during their flight from Communist North Korea during the Korean War in 1950. She must take care of her brother and together find their way south. Fiction

Lee, Stacey. *The Downstairs Girl*. Putnam, 2019. ISBN: 9781524740955. A historical tale (1890 Atlanta) of a Chinese American who writes a popular advice column, using a pseudonym and a lot of word play and witty observations of the times. Author of the popular *Outrun the Moon* (2016. Fiction

Lemire, Jeff. *Ascender, Volume 1*. Art by Dustin Nguyen. Image Comics, 2019. ISBN: 978-1534313484. Magic has replaced machines as the rulers of the Universe. Andy and Mila are leaving the planet Sampson. GN -Fiction

Lemire, Jeff. *Black Hammer: The Event, Volume 2*. Illus. by Dean Ormston and David Rubin, 2018. Dark Horse, ISBN: 9781506701981. Abraham Slam, Golden Gail, Colonel Weird, Madame Dragonfly, and Barbalien, former superheros, are trapped, in life in a rural town. Picking up where volume one ended, readers find out what caused all of the superheroes to end up where they are now. GN -Fiction

Lemire, Jeff. *Descender, Volume 5: Rise of the Robots*. Illus. by Dustin Nguyen, 2018. Image Comics, ISBN: 9781534303454; *Descender, Volume 6: The Machine War*. Illus. by Dustin Nguyen, 2018. Image Comics, ISBN: 9781534306905. In these final volumes of Descender's first story arc, Tim-21 and crew find themselves in the middle of the robot revolution. GN -Fiction

Lemire, Jeff. *Royal City, Volume 2: Sonic Youth*. Illus. by the author, 2018. Image Comics, ISBN: 9781534305526; Volume 3: We All Float On, 2018. Image Comics, ISBN: 9781534308497. The story of the Pike family, the loss of Tommy Pike's older brother, Patrick's death, and his father's stroke, give readers a glimpse this teen's life in 1993, and an exploration of loss, grief, family, and being accepted. GN -Fiction

Lemire, Jeff. *Sentient*. Art by Gabriel Hernandez Walta. TKO Studios, 2019. ISBN: 9781732748545. A gothic-space horror, pits children against adults. Artificial Intelligence plays into the story. GN -Fiction

Lendler, Ian, 2019. *The First Dinosaurs: How Science Solved the Greatest Mystery on Earth*. Illustrated by C. M. Butzer. Margaret K. McElderry Books/S&S. ISBN: 978-1534427006. A fascinating history of how the scientific study of dinosaurs began – the history of the science and of the dinosaur. Information/Nonfiction

Lenoir, Axelle. *Camp Spirit* Top Shelf Productions / IDW Publishing, 2020. ISBN: 9781603094658. Elodie is working as a camp counselor (1994), when the kids and a fellow counselor uncover something strange going on in the woods. GN -Fiction

Leong, Sloane. *A Map to the Sun*. First Second / Macmillan, 2020. ISBN: 9781250146687. A chance encounter on the beaches brings Luna and Ren to develop a friendship. Luna returns years later. Is the friendship worth rebuilding? GN -Fiction

Levy, Debbie. *Becoming RBG: Ruth Bader Ginsburg's Journey to Justice*. Art by Whitney Gardner. Simon & Schuster Books for Young Readers / Simon & Schuster. 2019. ISBN: 9781534424562. Biography of Supreme Court Justice Ruth Bader Ginsburg-her childhood and her inspiration. GN -Nonfiction

Lewis, Sean. *Coyotes, Volume 1*. Illus. by Caitlin Yarsky, 2018. Image Comics, ISBN: 9781534306479. Analia aka Red, was orphaned when coyotes plague the City of Lost Girls and killed her sister and mother. She and others band together to get rid of the coyotes and save others. GN -Fiction

Lewis, Sean. *Coyotes, Volume 2*. Art by Caitlin Yarsky. Image Comics, 2019. ISBN: 978-1534310315. Men in wolf pelts have terrorized and killed women for years. Eleven-year-old Red is determined to rid the men of their dominance but goals conflict with other women who want to rehabilitate. GN -Fiction

Leyh, Kat. *Snapdragon*. Illustrated by the Kat Leyh. First Second, 2020. ISBN: 9781250171115. Snapdragon connects loving yourself and magic. Fiction

Leyh, Kat. *Snapdragon*. First Second / Macmillan, 2020. ISBN: 9781250171115. When Snap's dog goes missing, she discovers that witches may be real after all. GN -Fiction

LeZotte, Ann Clare. *Show Me a Sign*. Scholastic Press, 2020. ISBN: 9781338255812. Based on true accounts of the Deaf community that existed on Martha's Vineyard during the 1880s. Mary's life is rather typical until a prejudice scientist arrives on the island and focuses on studying Mary and her supposed disability, without her cooperation. Fiction

Libenson, Terri. *Truly Tyler*. Balzer+Bray, 2021. ISBN: 97800628994571. The first book in a series: Emmie and Friends. Cliques, crushes, and comics. Four more titles in the series will share more about Emmie and friends: *Invisible Emmie, Positively Izzy, Just Jaime, Becoming Brianna*, and *You-Niquely You: An Emmie & Friends Interactive Journal*!

Liu, Marjorie. *Monstress, Volume 3*. Illus. by Sana Takeda, 2018. Image Comics, ISBN: 9781534306912. Fleeing from her enemies, Maika Halfwolf seeks refuge in a neutral city but must convince the others that survival rests on the strength of her shaman-empress heritage. GN -Fiction

Lloyd-Jones, Emily. *The Bone Houses*. Little, Brown, 2019. ISBN: 9780316418416. When Ellis, a mapmaker, arrives in town, the bones houses start causing concern for Ryn, the graveyard manager. Fiction

Locatelli-Kournwskcy, Loic. Persephone. Illus. by the author, 2018. Archaia, ISBN: 9781684151752. Persephone goes through the gates of Hades and finds herself in the middle of a quest to find an ultimate power. GN -Fiction

Locke, Katherine, and Silverman, Laura, eds. *It's a Whole Spiel: Love, Latkes, and Other Jewish Stories.* Knopf, 2019. ISBN: 9780525646167. A collection of stories in a variety of voices. Fiction

Lowry, Lois. *The Giver: Graphic Novel*. Art by P. Craig Russell. HMH Books for Young Readers, 2019. ISBN: 978-0544157880. Jonas (age 12) is the "Receiver of Memory," keeping the secrets and memories of his entire community. He realizes that changes must be made. GN -Fiction

Macaione, Giulio. *Alice: From Dream to Dream*. Illus. by Giulia Adragna. BOOM! Box, 2018. ISBN: 9781684151806. Alice has the ability to enter other people's dreams. Will the secrets of her life remain dreams, or will it all become a nightmare? GN -Fiction

Macaulay, David. *Crossing on Time: Steam Engines, Fast Ships, and a Journey to the New World.* Roaring Brook Press, 2019. ISBN: 9781596434776. In his usual stunningly detailed illustrations, Macaulay shows us all the nooks and crannies of the steamship interwoven with the history of steamships with a focus on the SS United States. Information/Nonfiction

Machado, Carmen Maria, *The Low, Low Woods* . Art by DaNi. Hill House Comics / DC Comics, 2020. ISBN: 9781779504524. Horrifying secrets about their community, from generations back, are discovered by El and Vee. GN -Fiction

Maclear, Kyo. *Operatic*. Art by Byron Eggenschwiler. Groundworks Books, 2019. ISBN: 978-1554989720. Charlie and other 8th graders are asked to find their song. Charlie's friend Luka has been the victim of homophobic bullying and the quest for their song-and the friendship of Charlie and Luka merge into a story of coping. GN -Fiction

Mafi, Tahereh. An Emotion of Great Delight: A Novel. HarperCollins Childrens Books, 2021. ISBN 9780062972415. War on Iraq has been declared by the USA, and Shadi's Muslim family is targeted by bullies. The year is 2003, and Shadi's father is dying, her brother already dead, her mother is having a breakdown, and her best friend has retreated. Shadi's own life is totally in shabbles. Then… she explodes. Forging a new place, finding love and hope. Fiction

Marks, Janae. *From the Desk of Zoe Washington*. Illustrated by Mirelle Ortega. HarperCollins/Katherine Tegen, 2020. ISBN: 9780062875853. A coming of age novel. Zoe Washington navigates a summer bakery internship, a fight with her best friend, and building a relationship with her wrongfully incarcerated father. Fiction

Marrin, Albert. A Light in the Darkness: Janusz Korczak, His Orphans, and the Holocaust. Alfred A. Knopf, 2019. ISBN: 9781524701208. A look at the history of the Warsaw Ghetto, told by comparing the philosophies of Doctor Janusz Korczak, who championed children's rights, and Adolf Hitler. Good vs. evil. Nonfiction

Maurel, Carole, and Tamaki, Mariko. *Luisa - Now and Then.* Illus. by the authors, 2018. Humanoids, ISBN: 9781594656439. A moving story about self-discovery, Luisa as a teen meets her adult self and must make tough decisions about the kind of person she wants to be. GN -Fiction

Mccoonis, Dylan. *Queen of the Sea.* Art by the author. Candlewick, 2019. ISBN: 978-1536204988. Raised by nuns on a small, remote island, Margaret, a spirited young orphan, spends her time exploring her surroundings, and discovers the island's true purpose, the truth of her own past, and the grave danger she is in. GN -Fiction

McCranie, Stephen. *Stephen McCranie's Space Boy, Volume 1.* Illustrated. Dark Horse Books, ISBN: 9781506706481. *Vol. 2* ISBN:9781506706801; *Vol. 3.* ISBN:9781506708423; *Vol. 4*, ISBN:9781506708430. *Vol. 5,* 2019) ISBN: 9781506713991. *Vol. 6.* ISBN: 9781506714004. *Vol. 7,* ISBN: 9781506714011. *Vol. 8.* ISBN: 9781506714028. Dark Horse Books, 2018-2020. After spending thirty years cryogenically frozen on a space flight to Earth, throughout the series, Amy continues to search for answers to the mysterious events involving her classmates, on the planet earth. GN -Fiction

McGinnis, Mindy. *Heroine.* HarperCollins/Katherine Tegen, 2019. ISBN: 9780062847195. After a serious car crash, star athlete Mickey Catalan becomes addicted to pain medication, and finds herself lying, stealing, and shooting up. A 2020 Top 10 Quick Pick for Reluctant Readers. Fiction

McGuire, Seanan. *Spider-Gwen: Ghost-Spider, Volume 2: Impossible Year.* Art by Takeshi Miyazawa, Rosi Kampe. Marvel Comics, 2019. ISBN: 978-1302914776. Gwen Stacy strives to maintain a balance in her life when her superhero status brings her attention. GN -Fiction

McKeever, Sean Kelly. *Outpost Zero.* Art by Alexandre Tengfenki, Jean-François Beaulieu, 2019. *Vol. 1, The Smallest Town in the Universe.* Image Comics. ISBN: 978-1534306929. *Vol. 2, Follow it Down* (2019); *Outpost Zero, vol. 3,* (2020). ISBN: 978-1534312166, Image Comics. Welcome back to the smallest town in the universe! Sam and Lyss find an unexpected opportunity to prove their worth and uncover greater mysteries buried beneath the ice surface and what was really behind their friend Stephen's death. GN -Fiction

Meyer, Joanna Ruth. *Echo North.* Page Street, 2019. ISBN: 9781624147159. Retelling of Norwegian fairy tale "East of the Sun, West of the Moon," featuring a disfigured Echo, who must save her father by living with a mysterious wolf for a year. Fiction

Meyer, Marissa. *Wires and Nerve: Gone Rogue, Volume 2.* Illus. by Stephen Gilpin, 2018. Feiwel & Friends, ISBN: 9781250078285. Android Iko is determined to help the queen of Luna, with the problem of hybrid wolfmen sabotaging Luna's fragile friendship with Earth. GN -Fiction

Mirk, Sarah. *Guantánamo Voices: True Accounts from the World's Most Infamous Prison.* Art by Gerardo Alba, Kasia Babis, Alex Beguez, Tracy Chahwan, Nomi Kane, et al. Abrams ComicsArts / Abrams Books. 2020. ISBN: 9781419746901. Anthology of tales from the prisoners, by multimedia journalist Sarah Mirk and a team of talented artists. GN -Nonfiction

Mizukami, Satoshi. *Spirit Circle.* Illus. by the author. Seven Seas, V.1, 2017. ISBN: 9781626926011; V.2, 2018. ISBN: 9781626926806; V.3, 2018. ISBN: 9781626927292; V.4, 2018. ISBN: 9781626928329; V.5, 2018. ISBN: 9781626929241. Fuuta has to discover what exactly happened between herself and Ishigami, in their previous lives to cause such hatred in a middle school girl. GN -Fiction

Mohamed, Omar. *When Stars are Scattered.* Art by Victoria Jamieson. Dial Books for Young Readers / Penguin Random House. 2020. ISBN: 9780525553908. Brothers Omar and Hassan are fleeing Somalia, and in a refugee camp in Kenya. Every day Omar cares for his special-needs brother Hassan, cleans their tent, goes to school, and waits for a way out. And everyday they search the faces of any new refugees for the face of their mother. GN -Nonfiction

Monk, J.N. *Topside.* Art by Harry Bogosian. Graphic Universe/Lerner Publishing Group, 2019. ISBN: 9781512445893. Con-artists, bounty hunters, and a mechanic travel together topside to save the planet! GN -Fiction

Moore, Stuart, and Lu, Marie. *Batman: Nightwalker.* Art by Chris Wildgoose. DC Ink / DC Comics, 2019. ISBN: 9781401280048. Bruce Wayne, as a young man, gets caught up in a high-speed chase. Wayne begins to question: who is the real villain? GN -Fiction

Moreci, Michael. *The Lost Carnival: A Dick Grayson Graphic Novel.* Art by Sas Milledge. DC Comics, 2020. ISBN: 9781401291020. An acrobat in the circus meets Luciana and must choose between his family and the allure of the romance. GN -Fiction

Moreil, Roxanne. *The Golden Age, book 1.* Art by Cyril Pedrosa. First Second / Macmillan, 2020. ISBN: 9781250237941. Exiled by a coup led by her younger brother, Princess Tilda rescued by a loyal knight and his ward and then sets about to reclaim the throne. GN -Fiction

Morris, Brittney. *Slay*. Simon & Schuster/Simon Pulse, 2019. ISBN: 9781534445420. Marginalized individuals are often excluded but Kiera, a 17-year-old Black gamer, is not about to be ignored. All is good until a troll infiltrates the game. Fiction

Mosco, Rosemary. *Birding is My Favorite Video Game: Cartoons About the Natural World from Bird and Moon*. Illus. by the author. 2018. Andrews McMeel Publishing, ISBN: 9781449489120. A humorous look at informational notes about birds, bees, and the natural world, science cartoons. GN -Nonfiction

Moskowitz, Hannah. *Sick Kids in Love*. Entangled, 2019. ISBN: 9781640637320. Isabel has chronic rheumatoid arthritis and avoids dating because of being a sick kid but then she meets another sick kid. Then the question becomes should she break her one rule or not. A 2020 Sydney Taylor Silver Medalist. Fiction

Mullane, Hellen. *Nicnevin and the Bloody Queen*. Art by Dom Reardon and Matthew Dow Smith. H1 / Humanoids, 2020. ISBN: 9781643377131. Nicnevin finds herself in the midst of modern-day druids' effort in an attempt to solve the murders. GN -Fiction

Murdock, Catherine Gilbert. *Da Vinci's Cat*. Greenwillow Books, 2021. ISBN: 9780063015258. A time slip fantasy that binds together two friends: Federico from 16th century Rome and Bee in present day New Jersey. Linking them is Leonardo daVinci's cat, and his mysterious wardrobe. Can rewriting history save today? Science Fantasy - Fiction

Murphy, Jill. *Pumpkin*. Balzer+Bray, 2021. ISBN: 9780062880451. Murphy's final companion book about drag, prom, and loving who you are. Willowdean Dixon is a person all readers should know. *Dumplin'* (Balzer+Bray, 2015) - the first in the Dumplin' series of books about Willowdean Dixon who takes on her own self-confidence by entering the local beauty contest and then carries on through more titles. The book *Dumplin'* is the basis for a Netflix movie and starring Jennifer Aniston, Danielle Macdonald, and Dove Cameron, as well as a soundtrack from Dolly Parton! Fiction

Nagabe. *The Girl from the Other Side: Siúil A Rún*. Illus. by the author. Seven Seas, V.3, 2017. ISBN: 9781626925588; V.4, 2018. ISBN: 9781626927018; V.5, 2018. ISBN: 9781626928473. Left in the care of "Teacher," a young girl named Shiva must survive in a land filled with vicious beasts that curse others with a touch. A struggle ensues. GN -Fiction

Nazemian, Abdi, 2019. *Like a Love Story*. HarperCollins/Balzer+Bray. ISBN: 9780062839367. Love among three teens – an Iranian who cannot be open about his sexuality, a gay photographer, and another who must deal with an uncle's++ HIV positivity. All join together as activists in 1989 New York. Fiction

Neri, G. *Grand Theft Horse*. Illustrated by G. Neri. Lee & Low Books, Inc., 2018. ISBN: 9781620148556. A story of Gail Ruffu-a horse trainer who fought for fair treatment of her horse and herself; in the process she was arrested and tried for grand theft. GN -Nonfiction

Nguyen, Tung Le. *The Magic Fish*. Random House Graphic / Penguin Random House, 2020. ISBN: 9780593125298. Tiến must figure out how to come out of the closet, to his Vietnamese-American parents. GN -Fiction

Nicholas, Matt, and Rebmann, Chad. *Relics of Youth, Vol. 1* . Art by Skylar Patridge. Vault Comics, 2020. ISBN: 9781939424587. In the process of a group of teens seeking answers to mysterious tattoos, they encounter menacing forces on the island–an island that may be theirs as the true guardians. GN -Fiction

Nijkamp, Marieke. *The Oracle Code*. Art by Manuel Preitano. DC Comics, 2020. ISBN: 9781401290665. Barbara Gordon is paralyzed by a gunshot and goes to a center to recover but Barbara begins to see others disappear from the center. She sets out to find out why. GN -Fiction

Nogiri, Yoko. *Love in Focus Vol. 1-3*, Kodansha Comics, 2019. ISBN: 978-1632367686; ISBN: 978-1632367693.; ISBN: 978-1632367969. Mako, lives in an inn which also includes Mitsuru, and Mako's old friend, Kei. The three must deal with the relationships that develop. GN -Fiction

Nourigat, Natalie. *I Moved to Los Angeles to Work in Animation*. Art by the author. Boom! Box, 2019. ISBN: 978-1684152919. Follows the artist in her transition from comic book illustrator to a career in animation, and learning things like storyboarding, studio culture. GN -Nonfiction

Ogle, Rex. Free Lunch. Norton Young Readers, 2019. ISBN: 9781324003601. Ogle's sixth-grade year and his family's experience with poverty and how their poverty impacts relationships. Information/Nonfiction

Oima, Yoshitoki. *To Your Eternity*. Illus. by the author. Kodansha Comics, V.1, 2017. ISBN: 9781632365712; V.2, 2017. ISBN: 9781632365729; V.3, 2018. ISBN: 9781632365736; V.4, 2018. ISBN: 9781632365743; V.5, 2018. ISBN: 9781632365750. The main character has the ability to change forms as he travels the world – causing exploration and changes. GN -Fiction

Okorafor, Nnedi. *Shuri, Volume 1: The Search for Black Panther*. Art by Leonardo Romero. Marvel Comics, 2019. ISBN: 978-1302915230. When the superhero king of Wakanda disappears on a space mission, Shuri is called on, and pressured by her mother, to search for the king. Shuri agrees, but what does she want for herself? GN -Fiction

Okupe, Roye. *Iyanu: Child of Wonder, vol. 1.* Art by Godwin Akpan. YouNeek Studios, 2020. ISBN: 9780999830161. An orphan with no memories of her past, Iyanu, discovers powerful hidden abilities but those powers threaten the people of Yorubaland who threaten her. GN -Fiction

ONE. *Mob Psycho 100.* Art by the author. *Vol. 1.* Dark Horse Manga, 2018. ISBN: 978-1506709871.; *Vol. 2.* Dark Horse Manga, 2019. ISBN: 978-1506709888; *Vol. 3.* Dark Horse Manga, 2019. ISBN: 978-1506709895. Other than having superpowers, Mob is just an average 8th grader. But he only wants to be a normal kid and get the girl. GN -Fiction

Onyebuchi, Tochi. *War Girls.* Razorbill, 2019. ISBN: 9780451481672. Nigeria and Biafra are at war, in the year 2172. Onyii, a fierce Biafran warrior finds his relationship strained with his beloved adopted sister, Ify who must return to Nigerian and join the fight against the Biafrans. Fiction

Oono, Kousuke. *The Way of the Househusband. Vol. 1-4.* VIZ Media, 2019. ISBN: 9781974709403, ISBN: 9781974710447, ISBN: 9781974713462, ISBN: 9781974717675. A slapstick-comedy. Tatsu, "the Immortal Dragon," lives a normal life as a househusband. GN -Fiction

Osajyefo, Kwanza. *Black AF: America's Sweetheart.* Illus. by Jennifer Johnson, 2017. BlackMask Studio, ISBN: 9781628751918. Eli is black and has superpowers that her adoptive (and white) parents have kept a secret. This superhero story explores social themes. GN -Fiction

Oseman, Alice. *Heartstopper* Vol. 1-2. Graphix / Scholastic, 2020. ISBN: 9781338617436. ISBN: 9781338617474. Charlie and affable rugby player Nick form fall in love in this British romance. GN -Fiction

Ostertag, Molly Knox. *Midwinter Witch.* Art by the author. Scholastic Graphix, 2019. ISBN: 978-1338540550. *The Hidden Witch.* Illus. by the author, 2018. Graphix, ISBN: 9781338253757. An orphaned witch, Ariel, is in training but feels like an outsider and becomes entangled in dark magic when a new girl comes to the school. GN -Fiction

Ottaviani, Jim. *Astronauts: Women on the Final Frontier.* Art by Maris Wicks. First Second / Macmillan, 2020. ISBN: 9781626728776. Narrated by Astronaut Mary Cleave. History of female astronauts from the first woman in space (Valentina Tereshkova to NASA Astronaut Groups 8 and 9. GN -Nonfiction

Ottaviani, Jim. *Hawking.* Art by Leland Myrick. First Second, 2019. ISBN: 9781620103838. Tells the story of Stephen Hawking's life, focusing on his career in science. GN -Nonfiction

Owen, Margaret. *The Merciful Crow*. Holt, 2019. ISBN: 9781250191922. A quest tale involving a prince and Hawk warrior, ferocious magic, and a plot to kill the king. An action filled fantasy of adventure. Fiction

Ozaki, Kaori. *The Golden Sheep*. Vol.1-3. Vertical Comics / Kodansha USA, 2019. ISBN: 9781947194809. ISBN: 9781947194885, 2020. ISBN: 9781949980127. Tsugi Miikura, a teenage guitarist, returns to her hometown, and finds her childhood friends have strangely not changed. GN -Fiction

Pacat, C.S. *Fence, vol. 4: Rivals*. Art by Johanna the Mad. BOOM! Box / BOOM! Studios, 2020. ISBN: 9781684155385. Nicholas and Seiji are squabbling and must get it together for the King's Row fencing team to defeat a challenging rival. GN -Fiction

Page, Nathan. *The Montague Twins: The Witch's Hand*. Art by Drew Shannon. Knopf Books for Young Readers / Penguin Random House, 2020. ISBN: 9780525646761. In order to solve their current mystery Pete and Al are going to let their adopted family in on their secrets. GN -Fiction

Pak, Greg. *Mech Cadet Yu, Volume 1*, 2018. ISBN: 9781684151950; *Vol. 2*, 2018. ISBN: 9781684152537; *Vol.3*, 2019. ISBN: 9781684153374; Illustrated by Takeshi. Boom! Studios. Stanford Yu, when given the opportunity of a lifetime he must learn to trust his team and meet the challenge to keep the planet safe and fight the second Sharg war against alien invaders. GN -Fiction

Pak, Greg. *Ronin Island, Volume 1*. Art by Giannis Milonogiannis. Boom! Studios, 2019. ISBN: 978-1684154593. *Ronin Island, Vol. 2,* 2020. ISBN: 9781684155576. Set in Feudal time, on an Island in the China Sea, Hana (a Korean orphan) and Kenichi-chief rivals, are both graduating from warrior training and must learn to work together. Adventures do not disappoint. GN -Fiction

Panetta, Kevin. *Bloom*. Art by Savanna Ganucheau. First Second, 2019. ISBN: 978-1626726413. When an accident occurs in his family's bakery, Ari has to rethink his life – his band with four friends, and other happenings in his high school. GN -Fiction

Park, Linda Sue. *Prairie Lotus*. Houghton Mifflin Harcourt, 2020. ISBN: 9781328781505. The era is the 1880's. Hanna's mother was Chinese American, and after her death Hanna's white father moves the family to the Dakota Territory to start over. But the community is not too welcoming to the biracial teen, and Hanna struggles to find her own way amidst the new community. Fiction

Pascat, C.S. *Fence, Volume 1*. Illus. by Johanna the Mad, 2018. Boom! Box, ISBN: 9781684151929. Nicholas starts a rivalry with the unbeatable Seiji Katamaya and strives to earn a place as a fencer to live up to his family's reputation. GN -Fiction

Pascat, C.S. *Fence*. Art by Johanna the Mad.*Vol. 2-3*. Boom! Box, 2019. ISBN: 978-1684152971, ISBN: 978-1684153343. Seiji and Nicholas continue to vie for a spot on the King's Row school team. GN -Fiction

Patterson, James, and Alexander, Kwame. *Becoming Muhammad Ali*. Illustrated by Dawud Anyabwile. Jimmy Paterson, 2020. ISBN: 9780316498166. Told in the alternating verse and prose voices of Cassius Clay and his friend Lucky readers learn of the struggles and determination of a child growing up in the Jim Crow era, who has his eyes set on becoming a boxing champion. Fiction

Perkins, Mitali. *Forward Me Back to You*. Farrar, Straus Giroux, 2019. ISBN: 9780374304928. For lack of support after a violent sexual episode at her high school, Kat flees to a new place and new friends. Eventually she goes to India to work with trafficked girls and finds that in helping others she is able to help herself. A 2020 Rise: A Feminist Book Project Top 10. Fiction

Petrus, Junauda. *The Stars and the Blackness Between Them*. Dutton, 2019. ISBN: 9780525555483. When Audre's relationship with a woman is revealed, her mother sends her out of Trinidad. Audre goes to Minneapolis with her father – but there she meets up with Mabel who has a serious illness. Alternating viewpoints of love. A 2020 Coretta Scott King Author Honor Book. Fiction

Philippe, Ben. *The Field Guide to the North American Teenager*. HarperCollins/Balzer+Bray, 2019. ISBN: 9780062824110. Norris Kaplan follows his university professor mother from Montreal to Austin, Texas, and her new job. Adjusting to high school in Texas is no small feat. The 2020 William C. Morris Award winner. Fiction

Pilkey, Dav. *Dogman: Crime and Punishment*. Graphix, 2020. The ninth book in this graphic novel series about Dogman and his nemesis Petey (a cat). Continues the outrageous adventures of the duel. GN - Fiction

Pimienta, Jose. *Suncatcher* by Jose Pimienta. Random House Graphic / Penguin Random House, 2020. ISBN: 9780593124819. An erie tale Beatriz's dead grandfather's soul can only be released from his old guitar, if she plays the perfect song. Can she do that without destroying herself? GN -Fiction

Pool, Katy Rose. *There Will Come a Darkness*. Holt, 2019. ISBN: 9781250211750. A 100-year-old prophecy unfolds as the actions of a gambler, a disguised prince, an assassin, and a warrior cross paths with one another. A 2020 Morris Award finalist. Fiction

Prince, Liz. *Coady & the Creepies*. Illus. by Amanda Kirk, 2018. BOOM! Box, ISBN: 9781684150298. Coady and her sisters are not going to let a tragic accident keep them from being the first punk band ever to complete Pinmaggedon. GN -Fiction

Quintero, Isabel. *Photographic: The Life of Graciela Iturbide*. Illus. by Zeke Peña. 2018. Getty, $19.95 ISBN: 9781947440005. Mexican photographer Graciela Iturbide, her mentors and iconic photos. GN -Nonfiction

Recchioni, Roberto. *Orphans, Volume 1: The Beginning*. Illus. by Emiliano Mammucari, 2018. Lion Forge, ISBN: 9781942367178; Orphans, Volume 2: Lies, 2018. Lion Forge, ISBN: 9781942367529. An energy beam kills many of the earth's population--children are orphaned and drafted into an elite army charged with invading an alien planet. What are they fighting, and why? GN - Fiction

Reed, Christina Hammonds. *The Black Kids*. Simon & Schuster Books for Young Readers, 2020. ISBN: 978-1534462724. In the aftermath of the Los Angeles riots, April changes from just another teen to "one of the black kids" who finds their life and perspective of all that is part of their life changing.

Reedy, Trent. *Hunter's Choice*. Norton Young Readers, 2021. ISBN: 9781324011378. Twelve-year-old Hunter has looked forward to his very first hunting trip. He's taken classes and earned his hunting license. Now the weekend of his first hunt has come. In the end he is faced directly with the knowledge that he holds the power of life or death. His decision brings him to realizing what his relationship is to nature and wildlife. Fiction

Revoy, Antoine. *Animus*. By Antoine Revoy. Illustrated. First Second, 2018. ISBN: 9781626721838. Set in Kyoto, Japan, when an impossible tragedy befalls friends. Hisao and Sayuri set out on a quest to solve a fantastical mystery. GN -Fiction

Reynolds, Jason, and Kendi, Ibram X. *Stamped: Racism, Anti-Racism, and You: A Remix of the National Book Award-Winning Stamped from the Beginning*. Little Brown Books for Young Readers, 2020. ISBN: 9780316453691 Reynolds rewrite of Ibram X. Kendi's adult work exploring the history of racism, anti-Black ideas, and a call to teens to do what is right. Information/Nonfiction

Reynolds, Jason. *Long Way Down:The Graphic Novel*. Art by Danica Novgorodoff. Atheneum Books, 2020. ISBN: 9781534444959. Seven ghosts reveal truths about fifteen-year-old Will's murdered brother and changes the path of Will's revenge. GN -Fiction

Reynolds, Justin A. *Miles Morales Shock Waves (original Spider-Man Graphic Novel)*. Illustrated by Pablo Leon. Scholastic/Graphiz, 2021. ISBN: 9781338648034. Miles Morales juggles his middle school activities and his work in Brooklyn as Spider-Man. A disaster causes him to turn his attention helping his mother's homeland, Puerto Rico. But then strange things occur: the disappearance of a new student's father, connections between the disappearance and his fundraising efforts - now Miles is faced with a mystery that he feels compelled to solve. GN -Fiction

Rhodes, Jewell Parker. *Black Brother, Black Brother*. Little, Brown Books for Young Readers, 2020. ISBN: 9780316493819. Their private middle school deals in racism – and the darker-skinned brother feels it more strongly than his lighter-skinned brother. Some relief comes from the local Boys and Girls Club as they face off racist bullies. Fiction

Ribay, Randy. *Patron Saints of Nothing*. Penguin/Kokila, 2019. ISBN: 9780525554912. Jay, a high school senior, travels to the Philippines to try to uncover the truth behind his cousin's death. Fiction

Ries, Ariel Slamet. *Witchy*. Art by the author. Lion Forge, 2019. ISBN: 9781549304811. In In Hyalin, long hair equates to powerful magic but Nyneve's father is killed because his hair is too long. Nyneve is conscripted into the Witch Guard and trains with other young witches. GN -Fiction

Rocco, John. *How We Got to the Moon: The People, Technology, and Daring Feats of Science Behind Humanity's Greatest Adventure.* Crown Books for Young Readers, 2020. ISBN: 9780525647416. Years of work and organization to get to the moon. Information/Nonfiction

Rogerson, Margaret. *Sorcery of Thorns*. Simon & Schuster/Margaret K. McElderry, 2019. ISBN: 9781481497619. A foundling raised in one of the great libraries, Elisabeth, seeks to protect the world and gets caught up in magical sabotage. Fiction

Rothenberg, Jess. *The Kingdom*. Holt, 2019. ISBN: 9781250293855. A fantasist is a human-android hybrid engineered to serve guests of a high-tech theme park. But then Ana and her six fantasist sisters do not act as intended. Suicide and homicidal behavior. What is to become of the kingdom. Fiction

Rowell, Rainbow. *Pumpkinheads*. Art by Faith Erin Hicks. First Second, 2019. ISBN: 978-1626721623. On their final night of work at DeKnock's Pumpkin Patch, the workers (high schoolers) decide to make the final shift an adventurous one. GN -Fiction

Rowell, Rainbow. *Runaways: Find Your Way Home,* ISBN: 9781302908522; Runaways: Best Friends Forever, ISBN: 9781302911973: *Runaways: Vol. 3, That Was Yesterday*, ISBN: 978-1302914134. *Runaways: But You Can't Hide*, ISBN: 978-1302918019.
Runaways: Canon Fodder, ISBN: 9781302920289. Art by Andres Genolet, Kris Anka & David Lafuente. Marvel Comics, 2018- 2020. Years ago, a group of kids discovered that their parents were supervillains. In order to survive, the teens became a superhero team-and a family. Their adventures continue through five tales. GN -Fiction

Ruby, Laura. *Thirteen Doorways, Wolves Behind Them All.* HarperCollins/Balzer+Bray, 2019. ISBN: 9780062317643. A tale of heartbreak and tragedy, and hope after Frankie and her younger sister are left in a Chicago orphanage, during the Depression and into WWII. The secrets that are revealed by a ghost, make for an interesting historical perspective. A 2020 Rise: A Feminist Book Project Top 10. Fiction

Ruillier, Jerome. The Strange. Illustrated. Drawn & Quarterly, 2018. ISBN: 9781770463172. An immigration story featuring a "strange," character -he looks different, and speaks a different language. He needs a forged ID and smuggled into a new home. Once there he must find a way to survive so that his family can come to him. GN -Fiction

Rusch, Elizabeth. *You Call This Democracy? How to Fix Our Democracy and Deliver Power to the People.* Houghton Mifflin Harcourt Books for Young Readers, 2020. ISBN: 9780358387428. A nonpartisan look at gerrymandering, electoral college, and voter suppression and unequal representation. Information/Nonfiction

Russell, Mark. *Wonder Twins: Activate! Vol. 1;* and *Wonder Twins: The Rise and Fall of the Wonder Twins,* Vol. 2. Art by Stephen Byrne. Wonder Comics / DC Comics, 2019. ISBN: 9781401294649. ISBN: 9781779501790. Alien twins Zan and Jayna balance their high school lives in Metropolis and their future in solving problems in their town. GN -Fiction

Russo, Meredith. *Birthday*. Flatiron, 2019. ISBN: 9781250129833. Eric denies the truth – he wants to be a girl. Morgan is questioning his own truth – is he gay, what if Eric was a girl. From age 14 to 18 the two boys navigate through their tangled lives. Fiction

Ryan, Pam Muñoz. *Mañanaland*. Scholastic Press, 2020. ISBN: 9781338157864. Max's family are secret guardians who rescue refugees and guide them to "Mananaland." Max loves futbol, but his real goal is to join his dad's team and become part of the secret guardians. Fiction

Sabic-El-Rayess, Amra. *The Cat I Never Named: A True Story of Love, War, and Survival*. Boomsbury YA, 2020. ISBN: 9781547604531. Amra's life turns to disaster in 1992 when her homeland, Bosnia, is invaded by Servian troops. A Muslim teens' story through the Bosnian genocide and a stray cat that protected the family. Information/Nonfiction

Sakisaka, Io. *Ao Haru Ride*. Illus. by the author, 2018.V.1. VIZ Media LLC, ISBN: 9781974702657; V. 2. VIZ Media LLC, ISBN: 9781974702664. In her last year in middle school, Futaba Yoshioka finally finds a boyfriend, Kou Tanaka, who is not immature or annoying. But, then Kou disappears and only resurfaces in high school. Will their relationship be rekindled?
Vol.3-5. VIZ Media, 2019. ISBN: 978-1974702671, ISBN: 978-1974702688, ISBN: 978-1974702695. Futaba Yoshioka is torn between her friendship with Yuri, and the crush each of them have on Kou. GN -Fiction

Sakisaka, Io. *Love Me, Love Me Not Vol. 1-5*. VIZ Media, 2020. ISBN: 9781974713097. ISBN: 9781974713103, ISBN: 9781974713110, ISBN: 9781974713127, ISBN: 9781974713134. Akari and Yuna become best friends during high school, but their friendship is challenged when they discover their differences. GN -Fiction

Salazar, Aida. *Land of the Cranes*. Illustrated by Quang & Lien. Scholastic Press, 2020. ISBN: 9781338343809. Betita must survive in a cruel and inhuman deportation camp with her pregnant mother without her papi who has already been deported. She must rely on her Aztec heritage to give her hope. Fiction

Sanchez, Alex. *You Brought Me the Ocean* art by Julie Maroh. DC Comics, 2020. ISBN: 9781401290818. Jake Hyde has many secrets so when Jake finds himself attracted to the swim team captain, his world quickly turns upside down. GN -Fiction

Sandler, Martin W. *1919: The Year that Changed America*. Bloomsbury, 2019. ISBN: 9781681198019. From the Great Molasses flood, to prohibition, women's suffrage, the red scare, labor strikes and the red summer – which occurred when Black WWI soldiers returned home to a wave of discrimination. A pivotal yar that shows how far we've come – and how far we have yet to go. Information/Nonfiction

Sandler, Martin W. *Race Through the Skies: The Week the World Learned to Fly*. Bloomsbury Children's Books, 2020. ISBN: 9781547603442. The 1909 international air meet in Rheims, France. Great photographs and details about a spectacular event. Information/Nonfiction

Schneemann, Karen, and Williams, Lily. *Go with the Flow*. Illustrated by Lily Williams. First Second, 2020. ISBN: 9781250143174. A group of high school friends establish a much needed 'period manifesto'. Fiction

Schneemann, Karen. *Go with the Flow*. Art by Lily Williams. First Second / Macmillan, 2020. ISBN: 9781250305725. Abby, Brit, Christine, and Sasha decide to start a "menstruation revolution" to change maintenance of product vending machines in the school. Social media is utilized to impact change. GN -Fiction

Schrefer, Eliot. *The Darkness Outside of US*. Katherine Tegen Books, 2021. ISBN: 978-0062888280. Two guys – sworn enemies have embarked on a rescue mission. Alone in space Ambrose and Kodiak must put their feelings aside—it's Ambrose's sister whose life is stake; or must they — love might be their only chance at survival. Fiction

Searle, Sarah Winifred. *Sincerely, Harriet*. Art by the author. Graphic Universe, 2019. ISBN: 978-1541545298. Harriet Flores is a young girl dealing with an invisible disability. Over the course of a summer, she becomes friends with her neighbor Pearl and finds solace in reading and writing. GN -Fiction

Sebala, Christopher. *Crowded, Volume 1*. Art by Ro Stein, Ted Brandt, Triona Farrell, Cardinal Rae. Image Comics, 2019. ISBN: 978-1534310544. Anyone can turn resentment into a crowdsourced opportunity for revenge and Charlie Ellison is the latest target for assassination. GN -Fiction

Sepetys, Ruta. *The Fountains of Silence*. Philomel, 2019. ISBN: 9780399160318. A romantic relationship develops during the Spanish Civil war between Daniel, an 18-year-old American, and Ana, who has suffered, along with her family under the Franco regime. Fiction

Shah, London. *The Light at the Bottom of the World*. Disney/Hyperion, 2019. ISBN: 9781368036887. In this futuristic novel (end of the 21st century) humans are beneath the water. Leyla McQueen will be vying to win a 100-contestant obstacle course. The prize – her father's freedom from jail. She must win. Fiction

Shimura, Takako. *Sweet Blue Flowers*. Illustrated. V.1, ISBN: 9781421592985; V.2, ISBN: 9781421592992; V.3, ISBN: 9781421593005; V. 4, ISBN: 9781421593012. Viz Media, 2017-18. Akira and Fumi rekindle their BFF status in high school but Fumi starts to fall for the most popular girl at school. GN -Fiction

Shinkai, Makoto. *Your Name*. Illus. by Ranmaru Katone. Yen Press ; V.2, 2017) ISBN: 9780316412889; V.3, 2018) ISBN: 9780316521178. Two teens, Mitsuha and Taki, swap bodies in their sleep. They could not imagine the dark threads that bind them. GN -Fiction

Shippen, Lauren. *The Infinite Noise*. Tor Teen, 2019. ISBN: 9781250297518. Caleb is hopeful that therapy will help him control his mood swings, but instead he finds that he has a superpower and a connection to Adam, who just might be able to help him with that power. Fiction

Shirahama, Kamome. *Witch Hat Atelier, Vol. 4-6.* ISBN: 9781632368607. ISBN: 9781632369291. ISBN: 9781646510108. Kodansha Comics, 2019-2020. The apprentices Olfrey and Coco are involved in their level 2, witches exam when they are interrupted by enemies, and must seek safety. GN -Fiction

Shirahama, Kamome. *Witch Hat Atelier.* Art by the author, 2019. *Vol. 1.* ISBN: 978-1632367709. *Vol. 2.* ISBN: 978-1632368041; *Vol. 3.* ISBN: 978-1632368058. Coco dreams of being a magician but accidentally performs a spell that traps her mother in stone. To rescue her mother, Coco must become an apprentice to Qifrey and travel to a land far from home.
Witch Hat Atelier, Vol. 4-6. ISBN: 9781632368607. ISBN: 9781632369291. ISBN: 9781646510108. Kodansha Comics, 2020. The apprentices Olfrey and Coco are involved in their level 2 witches' exam when they are interrupted by enemies and must seek safety. GN -Fiction

Shirai, Kaiu. *The Promised Neverland.* Illustrated by Posuka Demizu. Viz Media, 2018. V.2. ISBN: 9781421597133; V.3. ISBN: 9781421597140; V.4. ISBN: 9781421597157; V.5. ISBN: 9781421597164; V.6. ISBN: 9781974701476. Orphans Emma, Norman, and Ray learn a terrible secret about the fate of the children raised in their orphanage and work hard to construct a plan to escape before it's too late. GN -Fiction

Sibson, Laura. *The Art of Breaking Things.* Viking, 2019. ISBN: 9780451481115. Drugs and alcohol help Skye to cope with the secret about her mother's fiancé – but all others see is her as a party girl. All Skye sees is the danger to her little sister. Fiction

Slade, Suzanne. *Exquisite: The Poetry and Life of Gwendolyn Brooks.* Illustrated by Cozbi A. Cabrera. Abrams, 2020. ISBN: 9781419734113. The biography of a Pulitzer-winning poet. Sibert Honor Book. Information/Nonfiction

Small, Davis. *Home After Dark.* Illus. by the author, 2018. Liveright Publishing, ISBN: 9780871403155. Russell's mom leaves and later his alcoholic dad disappears, too. Russell is left to fend for himself until the Mah family takes him in. GN -Fiction

Smith, Cynthia Leitich. *Sisters of the Neversea.* Heartdrum, 2021. ISBN: 9780062869975. Stepsisters, Lily (who is Native American), and Wendy, are best friends but their parents are feuding and plan to spend the summer apart. What is to become of them? What the sisters don't know is that the boy next door – the boy who calls himself Peter Pan, has plans – to take them to a place with wild animals, Merfolk, fairies, and kidnapped children – and pirates, and a giant crocodile. Fiction. (Note: This is a first book in the Native American imprint: Heartdrum. The author is an enrolled Muscogee Creek Native American)

Smith, James Otis. *Black Heroes of the Wild West.* Toon Books. 2020. ISBN: 9786976535210. Biographical chapters featuring Stagecoach Mary, Bass Reeves, Bob Lemmons and others. GN -Nonfiction

Smith, Kiersten. *Misfit City, Volume 2*. Illus. by Naomi Franquiz. BOOM! Box, 2018. ISBN: 9781684151721. The group continues on their hunt for Black Mary's treasure. Wilder's mom is possessed by the ghost of Black Mary; the group must solve clues to unlock the mystery. GN -Fiction

Smith, Niki. *The Deep & Dark Blue*. Brown Books for Young Readers / Little, Brown and Company, 2020. ISBN: 9780316486019. After a coup Hawke and Grayson attempt to save their kingdom. GN -Fiction

Solomon, Rachel Lynn. *Today Tonight Tomorrow*. Simon and Schuster, 2021. ISBN: 9781534440241. Rowan Roth and Neil McNair have been bitter rivals for all of high school. But Rowan does have a plan to beat her infuriating nemesis one last time.

Sook, Kim Hyun, and Estrada, Ryan. *Banned Book* Club. Iron Circus Comics, 2020. ISBN: 9781945820427. Books banned by their South Korean government, in the early 1980s, is the subject of the book club this group of teens form to discuss the forbidden – and they reveal much about their government. College years in 1983; civil protests. GN -Nonfiction

Soontornvat, Christina. *All Thirteen: The Incredible Cave Rescue of the Thai Boys' Soccer Team*. Candlewick Press, 2020. ISBN: 9781536209457. Miracles do happen. In 2018, twelve soccer players and their coach are trapped in a cave underwater. This is the story of their incredible rescue by hundreds of volunteers. Information/Nonfiction

Soontorvat, Christina. *A Wish in the Dark*. Candlewick, 2020. ISBN: 9781536204940. Life for those who are rich is much better than those who are not. Two lives interact: Pong, born in a prison – but escapes, and Nok, the disgraced warden's daughter who wishes to recapture Pong and restore her status. Newbery Honor Book. Fiction

Spears, Rick. *My Riot*, Art by Helen Emmett. Oni Press, 2020. ISBN: 9781620107768. Val's bored angst ends when she meets Kat, and they form a punk band. Set in 1991. GN -Fiction

Spillet, Tasha. *Surviving the City*. Art by Natasha Donovan. HighWater Press, 2019. ISBN: 978-1553797562. Miikwan and Dez are best friends-both with family issues. Miikwan is Anishinaabe; Dez is Inninew. When Dez disappears most think she is another of the Indigenous women that are murdered in their community. GN -Fiction

Steele, Hamish. *DeadEndia: The Watcher's Test*. Illustrated. Nobrow, 2018. ISBN: 9781910620472. Barney, the janitor at Dead End, discovers that the haunted house is not just a theme park attraction-it is also a portal to hell. GN -Fiction

Steinkeller, Emma. *The Okay Witch*. Illustrated. Aladdin, 2019. ISBN: 978-1534431461. Thirteen-year-old Moth Hush loves all things witchy and her own magical powers, but is to come of her charm (and her spells)? GN -Fiction

Stilton, Geronimo. *The Sewer Rat Stink (Geronimo Stilton Scholastic Graphic Novel Series #1)*. Illustrated by Tom Angleberger. Scholastic Paperback, 2020. Geronimo and Hercule – Geronimo's best friend, a private detective pair up to investigate the sewer world of Mouse Island in an effort to save the city from rat stink. A mentor novel for teen learners to create (write and draw) their own books. GN-fiction.

Stone, Nic. *Shuri: A Black Panther Novel (Marvel)*. Marvel Action/Scholastic, 2020. ISBN: 978-1338585476. The first of an original middle-grade series starring Shuri, T'Challa's youngest sister. The book showcases Shuri's lab and her inventions. Author of an earlier work, *Dear Martin* – a don't miss title about social injustice - for grades 9-12.

Sugiura, Misa.. *This Time Will Be Different*. HarperTeen, 2019. ISBN: 9780062473448. C.J. makes it her mission to protect her grandfather's flower shop from scammers who want to take advantage; and seeks to protect Emily, her best friend from the girl who outed her maliciously. Fiction

Sumino, Yoru. *I Want to Eat Your Pancreas*. Art by Idumi Kirihara. Seven Seas Entertainment, 2019. ISBN: 978-1642750324. When Yamauchi Sakura's friend finds out she was dying the fright is unavoidable. GN -Fiction

Tagame, Gengoroh. *My Brother's Husband, Volume 2*. Illustrated. Pantheon Books, 2018. ISBN: 9781101871539. Yaichi has been struggling to accept his brother's husband, Mike. But when Mike visits Japan, Yaichi and his daughter realize just how important he is to their family. GN -Fiction

Takai, Tsuyoshi. *Black Torch*. Illustrated. Viz Media, 2018. V.1. ISBN: 9781974700462.V.2. ISBN: 9781974701520. Jiro Azuma is a teen ninja who can talk to animals. One day, he rescues an injured cat, and embroils himself in a whole new world of the supernatural, attracting the attention of a top-secret anti-mononoke espionage unit called Black Torch. GN -Fiction

Takano, Ichigo. *Become You, Volume 1*. Seven Seas Entertainment, 2019. ISBN: 978-1642756852. Taiyou is the only remaining member of the music club. Taiyou must find a way to put his trauma of his past aside and achieve his musical dreams. GN -Fiction

Takei, George, Eisinger, Justin, and Scott, Steven. *They Called Us Enemy*. Art by Harmony Becker. Top Shelf Productions, 2019. ISBN: 978-1603094504. Before he was Sulu on the starship Enterprise George Takei was a little boy struggling to understand why his family was packing up and going to live in a horse stable. GN -Nonfiction

Tamaki, Mariko. *Harley Quinn: Breaking Glass*. Art by Steve Pugh. DC Comics, 2019. ISBN: 978-1401283292. While her mother works on a cruise ship Harleen Quinzel goes to Gotham City and lives with the city's best drag queen. Harley makes a new best friend in Ivy at Gotham High. GN -Fiction

Tamaki, Mariko. *Laura Dean Keeps Breaking Up with Me*. Art by Rosemary Valero-O'Connell. First Second, 2019. ISBN: 978-1626722590. Laura Dean cheats but Freddy keeps coming back despite that. After visiting a medium, Freddy seriously questions the relationship. GN -Fiction

Tamaki, Mariko. *SuperGirl Being Super*. Illus. by Joelle Jones, 2018. DC Comics, ISBN: 978-1401268947. A new origin story for Supergirl and new characters, Kara's friends Dolly and Jen enter the universe. GN -Fiction

Tamaki, Mariko. *X-23*. Art by Juann Cabal, Marcio Fiorito, Georges Duarte, Diego Oloregui, 2019. *Vol. 1, Family Album*. Marvel Comics. ISBN: 978-1302913083; *Vol. 2, X - Assassin*. Marvel Comics. ISBN: 978-1302916862. Among the clones, a kidnapping, and efforts to rescue the original X-23 clone, Laura Kinney, bring a fierce rivalry to the other clones. GN -Fiction

Telgemeier, Raina. *Guts*. Art by the author. Scholastic. 2019. ISBN: 978-0545852517. The autobiographical story of the author's struggles in fourth-grade, with anxiety and the resulting stomachaches and how she learns to cope. GN -Nonfiction

Templer, Hannah. *Cosmoknights: Book One*. Top Shelf Productions, an imprint of IDW Publishing, 2019. ISBN: 978-1603094542. Pan lives on planet Verdian and when she and her friend, Tara are presented a chance to rid Verdian of the archaic medieval-type jousting tradition they make plans. GN -Fiction

Terceiro, Rey. *Meg, Jo, Beth, and Amy: Little Women*. Art by Bre Indigo. Little, Brown Books for Young Readers, 2019. ISBN: 978-0316522885. Meg, Jo, Beth, and Amy is a modern retelling of Louisa May Alcott's 1868 novel Little Women. GN -Fiction

Thermes, Jennifer, 2019. *Manhattan: Mapping the Story of an Island*. Harry N. Abrams. ISBN: 9781419736551. The 400 year history of the island and its transformation created by humans, history, and natural events. A history that includes immigrants, the slave trade, and all who built New York City. Information/Nonfiction

Thomas, Angie, 2019. *On the Come Up*. HarperCollins/Balzer+Bray. ISBN: 9780062498564. After her mother loses her job, Bri seeks to make a name for herself as a rapper and make something on her own – away from the reputation of her famous but dead father. The second book in the two-book series that began with *The Hate U Give* (HarperCollins/Balzer+Bray, 2017. Fiction

Thomas, Angie, 2021. *Concrete Rose*. HarperCollins/Balzer+Bray. ISBN: 9780062846716. Set seventeen years before *The Hate U Give*, this is the story of seventeen-year-old Maverick Carter and his not-so-perfect life. He finds out he is a father and has to figure out his life outside of drug dealing and the gangs. Fiction

Thompson, Kelly. *Sabrina the Teenage Witch*. Art by Veronica Fish. Archie Comics, 2019. ISBN: 978-1682558058. In this reboot of Sabrina, the Teenage Witch, Sabrina Spellman has just moved to Greendale with her aunts Hilda and Zelda and their sassy talking cat (and former wizard), Salem. GN -Fiction

Thompson, Kelly. *Nancy Drew: The Palace of Wisdom*. Art by Jenn St. Onge. Dynamite Entertainment, 2019. $14.99. ISBN: 978-1524108496. Nancy is a 17-year-old super sleuth. A mysterious letter bringing up her mother's death takes her home to investigate. GN -Fiction

Thompson, Kelly. *West Coast Avengers*. Art by Daniele Di Nicuolo, Gang Yuk Lim, Moy R, Stefano Caselli, Triona Farrell, 2019. *Vol. 1, Best Coast*. Marvel Comics. ISBN: 978-1302913458. *Vol. 2, City of Evils*. Marvel Comics. ISBN: 978-1302913465. When the West Coast Avengers, relocate to LA, a dearth of superheroes are there. But strange occurrences make them question if others are plotting to take down the WCAs? GN -Fiction

Thummler, Brenna. *Sheets.* By Brenna Thummler. Illus. by the author, 2018. Lion Forge, ISBN: 9781941302675. Marj Glatt, a teen, who is running her family's laundromat is overwhelmed with taking care of the business, caring for her younger brother, going to school, and dealing with the meddlesome Mr. Saubertuck, who wants to take over the laundromat. GN -Fiction

Tynion, James, IV. *The Backstagers, Volume 2: The Show Must Go On.* Illus. by Rian Sygh, 2018. Boom! Box. ISBN: 9781684150571. Behind the scenes of their high school's theater department, a group of teen boys run stage crew. When the creator of the Magical stage reappears, havoc ensues. GN -Fiction

Ukazu, Ngozi. *Check Please! Book One, #Hockey.* Illus. by the author, 2018. First Second, ISBN: 9781250177957. Eric is at the university on scholarship and joins the ice hockey team but it's difficult to be part of the in group when you are a queer athlete who bakes. GN -Fiction

Usdin, Carly. *Heavy Vinyl.* Illus. by Nina Vakueva and Irene Flores, 2018. Boom! Box, ISBN: 9781684151417. Set in 1998, Chris's favorite band's lead singer, Rosie Riot, goes missing, the shop manager of the record shop where she works lets Chris in on their secret and they join forces to find the singer. GN -Fiction

Usdin, Carly. *The Avant-Guards, vol. 2.* Art by Noah Hayes. BOOM! Box / BOOM! Studios, 2020. ISBN: 9781684155682. A second volume, the Avant-Guards adventures, the team's winning streak ends, and new relationships develop. GN -Fiction

Usdin, Carly. *The Avant-Guards, Volume 1.* Art by Noah Hayes. Boom! Studios, 2019. ISBN: 978-1684153671. Charlie is done with basketball. But Liv has other ideas and wants to start a women's basketball league, at their college. And she wants Charlie to play. GN -Fiction

Vaughan, Brian K. *Paper Girls, Volume 4.* Illus. by Cliff Chiang and Matt Wilson, 2018); *Vol. 5.* (2018. ISBN: 978-1534308671. *Vol. 6.* (2019. ISBN: 978-1534313248. Image Comics, ISBN: 9781534305106. The Paper Girls travel through time. When Tiff arrives in the year 2000 she meets her future self. When the paper girls reunite they find more chaos. GN -Fiction

Vaughn, Sarah. *Sleepless, Volume 1* (2018), ISBN: 9781534306844; *Volume 2* (2019), ISBN: 9781534306844. Illus. by Leila del Duca. Image Comics. Lady Poppy's life is in danger as her uncle is crowned king of Harbeny, Poppy's only protector is Cyrenic. Poppy resolves to find a way to expose her attackers and finally to live in peace. GN -Fiction

Venable, Colleen AF. *Kiss Number 8.* Art by Ellen T. Crenshaw. First Second, 2019. ISBN: 978-1596437098. Amanda, a 16-year-old, discovers her father's secret and realizes that she may have a crush on her best friend, Cat. The event changes Amanda's life. GN -Fiction

Vieceli, Emma. *Life Is Strange, Vol 2. Waves* ,2019; *Vol. 3 Strings* (2020. Art by Claudia Leonardi. Titan Comics / Titan Books. ISBN: 9781787730885. ISBN: 9781787732070. Life gets strange as Max attempts to deal with a moral dilemma and with the relationship between Rachel and Chloe. GN -Fiction

Warga, Jasmine. *Other Words for Home.* Balzer + Bray/HarperTeen, 2019. ISBN: 978-0062747808. Twelve-year-old Jude and her pregnant mom flee Syria to come to the United States for safety, but adjusting to being an immigrant in a strange country challenges Jude to fit in. Story told in free verse. Fiction

Waid, Ward, and Osalyefo, Kwanza. *Ignited, Volume 1.* Art by Phil Briones, John Cassaday. Humanoids, 2019. ISBN: 9781534301894. After a shooter targets their high school six friends gain supernatural abilities and plan an appropriate response to the shooting. GN -Fiction

Walden, Tillie. *On a Sunbeam.* Illus. by the author, 2018. First Second, ISBN: 9781250178145. Mia becomes the newest member on a ship that travels through space reconstructing historical ruins for new use but her real purpose is finding her lost love. GN -Fiction

Walker, David F. *The Life of Frederick Douglass: A Graphic Narrative of a Slave's Journey from Bondage to Freedom.* Art by Damon Smyth, Marissa Louise. Ten Speed Press. 2019. ISBN: 978-0399581441. The story of Frederick Douglass's life from his slave days to public acclaim. GN -Nonfiction

Walker, Suzanne. *Mooncakes.* Art by Wendy Xu. Lion Forge, 2019. ISBN: 978-1549303043. Nova is a witch, completing her witchhood apprenticeship at home with her grandmothers but ends up helping her best friend (a non-binary werewolf) defeat the demon seeking him. GN -Fiction

Wallace, Sandra Neil, and Wallace, Rich. *The Teachers March! How Selma's Teachers Changed History.* Calkins Creek, 2020. ISBN: 9781629794525. Recounts the impact of the 1965 Teachers March for Black voting rights in Selma, Alabama. Information/Nonfiction

Waller, Sharon Biggs. *Girls on the Verge.* Holt, 2019. ISBN: 9781250151698. Yes, one can get pregnant in a first sexual encounter. An abortion seems to be her only option-so Camille, Annabelle, and her best friend, Bea set off to fix the problem. Fiction

Walz, Jason. *Last Pick.* (2018) *Last Pick: Born to Run* (2019). ISBN: 9781626728912; ISBN: 978-1626728936. First Second. Twins Sam and Wyatt try to survive on Earth and find their abducted parents; and when Sam goes missing; Wyatt find the resistance even more dangerous. GN -Fiction

Wang, Jen. *Stargazing.* Illustrated. First Second, 2019. ISBN: 978-1250183880. Christine Hong is a normal middle school girl-good grades, music lessons, helpful and polite in her family's Chinese American community. Moon Li, the new girl is quite the opposite, but their friendship blossoms and they find many connections. GN -Fiction

Wang, Jen. *The Prince and the Dressmaker*. Illustrated. First Second, 2018. ISBN: 9781250159854. Belgium's Prince Sebastian's parents want him to find a bride. He wants to find a good designer to transform into his alter ego, Lady Crystallia. GN -Fiction

Warga, Jasimine. *The Shape of Thunder*. Balzer+Bray, 2021. ISBN: 9780062956675. Being able to go back in time to save their siblings may be the only way that Cora and Quinn's friendship may return. It's Cora's twelfth birthday and Cora leaves the note on her friend's porch. They need the chance to go back before Cora's sister dies in a school shooting and Quinn's brother had not yet done what he did. Is the gap impossible to mend? Fiction.

Warner, Andy. *This Land is My Land: A Graphic History of Big Dreams, Micronations, and Other Self-Made States*. Art by Sofie Louise Dam. Chronicle Books. 2019. ISBN: 978-1452170183. Five chapters-intentional communities, micronations, failed utopias, visionary environments, and strange dreams. Thirty created spaces around the world. GN -Nonfiction

Waters, Shannon, and Leyh, Kat. *Lumberjanes, Volume 7: A Bird's-Eye View*. ISBN: 9781684150458; *Lumberjanes, Volume 8: Stone Cold*. Illus. by Carey Pietsch. ISBN: 9781684151325. Boom! Box, 2017-2018. In Vol. 7, a giant bird kidnaps the Grand Lodge along with their head counselor, Rosie, and the friends must save her. In Vol. 8, when the Lumberjanes find that Barney has been turned into stone they appeal to their former nemesis, Diane. But Diane did not do it; the Lumberjanes must find out who did. GN -Fiction

Weatherford, Carole Boston, 2020. *Box: Henry Brown Mails Himself to Freedom*. Illustrated by Michele Wood. Candlewick. Fifty-one emotionally intense poems telling the story of Henry "Box" Brown. Newbery Honor Book. Information/Nonfiction

Wein, Elizabeth. A Thousand Sisters: The Heroic Airwomen of the Soviet Union in World War II. Balzer+Bray, 2019. ISBN: 9780062453013. Russian aviators during World War II, pilots, mechanics, and navigators helped change history. Information/Nonfiction

Wexler, Django. *Ship of Smoke and Steel*. Tor Teen, 2019. ISBN: 9780765397249. A street thief, Isoka, is recruited to become a government spy and steal the ghost ship, Soliton. Soon Isoka is caught up in alliances formed just to survive. Fiction

Whitley, Jeremy. *The Unstoppable Wasp, Unlimited*. Art by Gurihiru, Alti Firmansyah. *Vol. 1, Fix Everything*. ISBN: 978-1302914264; *Vol. 2, The Unstoppable!* ISBN: 978-153214366. Illustrated by Elsa Charretier. Marvel Comic, 2018-2019. Ying literally has a time bomb on her head, and the scientists from the G.I.R.L labs must find a way to disarm it. Later, A new superhero team must stop a threat from a group of scientific girl genius supervillains who start attacking local labs. GN -Fiction

Williams-Garcia, Rita. A Sitting in St. James. Quill Tree Books, 2021. ISBN: 9780062367297. "There is no story without history." A woman who leaves Haiti with her Black but rich husband, for Louisiana. Three generations of family on a sugar plantation are impacted by decisions made by this slave-owning woman, and her rejection of her granddaughter (a quadroon). Fiction from the 18th century that will lead to discussions about the past. Historical fiction.

Williams, Alicia D. *Genesis Begins Again.* Atheneum/Caitlyn Dlouhy, 2019. ISBN: 9781481465809. Her father's alcoholism and always being called out of her name – Genesis finally gets some positivity from a music teacher who encourages her talent. A 2020 Coretta Scott King/John Steptoe New Talent Award winner, a 2020 Morris Award finalist, a 2020 Newbery Honor Book, and a 2020 Notable Children's Book. Fiction

Williams, Leah. *Gwenpool Strikes Back.* Art by David Baldeon. Marvel Comics, 2020. ISBN: 9781302919238. Gwenpool wants to unmask Spider-man and get some real superpowers. GN -Fiction

Wilson, G. Willow. *Invisible Kingdom.* Vol. 1-2. Art by Christian Ward. Berger Books / Dark Horse Comics, 2019. ISBN: 9781506712277. (2020. ISBN: 9781506714943. A conspiracy of a large religious group and a large employer in a far-away galaxy, catches those in the middle. GN -Fiction

Wilson, G. Willow. *Ms. Marvel, Volume 8: Mecca.* Illus. by Marco Failla and Diego Orlortegui, 2017. Marvel, ISBN: 9781302906085; *Ms. Marvel, Volume 9: Teenage Wasteland.* Illus. by Nico Leon, 2018. Marvel, ISBN: 9781302910787. Havoc ensues when Jersey City's new mayor begins to arrest anyone with superpowers. Kamala Khan, teenage superhero, Ms. Marvel, are in danger. GN -Fiction

Winters, Julian. *How to Be Remy Cameron.* Interlude, 2019. ISBN: 9781945053801. Remy is gay and black – a brother and a friend who searches for a way to be himself, without being defined by those labels. Fiction

Wittenstein, Barry. *A Place to Land: Martin Luther King Jr. and the Speech that Inspired a Nation.* Illustrated by Jerry Pinkney. Holiday House, 2019. ISBN: 978-0823443314. An illustrated version of the celebrated speech by Martin Luther King, Jr. Information/Nonfiction

Wolk, Lauren, 2020. *Echo Mountain.* Dutton Books for Young Readers. ISBN: 9780525555568. The mountain becomes the family's home, during the Great Depression. But when Ellie's father has a tragic accident and left unconscious, it is the neighbors and nature that help them survive. Fiction

Woodson, Jacqueline. *Before the Ever After.* Nancy Paulson Books, 2020. ISBN: 9780399545436. ZJ, a 12-year-old, must deal with his father's chronic traumatic encephalopathy (CTE), as a result of his football-star sports activities. He seeks community support. A novel in verse. CTE is the term used to describe brain degeneration likely caused by repeated head traumas. Fiction

Yamaguchi, Tsubasa. *Blue Period, vol. 1.* Kodansha Comics / Kodansha USA, 2020. ISBN: 9781646511129. A popular high school student floats through life until he finds a love for art that changes where he is going. GN -Fiction

Yamazaki, Kore. *Frau Faust.* Illus. by the author. Kodansha Comics, V.1, 2017. ISBN: 9781632364807; V. 2, 2017. ISBN: 9781632364814; V. 3, 2018. ISBN:

9781632365491. Marion agrees to help a strange woman in exchange for tutoring lessons, with no idea that he is actually assisting Dr. Faust, the fairy tale character known for selling his soul to a demon. GN -Fiction

Yang, Gene Luen. *Dragon Hoops*. First Second / Macmillan. 2020. ISBN: 9781626720794. Yang's true story of the phenomenal men's varsity basketball team at Bishop O'Dowd High School in Oakland, CA, as they attempt to win it all in the California State Championship. Part memoir, part action adventure. Alternating focus on the game, and the people (coaches and so forth) that interacted with the team. GN -Nonfiction

Yang, Gene Luen. *Superman Smashes the Klan.* Art by Gurihiru. DC Comics, 2020. ISBN: 9781779504210. In 1946, An action-packed adventure. When Roberta Lee is faced with harassment in their new home, she must work with friends to help Superman take down the Klan. GN -Fiction

Yang, Kelly. *Three Keys: A Front Desk Novel*. Scholastic Press, 2020. ISBN: 9781338591385. Mia's family and several of her friends are being threatened with deportation back to China if the proposed immigration law is passed. While the threat of deportation looms over the family, they must also work to save the hotel they recently purchased. Fiction

Young, Bryan. *Healer of the Water Monster*. Heartdrum, 2021. ISBN: 9780062990402. Nathan is visiting his Nani (grandmother), for the summer, on the Navajo reservation. No electricity or cell service but his Uncle Jet who arrives with his own problems. When Nathan becomes lost in the desert he must summon his courage to save himself, his new friend, and with the help of the Navajo Holy Beings, he manages to save the Water Monster and help his Uncle Jet heal from his own demons. (Note: One of the first books in the new Heartdrum imprint). Fiction.

Young, Scottie. *Middlewest: Book One*. Art by Jorge Corona, Mike Huddleston. Image Comics, 2019. ISBN: 978-1534312173. When his father turns into the monster he truly is, Abel, accompanied by a talking fox, sets out to find a cure before his father finds him. GN -Fiction

Yupechika. *Satoko and Nada, Vol. 3*. Seven Seas Entertainment, 2020. ISBN: 9781642751000. Satoko and friends attempt to facilitate a meeting between Nada and her Abdullah. But only Nada and Satoko are involved. What will become of any relationship between Nada and her Abdullah? GN -Fiction

Zentner, Jeff. *Rayne & Delilah's Midnite Matinee*. Crown, 2019. ISBN: 9781524720209. Delia and Josie run a late-night horror show on the local cable station, showing hokey horror movies and humorous banter and goofy antics. When Lawson enters the tale, a road trip begins, and Delilah gets the chance to find her missing father. A slice of small -town wit and unpredictable characters. Compare theme and wit with those in Zentner's *The Serpent King* (2016). Fiction

Zhang, Lun Zhang and Gombeaud, Adrien. *Tiananmen 1989: Our Shattered Hopes*. Art by Améziane. IDW Publishing. 2020. ISBN: 9781684056996. First-hand account of the June 4th, 1989, massacre in Tiananmen Square. GN-Nonfiction

Chapter III – A Patchwork of Ideas

A collection of ideas, strategies, and some fun trivia associated with young adult literature that might stimulate development of specific activities that will complement the goals and objectives within your classroom's/library's specific curriculum.

To begin with here are some quotes to use as inspirational signs in your literate environment.

Literary Quotes

"When I get a little money, I buy books, and, if any is left, I buy food and clothes." ~ Erasmus

"Time spent reading, like time spent loving, increases our lifetime." ~ Daniel Pennac

"Some books are undeservedly forgotten, none are undeservedly remembered." ~ W.H. Auden

"Libraries are reservoirs of strength, grace and wit, reminders of order, calm and continuity, lakes of mental energy, neither warm nor cold, light nor dark…." ~ Germaine Greer

"Anyone who says they have only one life to live must not know how to read a book." ~ Anonymous

"I have always imagined that Paradise will be a kind of library." ~ Jorge Luis Borges

"The library is the temple of learning, and learning has liberated more people than all the wars in history." ~ Carl Rowan

"I am a part of everything I have read." ~John Kieran

"Outside of a dog, a book is a man's best friend. Inside of a dog, it's too dark to read." ~ Groucho Marx

"People say that life's the thing, but I prefer reading." ~ Logan P. Smith

"No story ever really ends, and I think I know why." ~ George MacDonald

"A house without books is like a room without windows." ~ Horace Mann

"When you sell a person a book you don't sell just twelve ounces of paper and ink and glue; you sell a whole new life" ~ Christopher Morley

Reading and Vocabulary

It's no secret that there seems to be a definite link between reading and vocabulary – both ways. Reading exposes scholars to more vocabulary, while more vocabulary helps with a higher level of comprehension. It's a two-way street – read more, and the gains are two-fold. The following is a fun exercise to play a little with vocabulary.

Create a response sheet with these words and ask readers to either check that the word is spelled correctly – or if not spell it correctly. Slides projected with class interaction makes for a fun discussion. Project all eight words and ask students to decide what the correct spelling is. Then reveal one word at a time and discuss the definition – and then reveal the sentence. The rest of the words will be scrutinized a little ore closely after the first word/spelling and definition is revealed.

Vocabulary and You — See How You Read

Check the spelling (and be ready to define)

astroid
chrysal
harras
orignal
starlite
techology
warehous
windrow

Answer key:

Astroid is not a misspelling of asteroid but an adjective meaning 'star-shaped'.
Chrysal is not a misspelling of crystal but part of an archery bow. (Also called a fret.)
Harras is not a misspelling of harass but a herd of stud horses.
Orignal is not a misspelling of original but is another term for the American moose.
Starlite is not a misspelling of starlight but a blue zircon, a type of mineral
Tecnology is not a misspelling of technology but the study of children.
Warehous is not a misspelling of warehouse but the plural of warehou, a fish from the waters of Australia and New Zealand.
Windrow is not a misspelling of window but a row of hay, raked together to dry.

Thematic Lists

Lists of related books provide readings for groups of readers who wish to discuss, the theme. In these discussions the focus is on how the book read fits into the theme. Specific examples of the author's techniques to present the main connection for the thematic focus of the list/connection. The following list provides an example of one list – the list could include many other titles connected to the theme.

A List — Thinkers and Inventors

Each of these books will provide readers with a snapshot of a person's life. Choose a book and find it in a local library – and read it. It is your assignment to find out more about the person's accomplishments and to create an interesting focus and write an article for a newspaper or periodical publication. Make sure you use the first sentences of your writing to "hook" the reader and show us (not tell) interesting information about your subject. The article could take any form you wish, e.g. TikTok, YouTube video, written newspaper article, a booklet about the person. Choose wisely and be creative.

- Becker, Helaine. *Counting on Katherine: How Katherine Johnson Saved Apollo 13*. Illustrated by Dow Phumiruk. Holt, 2018. ISBN: 9781250137524. Katherine Johnson is the subject of this book.
- Cline-Ransome, Lesa. *Counting the Stars: The Story of Katherine Johnson, NASA Mathematician*. Illustrated by Raúl Colón. S. & S./Paula Wiseman Bks, 2019. ISBN 9781534404755. Picture book biography spotlights Katherine Johnson's unquenchable curiosity, as well as her persistence in the face of discrimination against women and African Americans.
- Harrington, Janice N. *Buzzing with Questions: The Inquisitive Mind of Charles Henry Turner*. Illustrated by Theodore Taylor III. Calkins Creek. 2019. ISBN 9781629795584. Born in 1867, Charles Henry Turner's curiosity made him a very successful African American scientist and teacher. Turner's enthusiasm comes through clearly.
- Johnson, Jen Cullerton. *The Story of Environmentalist Wangari Maathai*. Illustrated by Sonia Lynn Sadler. Lee & Low. ISBN 9781643790121. Wangari Maathai is well noted for her efforts as an environment. She is an inspiration for all those who want to make a difference.
- Lord, Michelle. *Patricia's Vision: The Doctor Who Saved Sight*. Illustrated by Alleanna Haris. Sterling. ISBN 9781454931379. An inspirational profile of Dr. Patricia Bath, she worked hard and never gave up on her dream to help the blind community
- Lyons, Kelly Starling. *Dream Builder: The Story of Architect Philip Freelon*. Illustrated by Laura Freeman. Lee & Low. ISBN 9781620149553. Philip Freelon was an artist, an architect, and a dreamer. Lyons highlights his

masterwork as the architect of the Smithsonian National Museum of African American History and Culture.

Mangal, Mélina. *The Vast Wonder of the World: Biologist Ernest Everett Just*. Illustrated by Luisa Uribe. Lerner, 2018. ISBN 9781512483758. Winner of the first NAACP Spingarn Medal, Just's accomplishments are not limited to the title of a scientist. He was first a professor at Howard in the English department before becoming head of the Biology department, he wrote poetry, and he cared deeply about the experiences of his students.

Mosca, Julia Finley. *The Doctor with an Eye for Eyes: The Story of Dr. Patricia Bath*. Illustrated by Daniel Rieley. Innovation Pr. ISBN 9781943147311. A picture book details the life and accomplishments of Dr. Patricia Bath, an ophthalmologist who broke down color and gender barriers.

Mosco, Julia Finley. *The Girl with a Mind for Math: The Story of Raye Montague*. Illustrated by Daniel Rieley. Innovation Press, 2019. ISBN 9781943147427. A picture book biography on the life and work of engineer and computer analyst Raye Montague. In 1971, she used a computer program she had written to design a submarine, completing a task that had previously taken months in under one day.

Moss, Caroline. *Work It, Girl: last Off Into Space Like Mae Jemison*. Illustrated by Sinem Erkas. Quarto/Frances Lincoln. (Work It, Girl). ISBN 9780711245150. Jemison loved science from the time she was a little girl. She watched the Apollo moon landings – and she wondered why there were no women astronauts. As an adult she changed that.

Shetterly, Margot Lee, and Conkling, Winifred. *Hidden Figures: The True Story of Four Black Women and the Space Race*. Illustrated by Laura Freeman. HarperCollins/Harper, 2018. ISBN 9780062742469. This essential purchase introduces young readers to the inspirational and groundbreaking stories of Dorothy Vaughan, Mary Jackson, Katherine Johnson, and Christine Darden, and their once-hidden contributions to science, aeronautics, and space exploration.

Slade, Suzanne. *A Computer Called Katherine: How Katherine Johnson Helped Put America on the Moon*. Illustrated by Veronica Miller Jamison. Little, Brown. ISBN 9780316435178. This appealing retelling of Katherine Johnson's achievements focuses on her path as a Black female mathematician.

Book Packages

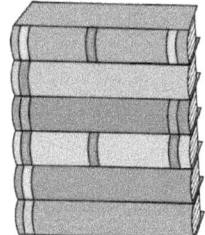 If you subscribe to the fact that readers learn more effectively when they already know something about a topic, you will want to consider "pairing" or creating book packages of books for readers to read.

Experiences or having read one book helps to build concepts in a particular area that mean something to them and to their particular background or culture. When a second book is linked to that first book the link helps the reader take in new information to complement their prior knowledge, the reader's interest and curiosity in activated and activities relating to either one of the books are infused with a sense of purpose. Some refer to this pairing (which may limit the selections to just two) or packaging as "bundling" which could conceivably include any number of titles but most often include four or five titles that relate in some way.

The packaging of related titles need not to be Nonfiction with fiction; the packaging might be several books of fiction with a similar theme, focus, or setting, for example. Other types of packages are appropriate as well: fiction-Nonfiction; fiction-fiction; Nonfiction-Nonfiction; fiction-film; Nonfiction-film; and so forth.

Longer lists are generally referred to as "thematic lists." By using one book (a familiar title perhaps) to activate a reader's prior knowledge sets the stage for enhancing comprehension, setting a purpose for reading/listening, and for providing new meaningful and challenging experiences and new reading.

The annotations/questions with the books in the book packages that follow should help you determine the "package" theme that will correlate with the curriculum or interests of specific readers. While each of these packages include a recent title, many are paired with titles that are classic titles that relate and provide a different perspective on the topic/person.

Each set of books can be expanded with addition titles related to the stated connection. For example, there are several other books that could be included in the Civil Rights package. If any of the three titles suggested are not available, a title with a similar theme might be included and used as a point of discussion.

This is an opportunity to develop collaboration between the classroom teacher and the library media specialist to develop and implement lessons regarding the library's holdings and the resources accessible to library patrons. Use the library catalog to identify and locate resources on specific topics and use the library databases to locate periodical articles that have been peer reviewed for accuracy and absence of inherent bias.

Civil Rights

Theoharis, Jeanne. The Rebellious Life of Mrs. Rosa Parks. Beacon Press, 2013.

Captivating History. African American History: A Captivating Guide to the People and Events That Shaped the History of the United States. Captivating History, 2020.

U.S. Government and the U.S. Supreme Court. Path Towards Equality: Anti-Discrimination Acts & Most Important Supreme Court Decisions Against Racism: Civil Rights Legislation…. Madison & Adams Press, 2017. (Note: only available as a Kindle edition but documents are available online at government sources).

Read, Think, Discuss

1. Complete a timeline of Park's life.
2. Select a name of a contemporary activist.
    a. Research the life of that individual
    b. Compare Rosa Parks to that individual who has was involved in a civil rights action.
    c. Cite three reasons why the two individuals are similar.
3. How does the 1866 Civil Rights Act apply to Rosa Parks. Defend Parks' position.
4. What reasons did Andrew Jackson cite for vetoing the 1866 Civil Rights Act?
5. Did the sources give conflicting information about events?
6. What events led to the passage of the Civil Rights Act of 1963
7. List the events that precipitated the passage of this act.
8. Explain how the events impacted the passage of the Civil Rights Act
9. Locate at least three credible sources (any format) that recounts the events of 2020, in regard to the protests seeking police reform and oversight – equal treatment for all. Do you think any changes have come about? Explain

What additional titles can you locate in the library that have information which could provide some additional information on this topic?

What learning did these books and the discussions bring to you?

Discrimination in America

Ebrahim, Zak. *The Terrorist's Son: A Story of Choice.* With Jeff Giles. Simon and Schuster, 2014.

Marrin, Albert. Uprooted: The Japanese American Experience During World War II. Knopf, 2016.

Lewis, John; Aydin, Andrew; and Powell, Nate. *March: Book One.* Top Shelf, 2013. (Note the existence of March: Book Two [2015] and March: Book Three [2016] are available.)

Reynolds, Jason, and Bendi, Ibram. Stamped: Racism, Antiracism, and You: A Remix of the National Book Award-winning Stamped from the Beginning. Little Brown Books for Young Readers, 2020.

Read, Think, Discuss

1. Zak's father's terrorist act impacted the life of Zak and his family. Explain the results of the act and identify three quotes from the book that verify your inference about the impact the act had on Zak and his family.
2. Many cite racism as the major reason leading to the internment of Japanese Americans during World War II. Provide evidence of this factor by finding quotes from the top U.S. political and military leaders that proves or disproves the racism factor regarding the internment.
3. In March: Book One, sit-ins are a focus. Those involved in the sit-ins had expectations for how whites would react to the action those sitting-in were taking. Did the white citizens react in that manner? What do you think the impact of the white behavior was on those who were sitting-in.
4. Stamped – An exploration of racism and antiracism in American

Note: What ideas do you glean from reading the narratives in each of these books? How do you see the treatment of individuals in the United States? How could any positive changes be made? What can you do?

Action

In 2020, the death of George Floyd caused by a Minneapolis police officer suffocating him, in a 9-minute, 29 seconds second encounter, where the officer pressed his knee against Floyd's air passage, fueled many days of protests and outrage across the country. Those protesting cited not only this murder at the hands of officers who are supposed to protect and serve, but the protest was a reaction to the many murders of many other black citizens as well: Breonna Taylor (Kentucky health care worker, shot in her own apartment during a forced entry raid at the WRONG apartment), for Ahmaud Arbery, who was jogging in a Georgia neighborhood, murdered by whites who thought he did not belong in their neighborhood, and for many others including William Till who was lynched for supposedly showing an interest in a white woman. How did the history of discrimination in the United States fuel the actions that evolved in 2020. And what lasting impact do you think the past has had on our culture today?

Family Dynamics

Holt, K. A. *Rhyme Schemer*. Chronicle Books, 2014.
Grimes, Nikki. *Words with Wings*. Woodsong, 2013.
Ng, Celiste. *Everything I Never Told You*. Penguin Random house, 2014.

Read, Think, Discuss

1. *Rhyme Schemer* focuses on Kevin's relationship with his brothers. Find three examples of how that relationship impacts Kevin's behavior at school.
    a. Identify two quotes from the book that provide insight into Kevin's relationship with his parents.
    b. What was the pivotal moment in Kevin's identity and how did Kevin's character evolve from the beginning to the end of the book?

2. Grimes uses poems to tell the story of Gabby in her book *Words with Wings*. Gabby is dealing with her parents' divorce and her move to a new school.
    a. Compare/contrast the impact of relationships on Kevin (*Rhyme Schemer*) and Gabby (*Words with Wings*).
    b. How are the stories of each of the characters like one another? Different? Cite evidence to support your inferences.
3. In *Everything I Never told You*, Lydia feels immense pressure to please her parents. How do you feel you react to the expectations your parents have for you? Or the non-expectations? Do you think it would be more challenging to be treated as a favorite child or to be ignored as her siblings were? Write a 2-3 paragraph reflection on which status you prefer and explain why that is so … favorite child or ignored child? Or something in-between.

Finding Who We Are

Oshiro, Mark. *Anger Is a Gift*. Tor Teen, 2018.
Rowell, Rainbow. *Carry On: A Novel*. St. Martin's/Griffin, 2015.
Russo, Meredith. *Birthday: A Novel*. Flatiron Books, 2019

Read, Think, Discuss

1. *Anger is a Gift* – In the midst of struggling with his identity, and with institutionalized racism, Moss Jeffries fights to find his place in his community; deals with his father's murder (six years ago), and falls in love.

2. *Carry On* – A book of fantasy – but half the time Simon can't make his wand work, and the other half of the time he starts something on fire. His mentor is avoiding him, and his nemesis, Baz, completely plague him during the last year at the Watford School of Magicks.

3. *Birthday* – Eric and Morgan share a birthday, and after six years of sharing that birthday as best friends, their destiny is revealed, and they discover who they are meant to be.

Note: These books are on several lists promoted as being among those that are recommended for all teen readers; books that will provide LGBTQ teens with a mirror to validate their own experiences. The books will provide a window for other teens who need to realize the challenges LGBTQ teens might be experiencing. All the while these teens are experiencing the normal (and sometimes extraordinary) trials and tribulations of being a teen.

On the Homefront – World War II

> Green, Amy Lynn. *The Lines Between US*. Bethany House, 2021.
> Ramos, Jason, and Smith, Julian. Smokejumper: A Memoir by One of America's Most Select Airborne Firefighters. William Morrow, 2016
> Stone, Tanya Lee. Courage Has No Color, The True Story of the Triple Nickels: America's First Black Paratroopers. Candlewick, 2013.
> Weeks, Linton. (2015, January 22). *How Black Smokejumpers Helped Save the American West.* National Public Radio (NPR) History Department. http://bit.ly/smokejumpersWWII

Read, Think, Discuss

1. *The Lines Between US* – A fictionalized tale of conscientious objectors who battled wildfires in the North West from 1943-45. Fewer than 300 Conscientious objectors served in this way. But the increase in blazes in 1945 caused much concern – and a mystery that called for teamwork with members of the military. The Triple-Nickels are involved.
2. *Courage Has No Color* – Nonfiction that tells the story of America's first black paratroopers. Their courage and bravery earned them a lasting page in the annals of American history.
3. *A Memoir by One* ... This title does not take place during WWII but does provide a look into the dangers and challenges faced by the smokejumpers who endanger their lives every time they jump into push back a dangerous fire.
4. *How Black Smokejumpers* ... A brief summary of how the Triple Nickels became involved in smokejumping, and provides some summary and introductory information from Tanya Lee Stone's books *Courage Has No Color*.

Note: Who knew that smokejumpers played such an important part in World War II. In fact, why were they even necessary? And as important as their mission was, how did Black paratroopers enter into the picture? A slice of World War II history that needs to be shared.

Black Panthers and Their Voice in America's Culture

Magoon, Kekla. *Revolution in Our Time: The Black Panther Party's Promise to the People.* Candlewick, 2021.
Magoon, Kekla. *The Rock and the River.* Aladdin, 2009.
Magoon, Kekla. *Fire in the Streets.* Aladdin Hardback.
Williams-Garcia, Rita. *One Crazy Summer.* Aladdin, 2009.

Read, Think, Discuss

1. Kekla Magoon's *The Rock and the River* mainstream novel for young people featured the Black Panther Party as did Magoon's companion novel, Fire in the Streets. Both inspired Magoon to begin the research process for *Revolution in Our Time*.
2. *Revolution in Our Time* follows the movement from the early days of Blacks in America (slavery) to the emergence of the Black Lives Matter emphasis in the 2020s.
3. *Fire in the Streets* After Dr. King's assassination in 1968, Maxie, a fourteen-year-old in Chicago joins the Black Panthers over her family and boyfriend's objections. She is soon caught up in the anti-war and civil rights demonstrations.
4. *The Rock and the River* Set in 1968, in Chicago, fourteen-year-old Sam Childs is caught between his father's belief in Dr. King's non-violent approach to civil rights and his brother who has joined the more aggressive Black Panther Party.
5. *One Crazy Summer* – Set in the same time period (1968) as Magoon's novels, this one is decidedly for a younger middle-school audience. Three sisters leave their New York home to travel to Oakland, California to stay the summer with their mother who had abandoned them (with their father and grandmother) to work with the Black Panthers in Oakland, California. The story of the 1960s and the Gaither Sisters: Delphine, Vonetta, and Fern continue in *P.S. Be Eleven* (Quill Tree Books Reprint edition, 2015), and *Crazy Summer in Atlanta* (Quill Tree Books Reprint edition, 2016).

Notes: Construct a timeline beginning with the emergence of the Black Panther movement in 1966; their involvement and influence on the Civil Rights Movement, and up to the emergence and involvement of the Black Lives Matter movement which began in 2020. Note: the positive gains made by these actions, and the areas where improvement needs yet to be made.

Capsule Packages

The following titles have the potential for connections and common questions and broad discussions regarding those connections. Depending on the reader's prior experiences the connections may be something different than the connection made by another reader. The packages are suggested as having a commonality ready to be discovered and discussed by readers.

Time Warp Titles

Murdock, Catherine Gilbert. *Da Vinci's Cat.* Greenwillow Books, 2021. ISBN: 9780063015258.
- A time slip fantasy that binds together two friends: Federico from 16th century Rome and Bee in present day New Jersey. Linking them is Leonardo daVinci's cat, and his mysterious wardrobe. Can rewriting history save today?
- Compare and contrast to the plot and friendships prevalent the two following classics:

Stead, Rebecca. *When You Reach Me.* Wendy Lamb Books, 2009.. Miranda, a sixth grader tries to make sense of her life and the laughing man that lives near her apartment. She turns to what she knows and that is Madeleine L'Engle's *A Wrinkle in Time.* For those who know L'Engle's book the hints at fantasy and descriptions will be obvious.

L'Engle, Madeleine. *A Wrinkle in Time.* Dell, 1962. Various editions are now available including a graphic edition

Coming of Age – Dealing with Sexual Violence, Racism, Poverty ...

Brown, Echo. *Black Girl Unlimited: The Remarkable Story of a Teenage Wizard.* Macmillan, 2020.
Based on much of her own life, Echo Brown writes a tale that intertwines poverty, sexual violence, depression, racism, and sexism in a not to be missed coming of age tale. Fiction.

Compare and contrast the chief protagonist in *Black Girl Unlimited* ... to the chief protagonist in each of the following two titles. What are obstacles for each of. them and what might help them overcome, prosper, and succeed:

Watson, Renee. Piecing Me Together. Bloomsbury, 2018. Everyday Jade leaves her friends behind and goes off to a private school where she intends to seek every advantage afforded her. But she is tired of being identified as someone who is in need of help.

Zoboi, Ibi. American Street. Balzer+Bray, 2018. ISBN: 9780062473059. When Fabiola's mother is detained at the border, Fabiola is left on her own to navigate among her three loud cousins, the unknown on Detroit's west side, a new school, and a romance.

Soldiers & Spies in Plain Sight – Revolutionary War

Rockwell, Anne. *A Spy Called James: The True Story of James Lafayette, Revolutionary War Double Agent.* Illustrated by Floyd Cooper. CarolRhoda Books, 2016.
Story of James Lafayette who was a double agent during the Revolutionary War, and who helped Washington defeat Cornwallis. When the war ended he was denied his freedom. His petition to the Virginia General Assembly was denied. Eventually General Lafayette intervened and James became James Lafayette, a free man when the general assembly reconsidered.

African Americas, Jewish soldiers, and Women were among the soldiers that fought and helped the colonists win the American Revolution. Write a brief paragraph about the contributions of an "unexpected" Revolutionary soldier.

Krensky, Stephen. *Hanukkah at Valley Forge.* Illustrated by Greg Harlin. Dutton. 2006. (Available in paperback only)

Anderson, Laurie Halse and Faulkner, Marr. Independent Dames: What You Never Knew About the Women and Girls of the American Revolution. Simon and Schuster, 2008.

Hidden Secrets – Forbidden Records

Tate, Don. *William Still and His Freedom Stories: The Father of the Underground Railroad.* Peachtree Publishing, 2020.
William Still was the son of enslaved people who had escaped to the North. William worked hard and earned a job with those helping others who were seeking freedom. Those who came through his office were recorded – and the book hidden away so as not to get anyone in trouble. The intent was to help reunite families who escaped at different times – little did he know that his efforts would reunite his own.

Throughout history there have been secrets that if released would endanger others. That was true during the period of slavery and in World War II during the Holocaust. The following two books take place during World War II and the Holocaust, but they too have hidden secrets and forbidden records. Read these books and compare and contrast the historical events and how they impact the outcome throughout the world. Compare the secrets and the hidden records to those collected by William Still. With each of these people – what was their most significant contribution? Explain why.

Vaughan, Marcia. *Irena's Jars of Secrets* by Marcia Vaughan, illustrated by Ron Mazellan. Lee and Low Books, 2011.

Sis, Peter. Nicky & Vera: The Quiet Hero of the Holocaust and the Children He Rescued. Norton Young Readers, 2021.

Instead of Book Talks - Instead of Book Reviews Instead of Anything Else

Literary Triads

Literary Triad

The procedure for this activity includes grouping participating students into groups of three. Group members are then asked to discuss the books they are reading. The students do not need to have finished the book, and ideally each individual in the group is reading a different title. The discussion should not b of the round-table type but should be structured more like the discussion of a good movie—it should be light and friendly. Students should not each have a designated turn – there should be interaction with comments – and questions. Say, "You will have limited time for discussion so make sure you get your book and your voice in the discussion – even if you have to politely interrupt." Allow the discussion to go on for three to five minutes. If the discussion seems to be winding down sooner, end the discussion immediately. The discussions should end while each participant still has something to say.

Number the students 1-2-3. At this time #1 should write a letter to #2 and #2 should write to #3, and #3 should right to #1. The letter should follow up on the discussion just interrupted. After three to five minutes, stop the writing before all have finished. When the STOP announcement is made - -a word may be finished but not the rest of the sentence. It's a freeze stop.

Pass the letters to the recipient, and the recipient should read the letter they have just been handed.

After reading their letter each recipient should answer the letter with their own letter written back to the letter writer: #1 back to #3, #2 back to #1, and #3 back to #2.

After three to five minutes, declare a freeze stop. Hand the letters back to the original writer to read. This triad discussion/writing time will mix talk and writing to introduce new titles to students and allows each student to share books they like or are enjoying (and sometimes books that they aren't finding too enjoyable).

As the procedure is utilized more often the writing/talking sessions will become more involved and the time spans may be expanded as appropriate. Just make sure the individual sessions are interrupted before students completely exhaust what they have to say—always leave room for more information to be shared.

©2019-2021 McBookwords

Quotes – What Do You Make of It?

1. Choose a fiction book that focuses on an era that you are studying. In this case I choose *Odette's Secret* - A story of a girl during World War II. Macdonald, Maryann. *Odette's Secret* by Maryann Macdonald. Bloomsbury, 2013. ISBN: 978159990-750-5.
2. Ask students to read the book they select, and to generate quotes from the book; or their own reaction to the book. These are examples from Odette's Secret.

Brief quotes from the book, or quotes from my mind that …came as a result of reading the book - Macdonald, Maryann. *Odette's Secret* by Maryann Macdonald. Bloomsbury, 2013. This is a list from *Odette's Secret*.

- "Twist vegetables from their stem."
- At night: "I imagine my mother's face. It floats in the air just outside my window."
- Father is a prisoner.
- Dark hole dug deep into the earth.
- A measure of poverty — "And I will get used to it. She's right. I do."
- "A farmer lets me cut hay with a sickle."
- far up in the hills, / all alone
- …retreats into her own solitude.
- but lured back by poetry… it even lures her to return to school with the village children.
- poetry sustained her father, too, as he traveled 8 mos. from his liberated POW camp home to Paris.
- brought her, not a pearl necklace, but a leather-bound notebook.
- The story of all the secrets I kept and the story of my lost-and-found heart.

3. Pass the quotes to another student and ask the recipient to write a 2-3 paragraph reaction to the quotes, exploring what the book might be about, era, what happens, and so forth. Make sure the reference to the book is included. Make of these what you will.
4. As a follow-up ask the second student to read the book and compare their original 2-3 paragraphs with what they thought of the book and its story line.

Book Pairings

After reading a book that has been particularly enjoyed, ask readers to recommend another book that they feel any reader of the book will enjoy as a second book to read. The selected book could be a picture book, a book of information, a fiction book, a biography perhaps, or any book that the reader can articulate a connection to.

As an example - I used the same book as above: Macdonald, Maryann. *Odette's Secret* by Maryann Macdonald, in conjunction with a picture book *Irena's Jars of Secrets* by Marcia Vaughan, illustrated by Ron Mazellan (Lee and Low Books, 2011).

Irena Sendler saved many children from the Warsaw ghetto and kept their names in a jar. For more information about the books:

Odette's Secret by Maryann Macdonald http://bit.ly/OdettesSecrets
Irena's Jars of Secrets by Marcia Vaughan http://bit.ly/sendler

But We Have to Teach the Classics

Well yes, you probably do, if your school curriculum mandates that – otherwise I would assess the goals and objectives and decide if the classics are the best choices or if they are being taught just because "we've always done it that way." But the relevance of any assigned book must always be dealt with. If the classics are to be taught perhaps pairing them with more contemporary titles that share similar themes, plots, and so forth will create some relevancy, provide compare/contrast experiences, and help readers see the commonality of themes/plots across time. Perhaps these suggestions will be of some help – and likely there are others you could add to this list.

Classic: *Romeo and Juliet* by William Shakespeare

- Contemporary: *The Fault in Our Stars by John Green (Dutton 2012)*
  Notes: Star Crossed Lovers
- Contemporary: *The Sun Is Also a Star by Nicola Yoon (Delacorte Press, 2016)*
  Notes: responsibility to family, fate vs free will, love and relationships

Classic: *Macbeth* by William Shakespeare

- Contemporary: *Beautiful Creatures by Kami Garcia and Margaret Stohl (Little, Brown, 2010)*
  Notes: *Beautiful Creatures* contain many allusions to Macbeth – family prophecies, fantastical world and intrigue.

Classic: *To Kill a Mockinbird* by Harper Lee

- Contemporary: *The Girl Who Fell from the Sky* by Heidi W. Durrow (Algonquin, 2010)
  Notes: Alternative views on racial issues and prejudice, and friendship
- Contemporary: *Dear Martin* by Nic Stone (Crown Book, 2017)
  Notes: Alternative views on racial issues and prejudice, and friendship, coming of age
- Contemporary: *Just Mercy: A True Story of the Fight for Justice* (Young Adult Version) by Bryan Stevenson (Delacorte, 2018)
  Notes: Racial issues and prejudice, equality, and friendship, coming of age

Classic: *1984* by George Orwell

- Contemporary: *Stronger, Faster and More Beautiful* by Arwen Elys Dayton (Delacorte, 2018)
  Notes: Technology in culture, conflict of morals and values, human and civil rights

Classic: *The Great Gatsby* by F. Scott Fitzgerald

- Contemporary: *Great* by Sara Benincasa (Harper Teen, 2014)
  Notes: Both deals with issues of class sexuality, and ambition, in America. Benincasa's book is an update of *The Great Gatsby* but with a almost totally female cast (countering the predominate male presence in all the classics).
- Contemporary: *We Were Liars* by E. Lockhart (Delacort, 2014)
  Notes: Both deal with family and relationships, morals and values in conflict, social class and expectations.

Classic: *The Scarlet Letter* by Nathaniel Hawthorne

- Contemporary: *The Boyfriend List* by E. Lockart (Delacorte, 2006)
  Notes: Both demonstrates sexual double standards and mores (then and now)

Classic: *Lord of the Flies* by William Golding

- Contemporary: *The Hunger Games* by Suzanne Collins (Scholastic, 2010)
  Notes: Both take place in a world where teenagers are in combat with one another, to the death, in order to survive. Morality, sacrifice, and survival.
- Contemporary: *Wilder Girls* by Rory Power (Random House/Ember, 2020)
  Notes: Each take place in a world where teenagers are in combat with one another, to the death, in order to survive. Morality, sacrifice, and survival.

Classic: *Of Mice and Men* by John Steinbeck

- Contemporary: *Perfect Escape* by Jennifer Brown
  Notes: Focuses on sibling relationship – one fleeing economic hardship or a cheating scandal – the other dealing with the realities of mental illness.

Classic: *The Kite Runner* by Khaled Hosseini

- Contemporary: *The Things She's Seen* by Ambelin Kwaymullina and Ezekiel Kwaymullina (Knopf, 2019)
  Notes: Culture void/diversity, grief and dying, seeking justice

Classic: *The Odyssey* by Homer

- Contemporary: *Rickety Stitch and the Gelatinous Goo* by Ben Costa & James Parks (Knopf, 2017)
  Notes: Both are built around a plot involving an epic quest and includes a major motif -- good vs evil

Classic: *Catcher in the Rye* by J.B. Salinger

- Contemporary: *I Am Not Your Perfect Mexican Daughter* by Erika Sanchez (Knopf, 2017)
  Notes: Seeking acceptance and belonging, coming of age, responsibility to family, grief and suffering.
- Contemporary: *Kindness for Weakness* by Shawn Goodman (Delacorte, 2013)
  Notes: Seeking acceptance and belonging, coming of age, responsibility to family, grief and suffering.

Need more examples or suggestions?

There are many more listed by Julianne Daly in her article.

Daly, Julianne. (2018, March 22). #TBT/#TBR: YA Books to Pair with Classics. P¡QUE Beyond the Book. https://piquebeyond.com/2018/03/ya-books-with-classics/

Searching for Balance

In a final effort to encourage us to be inclusive in terms of books we select to use in the classroom/library, encourage scholars to read, or to use as research please check your book offerings (home, library, classroom). In your collection do you have a title that fits these descriptions? I think the results might speak volumes as to what each of us needs to do next.

1. Fiction book with an African American main character that is not dealing with civil rights or slavery.

2. A Nonfiction book about an African American that is not dealing with civil rights or slavery (and whose name is not a household name such as Martin Luther King, Jr. or Rosa Parks).

3. A Latino-American chief protagonist in a fiction book that is not dealing with migrant workers or crossing the border illegally.

4. A Nonfiction book showcasing the contributions of a Latino-American

5. A Native American chief protagonist in a contemporary fiction book that is dealing with teens in the present day.

6. An information book about Native Americans that show Native Americans as people without feathers and showing them in contemporary settings.

7. A nonfiction book showcasing the contributions of Native Americans in the present day.

8. An Asian American that doesn't have a character that is running a laundry or being the smartest kid in class.

9. A book that showcases inventors, explorers, politicians, any hero that are not of white European descent, and that do not refer to the subjects as "women astronauts," or "African-American heroes," – terms that designate the subject as "other" and totally unexpected, as if women cannot be astronauts, or African Americans cannot be heroes.

About the Author

Sharron McElmeel is a nationally known children's and young adult literature specialist and literacy advocate. She has authored more than 35 books for parents and educators, and has published more than 100 journal articles, in addition to having contributed more than 300 book reviews to professional journals. She has provided keynote or featured presentations at over 50 national and state conferences. She served on the 2007 Caldecott medal nomination committee. She completed a bachelor's degree in elementary education at the University of Northern Iowa and earned a master's degree in Library Science from the University of Iowa with educational administration and reading certifications at the elementary and secondary levels. She has taught at all levels from elementary through the university level. She continues to contribute to professional publications and maintains several blogs with reviews and articles. She has an active social media presence. During her time as an elementary classroom teacher, she was active in creating literacy models for promoting reading and writing in the educational environment, as well as, in the wider community. Later, as a librarian, her work to promote reading and literacy in schools earned her the honor of Iowa's Reading Teacher of the year. She remains the only librarian ever honored by the Iowa Reading Association as their Reading Teacher of the Year. In recognition of her contributions to literacy in the community, she was honored with Iowa's Celebrate Literacy Award. Other honors include being nominated as Iowa's Teacher of the Year and named as one of Top Ten Online Educators (Innovative Teaching).

Her research files, which support the professional resources and articles that she has written, are housed in her alma mater's (University of Iowa) Special Collections (MSC0991). The files are available for scholarly research, by request.

She is a life-long resident of Iowa. She and her husband live in a rural area, where their home clings to the edge of a small village. Their home at various times, has been shared with six children, a dog or two (actually they share the heated garage). Their home is filled with several thousand books and the laughter and antics of grandchildren who visit frequently.

www.ingramcontent.com/pod-product-compliance
Lightning Source LLC
Chambersburg PA
CBHW080341170426
43194CB00014B/2644